NOLO *Your Legal Companion*

"In Nolo you can trust." —**THE NEW YORK TIMES**

Whether you have a simple question or a complex problem, turn to us at:

NOLO.COM

Your all-in-one legal resource

Need quick information about wills, patents, adoptions, starting a business—or anything else that's affected by the law? **Nolo.com** is packed with free articles, legal updates, resources and a complete catalog of our books and software.

NOLO NOW

Make your legal documents online

Creating a legal document has never been easier or more cost-effective! Featuring Nolo's Online Will, as well as online forms for LLC formation, incorporation, divorce, name change—and many more! Check it out at **http://nolonow.nolo.com**.

NOLO'S LAWYER DIRECTORY

Meet your new attorney

If you want advice from a qualified attorney, turn to Nolo's Lawyer Directory—the only directory that lets you see hundreds of in-depth attorney profiles so you can pick the one that's right for you. Find it at **http://lawyers.nolo.com**.

ALWAYS UP TO DATE

Sign up for NOLO'S LEGAL UPDATER

Old law is bad law. We'll email you when we publish an updated edition of this book—sign up for this free service at nolo.com/legalupdater.

Find the latest updates at NOLO.COM

Recognizing that the law can change even before you use this book, we post legal updates during the life of this edition at **nolo.com/updates**.

Is this edition the newest? ASK US!

To make sure that this is the most recent edition available, just give us a call at **800-728-3555**.

(Please note that we cannot offer legal advice.)

Please note

We believe accurate, plain-English legal information should help you solve many of your own legal problems. But this text is not a substitute for personalized advice from a knowledgeable lawyer. If you want the help of a trained professional—and we'll always point out situations in which we think that's a good idea— consult an attorney licensed to practice in your state.

FIRST EDITION	JUNE 2008
Cover Design	JALEH DOANE
CD-ROM Preparation	ELLEN BITTER
	MICHAEL SANDER
	ERIC WORKMAN
Proofreading	ANI DIMUSHEVA
Index	MEDEA MINNICH
Printing	CONSOLIDATED PRINTERS, INC.

Stim, Richard.
  Ebay business start-up kit : with 100s of live links to all the information & tools you need / by Richard Stim. -- 1st ed.
     p. cm.
  This is an interactive kit that connects you directly to eBay.
  ISBN-13: 978-1-4133-0865-5 (pbk.)
  ISBN-10: 1-4133-0865-1 (pbk.)
  1. eBay (Firm) 2. Internet auctions. 3. New business enterprises--
Management. 4. Electronic commerce--Management. 5. Small business--
Management. I. Title.
  HF5478.S75 2008
  658.8'7--dc22
                                    2007051630

Quantity sales: For information on bulk purchases or corporate premium sales, please contact the Special Sales Department. For academic sales or textbook adoptions, ask for Academic Sales. Call 800-955-4775 or write to Nolo, 950 Parker Street, Berkeley, CA 94710.

1st edition

eBay Business Start-Up Kit

With 100s of Live Links to All the Information & Tools You Need

By Attorney Richard Stim

Acknowledgments

Thanks to:

- Terri Hearsh for her layout and production of this book
- Paul Dodd and Peggi Fournier of 4D Advertising for conspiring with me on the idea of a disc-driven eBay book, and for coming up with the original design and layout, and
- The Applications Development crew at Nolo—Ellen Bitter, André Zivkovich, and especially Mike Sander—for all their work on making the disc come alive.

About the Author

Richard Stim is a Nolo editor and author who writes about small business and related topics. Among his books are *Wow! I'm in Business, Profit From Your Idea*, and *Retire Happy*. He lives in San Francisco where he spends more time than he should buying and selling audiobooks on eBay.

Table of Contents

What's So Special About This Book?

1 Welcome to eBay

The eBay Community 5

Your eBay Business Is an Extension of You 6

About This Start-Up Kit 7

2 Getting Started

What You Need to Start Selling 10

Check It Out: The eBay Home Page 12

Register as an eBay Member 15

Get Started Now! 18

I Want to Buy Something 19

I Want to Sell Something 19

eBay Selling Methods 20

Use a Tabbed Browser 21

My eBay 21

eBay Help 22

eBay Help Resources 22

Other eBay Companies 23

3 Is eBay Your Hobby or Your Business?

What's the Difference Between a Hobby and a Business?.................................28

If the IRS Audits You.................................29

You Have a Business If ….................................29

Use Depreciation to Show a Profit.................................32

4 What Will You Sell?

What Are People Buying on eBay?.................................34

Keep Track of Costs.................................39

Selling Strategies.................................39

5 List an Item for Sale

I'm New to eBay.................................45

Completing the Sell Your Item Form.................................48

The Fastest Way to List an Item for Sale.................................49

List an Item Using "Customize Your Listing".................................54

Categories Matter.................................54

Using "Create Your Listing" (All Options).................................56

Titles: The Rule of 55.................................56

What Condition Is Your Item In?.................................58

Getting It Picture Perfect.................................60

Tip: Photo Hosting Services.................................62

The Description: Use Words That Sell.................................63

Pricing.................................65

Choosing Your Price at eBay.................................65

Tech Tip: eBay Marketplace Research.................................66

Quantity.................................66

Timing and Duration.................................67

Keeping Track of Fees.................................68

Tech Tip: Fee Calculators.................................69

Additional Information (Terms and Conditions)................................71

Shipping Costs 72

Payment 72

Review and Submit..73

Revising or Terminating an Auction 74

6 Buy an Item

I'm New to eBay 76

Buying on eBay Motors..76

Tech Tools: The eBay Toolbar 76

Watch Before Bidding..77

Want It Now Listings..77

Tech Tip: eBay Marketplace Research................................79

Quicklist: Before You Bid..79

Bidding..83

7 Open an eBay Store

What is an eBay Store?..90

What's It Cost to Create and Run a Store? 95

How to Open a Store 97

eBay Basic Store Information Intake................................98

Just So You Know 100

ProStores: Beyond eBay Stores..101

8 PayPal Basics

What Is PayPal?..104

Getting Started With PayPal..104

PayPal Fees..106

Billing With PayPal..107

PayPal Auction Tools and Integration 107

9 Rules, Disputes, and Feedback

eBay Rules 110

Common eBay Frauds 113

Avoiding Auction Frauds 114

Resolving Common Disputes 115

Small Claims Court Usually Won't Work 119

Feedback 119

A Final Warning About Feedback 124

10 eBay Motors

What Is eBay Motors? 126

Selling on eBay Motors 126

Buying a Car on eBay Motors 128

Quicklist: Selling a Car on eBay Motors 130

11 Auction Management Tools

Desktop or Web-Based Tools 134

What Do Auction Management Tools Do? 134

What Software Tools Do You Need? 135

Quicklist: Software Tools 135

Popular Auction Management Programs 138

eBay 138

Vendio 139

Auction Hawk 139

Marketworks 140

Auctiva 140

InkFrog 140

More Information ... If You Want It 140

Yes, There Are More eBay Tools 141

12 Become a PowerSeller

The Elite World of PowerSellers 144

Ten Things PowerSellers Have in Common 145

Driving Traffic to Your eBay Store or Website 150

Borrowing Money to Grow 154

Warning: Don't Become a Power Debtor 156

13 Should You Quit Your Day Job?

Two Tips If You Decide to Quit 159

Avoid Problems With Your Current Employer 159

14 Business Entities: What Kind of Business Should Your eBay Business Be?

How Do You Know What Kind of Business Entity You Have? 172

What Is Limited Liability? 172

LLC or Corporation? 173

How to Create an LLC 175

Converting to an LLC 175

Why Choose a Corporation Instead of an LLC? 176

If Your eBay Business Is a Partnership 178

Odd Ducks: Limited Partnerships and S Corporations 180

Ways to Organize Your Business 180

15 Insurance

Basic Insurance Terminology 184

Basic Coverage 185

Coverage Through Your Homeowners' Policy 188

If Your Business Needs More Coverage 189

Lower Your eBay Insurance Costs 189

16 Recordkeeping

What Records Should You Keep? 194

eBay Accounting Software 197

Accounting Resources 199

Choose an Accounting Method 199

Keep Your Business and Personal Finances Separate 200

What Records Do You Need If You're Audited? 201

How Long Should You Keep Records? 203

17 Shipping and Returns

Shipping Tips 206

Shipping Solutions 208

Stay Away From Drop-Shipping 210

Shipping and Delays: The Legal Rules 211

Returns and Refunds 212

Terms and Conditions 213

18 Working from Home

Zoning, Lease, and Homeowners' Association Restrictions 216

Warning: Don't Let Your eBay Home Business Disturb the Neighbors 217

Can You Get the Insurance You Need? 217

Can You Separate Your Work From Your Home Life? 218

Tips for Maximum Home Office Efficiency 218

Leasing Space 221

Welcome Home 223

19 Hiring Help

What's the Difference Between an Employee and an
Independent Contractor?..226

Misclassifying Workers..228

How Does the IRS Decide Who Is an IC?...229

Before You Hire a Friend or Family Member for Your eBay Business.................229

Finding the Right Person for the Job...230

Employment Resources...232

Legal and Paperwork Requirements: ICs...232

Getting Started as an Employer...234

Legal and Paperwork Requirements: Employees...235

Set Up a Payroll System...236

20 Financial Forecasting

Break-Even Analysis..240

Profit and Loss Forecast...242

Cash Flow Projection..246

21 Business Licenses and Permits

EIN: IRS Form SS-4, Application for Employer Identification Number.................252

Local Business License...253

DBA: Register Your Fictitious Business Name...253

Get a Seller's Permit...255

Make Sure You Meet Local Zoning Requirements...256

22 Paying Your Taxes

This *Does* Apply to You...258

What Taxes Your eBay Business Will Have to Pay..259

What About Sales Outside the U.S.?..261

How Business Income Is Taxed...261

Paying Estimated Taxes..263

23 Tax Deductions

What's a Tax Deduction Worth?...266

Basic Categories of Tax Deductions...267

Operating Expense: Deducting Home Office Costs 269

Additional Tips: Home Office Deduction 273

Operating Expense: Deducting Vehicle Costs..274

Operating Expense: Deducting Travel Costs..275

Operating Expense: Deducting Meals and Entertainment Costs............................276

Capital Assets: Deducting the Costs of Long-Term Assets...277

Section 179 277

Depreciation 278

Special Rules for Computers, Cell Phones, and Other Potential Toys....................279

Inventory Expense: Deducting the Cost of Goods Sold...280

Commonly Overlooked eBay Deductions..282

Quicklist: Tax Deductions 283

A Appendix: How to Use the CD-ROM

Installing the Files Onto Your Computer..289

Using the HTML Version of This Book..290

Using the Word Processing Files to Create Documents 291

Using the Spreadsheets..293

Files on the CD-ROM..295

Index

What's So Special About This Book?

Why choose this book over the dozens of other eBay books? Because this book includes something you may find indispensable: a disc that links to hundreds of eBay resources and related websites. That's right. Not only does the disc contain all of the text within this book, it also includes hundreds of direct links to the eBay information you need.

Once you put the disc into your computer and connect to the Internet, you will be able to click through to online resources, download forms, and find information quickly. To give you an idea, here are just a few of the things you can do with the disc:

- **Easy eBay access.** You can quickly access eBay resources—for example, you can find all the eBay community resources, such as announcement boards, the answer center, discussion boards, community help boards, chat rooms, reviews and guides, and eBay groups, all easily grouped on one page.
- **Links to government forms.** Need to fill out the form for an employer-identification number (EIN)? It's one click away. No more searching through pages of Google results for the right form. With the disc, you can find all of the appropriate tax forms and information you need and download them directly to your computer.
- **Connect to eBay-related services and sites.** You can quickly locate eBay partners, eBay owned companies, and eBay gadgets. For example, you can click through to auction calculators that will enable you to determine your profit margin and fees.

- **Business and legal services at your fingertips.** Need help finding services? Not a problem. Essential services have been filtered to save you time. For example, you can connect directly to your state government website to obtain LLC information or connect to a reliable LLC formation service.
- **Hand-holding assistance for first-timers.** If you're new to eBay, you'll find links for each step in the eBay listing and buying process.

For detailed information about using the disc, see the appendix at the end of this book.

You'll find this book helpful even without the disc. Not only does it mirror the information on the disc (every time you see an underlined word, check the corresponding section on the CD for a clickable resource), but it also includes fill-in forms to help you get started. And of course, the book allows you to learn about eBay without having to sit in front of your computer—for example, when you're in the tub, on a bus, or on an airplane (although you'll soon be able to manage your eBay business in the air as well). Whatever way you choose to use this kit, it's been designed to get you up and running ASAP. So, let's get started! ●

Welcome to eBay

The eBay Community.. 5

Your eBay Business Is an Extension of You 6

About This Start-Up Kit... 7

C hances are good that you've bought or sold something on eBay. After all, at any given moment, there are <u>100 million listings</u> on the eBay site, and the company receives 6 to 7 million listings a day. No wonder eBay averages over <u>a billion dollars a quarter</u> in profits.

But just as eBay profits, so do hundreds of thousands of entrepreneurs who have grown from occasional eBay users into eBay businesses. In fact, at least <u>724,000 people</u> in the U.S. rely on eBay for either their primary or secondary source of income. An estimated 14% of eBay sellers have retired from their jobs to work full time on eBay (and an additional 12% were considering doing so).

This start-up kit is designed to help you move from being an occasional eBay user to starting and operating an eBay business, with the goals of increasing your income and providing you with more independence.

eBay offers you a great chance to achieve both goals, but there's a lot of work involved. As chief cook and bottle washer of your eBay business, you'll have many other tasks besides buying and selling. Additionally, working from home can also become a challenge—especially when you've filled up the closets and bathrooms with excess inventory.

The good news is that many people have already paved the way with their eBay businesses, and this start-up kit summarizes much of the advice about the challenges involved. Whether you are starting a new business from scratch or are seeking to expand your retail operation to the Web, *The eBay Business Start-Up Kit* will help answer many of the questions that arise in the process. You should find this start-up kit easy to use; it's designed like a website with links to many other helpful resources (therefore, it will help if you're connected to the Internet while using it).

Before embarking on your journey, though, please keep this in mind: eBay success is based on two underlying factors—community and personality.

As you'll see below, the key to eBay member loyalty is the site's rich sense of community. And as you explore eBay, you will also discover that the eBay entrepreneurs who invest their personality into their business often have the best chance for success and longevity.

The eBay Community

Several companies have unsuccessfully challenged eBay's dominance in the online auction market. The uniquely distinguishing aspect of eBay—and, some might argue, the key to eBay's continuing success—is that eBay operates as a community of members, not as a store, franchise, or company.

eBay is a self-policing, self-helping, and, to some extent, self-governing sales universe. The eBay community, which includes eBay members and eBay staff, abides by certain community values, including simple principles such as "We believe people are basically good" and "We encourage you to treat others the way you want to be treated." This sense of community should never be taken lightly by users, because the power of eBay community opinion is substantial. Failing to abide by community rules can get you suspended or banned from eBay. Conversely, the eBay community is also supportive—eBay and its members offer a lot of free advice and help to those getting started, which in turn engenders more loyalty to the site. To get a sense of this support, review some of eBay's rich collection of resources and help, including the following:

eBay Community Resources	
announcement boards	Look here for general announcements.
answer center	Look here for answers to eBay questions.
discussion boards	Look here for posted discussions on hundreds of eBay topics.
community help boards	Look here for help from other eBay members.
chat rooms	Look here for live discussions among eBay members.
reviews and guides	Look here for community-created handbooks on hundreds of eBay topics—for example, collecting Harry Potter books.
eBay groups	Look here to exchange information with like-minded eBay members.

Your eBay Business Is an Extension of You

The other underlying factor that contributes to the success of an eBay business is a strong sense of personality. As most brick-and-mortar retailers quickly learn when they try to move their businesses online, eBay is a whole different ballgame. While it may seem counterintuitive, sales transactions on eBay tend to be more personal, and customers expect a heightened level of service and attention. However, the rewards from these personal interactions can be great, because those interactions lead to trust—and trust leads to increased business.

As you peruse eBay stores and online auctions, you will see this personal touch over and over. Keep in mind that eBay is a global marketplace where many sellers have access to similar merchandise. When prices are similar, buyers rely on personal and sometimes intangible factors to distinguish among sellers.

As you will see, many of the decisions you make when setting up your eBay business require a personal touch—for example, the name of your eBay store, the colors you choose for the background of a particular auction, the type of merchandise you sell, the size of the lettering in your listings, the quality of your images, and even your choice of username. From top to bottom, each eBay business is a unique mix of branding and personal identity. When in doubt as to what course to take with your eBay business, it's always best to choose the route that's most comfortable for your personality. Your choices may not always lead to short-term profits, but letting your business reflect who you are is more likely to provide personal satisfaction, steady income, and longevity as a business.

About This Start-Up Kit

The start-up kit includes this book and a disc. With the exception of some of the forms and introductory material, the disc includes all of the material in the book. The difference is that the disc operates as a website. When you insert it in your CD-ROM drive it will install on your computer. Once installed, you'll be able to use it to learn about eBay as if you were on the Web, clicking live links that give you direct access to hundreds of eBay, government, and related auction resources.

Internet connection needed. Ideally, you should be connected to the Internet while using the disc. If you are not connected, you can still use the program on your computer, but ultimately you will need the Internet connection if you want to use eBay.

Getting around. You can get around the program as you would on any website. You can access links to additional resources by clicking on any underlined term. Additionally, there are drop-down menus on each Web page as well as a navigation bar on the left side of each page. ●

Getting Started

What You Need to Start Selling 10

Check It Out: The eBay Home Page 12

Register as an eBay Member 15

Get Started Now! 18

I Want to Buy Something 19

I Want to Sell Something 19

eBay Selling Methods 20

Use a Tabbed Browser 21

My eBay 21

eBay Help 22

eBay Help Resources 22

Other eBay Companies 23

F irst, the bottom line: Chances are that many of you are already familiar with eBay and won't need much of the basic information about getting started. But in case you've had little exposure to the world's greatest auction site, this chapter provides straightforward information about registering, navigating around the eBay site, getting started as a seller and buyer, getting help, and learning about the specialty sites owned by eBay.

Need Help Bringing Your Business into eBay? If you want business solutions, advice on buying packing material and mailers in bulk, or tips for locating items to buy and resell—then check out eBay Business, a portal for businesses seeking advice about eBay.

What You Need to Start Selling

File this information as "obvious" … but we'll go ahead and tell you anyway. Listed below are the essential items needed to operate an eBay Business. If you are all set up, skip this list.

- **Computer.** Just about any computer that can get you on the Internet—PC, Mac, or Linux—will work fine for eBay, but you'll be most efficient with a computer manufactured within the past three or four years. Older computers, particularly with older operating systems (such as Windows 98), may not perform as well or as quickly and may prevent you from using certain auction management tools. Expect to pay anywhere from $500 to $2,500 for a new computer.
- **Broadband connection.** There's no way around it. eBay buyers and sellers need a broadband connection (also known as a "high speed" connection). Some eBay members operate with dial-up modems, but most eBay businesses find dial-up too slow to process a meaningful number of sales. Broadband is commonly provided by cable television companies, telephone companies (known as "DSL"), and satellite Internet services companies. CNET offers a guide that can help you locate

broadband providers. Expect to pay $30 to $50 per month for broadband depending on the connection speed.

- **eBay membership.** You must be an eBay member (with your own unique eBay ID) in order to buy or sell. See below for registration and ID information. eBay membership is free.
- **Digital camera and/or scanner.** You will need digital pictures of the merchandise you are selling. eBay supplies pictures for most media merchandise (covers of popular DVDs, CDs, and books), but for all other items, you'll need to create your own pictures. We discuss cameras and photography in Chapter 5, *List an Item for Sale.* Expect to pay between $100 to $300 for a digital camera and $50 to $200 for a scanner.
- **Something to sell.** For information about tracking down suitable merchandise, read Chapter 4, *What Will You Sell?*
- **Shipping supplies.** Bubble wrap, anyone? You'll need packing material, mailing envelopes, and whatever else is required to guarantee safe delivery of your merchandise. Your shipping performance is a crucial aspect of your reputation in the eBay community. Badly packed items can ruin your feedback ratings—the opinion provided by other members about your transactions. For more, see Chapter 9, *Rules, Disputes, and Feedback.*
- **Credit (or merchant) card account and PayPal membership.** Most eBay members consider essential both PayPal membership and the ability to accept credit cards from buyers. (For more information on PayPal, read Chapter 8, *PayPal Basics.*) Note that you can operate on eBay without credit cards or PayPal (for example, instead of providing a credit card to register as a seller, you can participate in <u>ID Verify</u>), but it is not recommended. Buyers feel safer and prefer to work with sellers who have credit card and PayPal capacity. There is no charge for joining PayPal, though there may be transaction charges.

Check It Out: The eBay Home Page

You can get to the eBay home page by typing www.eBay. com into your browser (your browser is the program you use to access the Internet). The eBay home page consists of five major components: a navigation bar, a search box, a My eBay section, advertisements, and side menus.

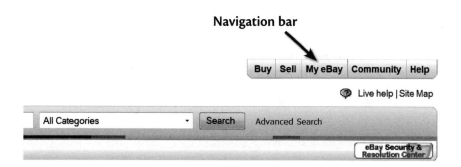

Navigation bar

Navigation bar. Use the top navigation bar to launch pages for buying and selling and to reach a customizable My eBay page, the eBay Community page (for accessing other members), and the main Help page.

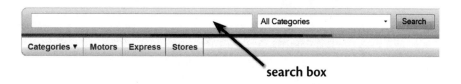

search box

Search box. You can use the search box to find items currently offered for auction (click "Advanced Search" for more searching choices).

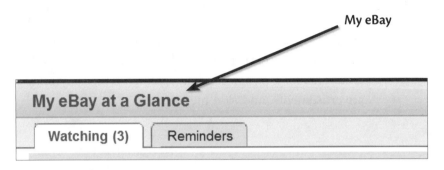

My eBay. When you sign in on the home page, eBay provides a window to your eBay account, known as My eBay, including buying, selling, and watching reminders.

Advertisements. Advertisements for eBay merchandise or special eBay member offers are peppered throughout eBay, including the home page.

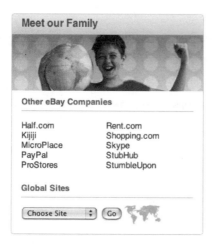

Side menus. Use the side menus to find eBay's specialty sites, eBay categories, and other eBay services, some of which are described in more detail below.

Register as an eBay Member

The first step to buying and selling on eBay is to register as a member. You'll need to be at least 18 years of age, and you must have a valid email address. If you have already registered, skip this step.

To start, click the Register button near the top navigation bar.

Then, fill out the form on the "Register: Enter Information" page (below).

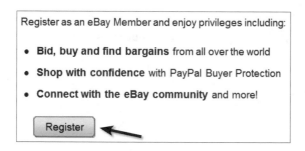

Hi! Ready to register with eBay?

It's your typical registration - free, fairly simple and we won't share your information with anyone else.

Already registered or want to make changes to your account? Sign in.
Want to open an account for your company?

Tell us about yourself - All fields are required

First name

Last name

Street address

City

State / Province   ZIP / Postal code   Country or region
-Select-   United States

Primary telephone number
[ ] - [ ] - [ ]   ext.: [   ]

Email address

Re-enter email address

We're not big on spam. You can always change your email preferences after registration.

Choose your user ID and password - All fields are required

Create your eBay user ID

← **eBay user ID**

Check if your user ID is available
Use letters or numbers, but not ( ) < > & @. How to pick a great user ID.

Create your password

← **eBay password**

Re-enter your password

Use 6 or more characters or numbers. How to choose a secure password.

Pick a secret question
Select your secret question...

Your secret answer

If you forget your password, we'll verify your identity with your secret question

Date of birth
--Month--   --Day--   Year [   ]
You must be at least 18 years old to use eBay.

The not-so-fine print

☐ I agree that:

- I accept the User Agreement and Privacy Policy.
- I may receive communications from eBay, and can change my notification preferences by visiting My eBay.
- I'm at least 18 years old.

[Register]

Your eBay User ID. You will have to choose a unique user ID— the name by which you're known in the eBay community—and you will need a password. There are <u>rules</u> for choosing a user ID—for example, you can't use the word "eBay" as part your user ID. Keep in mind that your user ID is the first piece of information that buyers receive about your business, so choose one that expresses something about your philosophy or business. It's easy to <u>change your user ID</u> later, but you can only do so once per 30-day period.

eBay's User Agreement. You must also agree to the terms of eBay's <u>user agreement</u> and the <u>eBay privacy policy</u>. You will be happy to know that eBay does not sell or rent your personal information.

Check your email. After you complete the form, you will receive an email confirmation. Open your email and click on the link. You should then receive a final confirmation.

Maintain two accounts. It's possible for you to maintain two accounts—for example, if you are selling two distinct types of merchandise. However, both accounts must have different User IDs with different email addresses, and they cannot be used in the same listing. If you wish, you can always <u>merge</u> these accounts later.

Get a seller's account. In order to sell on eBay, there's one more step. You will need to <u>establish a seller's account</u> by providing your credit or debit card, or, if you don't have a credit card, you must establish proof of your identity using eBay's <u>ID Verify process</u> (there's a $5 fee for this service).

Modify your About Me page. When registering, you may also want to address the About Me page. This personalized page lets you tell your story, provides a place to list special items, and can link to your eBay store or related website. Like your User ID and the design of your auctions or eBay store, the About Me page gives you the opportunity to distinguish yourself by providing buyers some information about your philosophy and personality. It's easy to create one. Go to the About Me sign-in page (see below) and click "Create Your Page." Note that eBay has guidelines for About Me pages. For example, you may not promote outside-of-eBay sales or prohibited items.

The eBay About Me Sign-in Page

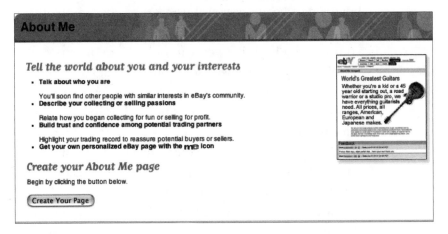

Get Started Now!

All set? Go to the eBay home page and take a look around. Go ahead and start buying or selling if you feel comfortable (or adventurous). If you're using the disc that accompanies The eBay Start-Up Kit, keep the program open in a separate window and return here if you need assistance. Below, we explain the basic things you can do on the eBay home page.

I Want to Buy Something

If you're registered, go ahead! Adam Ginsberg, eBay PowerSeller and author of *How to Buy, Sell, and Profit on eBay* (Harper Collins) recommends buying something as soon as you register as a member of eBay. He says that a quick initial buy does two things: It familiarizes you with the eBay site navigation, and it is a fast way to increase your feedback score.

If you're not quite ready to shop and have registered as a new member, read Chapter 6, *Buy an Item*. Keep in mind that you will get the best deals on eBay by doing research—for example, checking what similar items are selling for, researching what similar items have sold for, and reviewing the seller's feedback ratings.

I Want to Sell Something

If you're ready to sell something and have registered as a new member, you will then need to <u>establish a seller's account</u>. That's as easy as furnishing eBay with some credit card information.

- For more information on selling at eBay auctions, read Chapter 5, *List an Item for Sale*.
- For information on selling via an eBay store, read Chapter 7, *Open an eBay Store*.

eBay has several <u>formats</u> for listing items for sale—Standard Auction, Standard Auction with Buy It Now, Fixed-Price Item, Multiple Item Auction, Fixed Price with Best Offer, and Store Inventory, to name a few. It may seem confusing to have so many formats—we explain most of them in more detail in Chapter 5, *List an Item for Sale* (and you can find definitions in <u>eBay's glossary</u>)—but keep in mind that the vast majority of transactions are completed by means of a standard auction listing. These auctions are open for fixed time periods—typically five to seven days—and the highest bidder at the end of that time period purchases the merchandise. (Note: You cannot sell everything on eBay. Some items—for example, alcohol, firearms, lock-picking equipment, body parts (yes, it has been tried)—are <u>restricted</u>.)

Below, we list the various ways to sell on eBay.

eBay Selling Methods

Standard Auction Listing	This is the most common eBay format. Auctions have fixed time periods—commonly five to seven days. The highest bidder at the end of the time period buys the merchandise.
Standard Auction With BIN Listing	This is a standard auction with a purchasing twist; a buyer can purchase the item at the Buy-It-Now price offered by the seller, but only before the first bid is placed. Once someone bids on the item, the Buy It Now feature disappears.
Multiple Item Auction Listing	This is the same as the standard auction, above, except the seller offers multiple quantities of the same item (sometimes referred to as a Dutch auction). There are <u>special bidding rules</u> for multiple item auctions—for example, all winning bidders pay a price equal to the lowest winning bid.
Fixed Price Listing	This is a Buy-It-Now arrangement without the auction; the buyer can purchase the item immediately at the price set by the seller. Fixed price listings can include multiple quantities of the same item.
Fixed Price Listing with Best Offer	This is the same as the fixed price listing, above, with a buying option; the buyer can suggest a "<u>best price</u>" offer and the seller can choose to accept or reject it.
Store Inventory	You must have an <u>eBay store</u> to sell store inventory. This is really the same as the fixed price listing, except that it originates from your eBay store. Store listings appear for a longer period of time than auction listing and may include a best offer option.

Use a Tabbed Browser

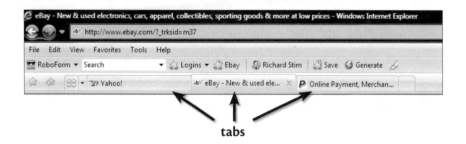

tabs

Tabbed browsers are great for eBay. (Your browser is the program that you use to get around the Internet.) A tabbed browser allows you to auction your folding bike in one window, search for classic cartoons in a second one, and view this program in a third. Mozilla *Firefox*, Apple *Safari*, and Microsoft *Internet Explorer 7* are tabbed browsers. *Internet Explorer 6* is not.

My eBay

Every eBay member has a private My eBay page, which tracks recent transactions and advises you when action is needed—for example, when you need to provide feedback or respond to a seller inquiry.

Consider the My eBay page a basic auction management tool. eBay provides an overview of how to <u>manage your My eBay</u>. If you're a medium-to-high volume seller, you may find it limiting because it cannot automate common transactions. For example, it does not provide templates for email responses or allow you to print invoices in bulk. In that case, you may wish to subscribe to one of the management programs described in Chapter 11, *Auction Management Tools*.

Some of the more popular tools are Selling Manager and its upgraded version, Selling Manager Pro, both subscription services owned by eBay. If you subscribe, Selling Manager will replace your basic My eBay page information with its more advanced template, which operates like a dashboard for your eBay activities.

eBay Help

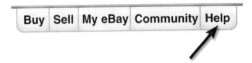

Whenever in doubt, click "Help." That will take you to eBay's <u>Help home page</u> where you can explore numerous eBay help topics.

eBay Help Resources

Ebay Help Resources	
learning center	Look here if you're starting out on eBay (or if you've been using eBay for a while and are starting a new activity).
search help	Look here for specific topics. Just type in your search query as you would with any search engine.
top questions	Look here for the most common questions about eBay, such as, "Can I retract or cancel my bid?"
a-z index	Look here for an alphabetical listing of eBay topics.
eBay acronyms	Look here for an explanation of acronyms such as BIN and FVF.
eBay glossary	Look here for an alphabetical listing of common eBay terms such as proxy bidding or User ID.
contact us	Look here if you want to write a question or report a problem to eBay.
eBay university	Look here for eBay subjects that you can take courses on at a nearby city or online or can learn about using an instructional DVD.

The Learning Center has tutorials and audio and audiovisual programs to learn all of the eBay basics.

Other eBay Companies

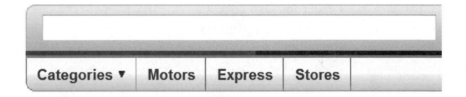

Below the eBay search box you will find tabs for three additional eBay-owned selling services—Motors, Express, and Stores.

eBay Motors. Over two million passenger cars have been sold on eBay Motors, one of the most popular eBay-owned websites. The rules for selling and buying at eBay Motors are basically the same as for regular auction items.

eBay Express. eBay Express is an auction-less retail site owned by eBay. It's similar to retail websites such as Amazon where everything is at a fixed price and buyers use a shopping cart to acquire goods from merchants. Sellers at eBay Express must satisfy some special requirements.

eBay Stores. eBay Stores are cyber-stores where you can sell inventory at fixed prices. You can learn more about them in Chapter 7, *Open an eBay Store.*

Other eBay Companies

Half.com	Rent.com
Kijiji	Shopping.com
MicroPlace	Skype
PayPal	StubHub
ProStores	StumbleUpon

Global Sites

Choose Site ▾ Go

Other eBay Companies. The eBay companies listed on the side menu of the home page are eBay-owned websites that offer additional services, as follows:

- **Half.com.** Half.com is a bargain center for buyers—sort of an eBay Express with more aggressive pricing.
- **Kijiji.** Kijiji is a local and free classifieds site where you can buy and sell new or used goods, look for a car or a job, find local events, and meet local people.
- **MicroPlace.** MicroPlace is a social investing site where your investment dollars are used to provide loans to the working poor.
- **PayPal.** PayPal is an automated online payment system that enables anyone with an email address to make payments from across the country or around the world.
- **ProStores.** ProStores helps you create a web store.
- **Rent.com.** eBay's Rent.com is a free website where you can search for rental properties and roommates.
- **Shopping.com.** Shopping.com provides comparison shopping from a variety of online stores.

- **Skype.** With <u>Skype</u> you can talk—using your computer's Internet connection—to other Skype members anywhere at low rates. Some eBay services have been <u>integrated into Skype</u> as well.
- **StubHub.** At <u>StubHub,</u> you can buy and sell tickets for sports, music, and other events.
- **StumbleUpon.** <u>StumbleUpon</u> is a unique free service. It helps you locate unusual or interesting websites based on your personal preferences. ●

Is eBay Your Hobby or Your Business?

What's the Difference Between a Hobby and a Business? 28

If the IRS Audits You 29

You Have a Business If… 29

Use Depreciation to Show a Profit 32

    Ask the IRS to Wait One Year 32

First, the bottom line: There is a big difference tax-wise as to whether your eBay activity is a hobby or a business in the eyes of the IRS, with greater benefits arising from a business classification. However, treating eBay as your business when Uncle Sam concludes it is a hobby can result in back taxes and penalties. Don't fear the tax man, though—there are ways to demonstrate you are operating a legitimate eBay business.

What's the Difference Between a Hobby and a Business?

If your eBay work qualifies as a business, you can deduct your eBay losses from other income earned in the same year, including salary, your spouse's income, or interest and investment income. You can also carry over losses from your eBay business from year to year even if you don't expect big profits for some time.

If your eBay activity is considered a hobby, you can deduct your expenses from your eBay income only. For instance, if you lose $2,000 in your first year online, you can't deduct it from other income. Accountants refer to this restriction as the "hobby loss rule." Additionally, a hobbyist can't carry over losses to apply against future years' income; they are lost forever. Finally, hobby expenses are only deductible if you itemize deductions on your tax return, and if they, along with any other miscellaneous itemized deductions, exceed 2% of your adjusted gross income.

TIP

Nolo, the publisher of *The eBay Business Start-Up Kit* provides an article on hobby/business tax standards at its website, www.nolo.com, and you can find an explanation of IRS standards at www.irs.gov.

If the IRS Audits You

If the IRS questions the treatment of your eBay activities as a business, you must demonstrate that your primary motive in operating your business is to earn a profit and that you have continuously and regularly engaged in your business over a substantial period. Below is a worksheet to help determine whether the IRS would agree you are operating a business instead of enjoying a hobby.

You Have a Business If ...

- If you earned a profit from your eBay activity in any three of the last five years, the IRS is unlikely to question your classification.
- Even if your eBay business didn't earn a profit in three of the last five years, you can still claim business status by showing profit-seeking behavior, which the IRS measures by looking at the five factors below. Studies show that taxpayers who satisfy the first three factors—you act like you're in business, demonstrate expertise, and expend time and effort—are routinely classified as businesses even if they don't expect to profit for years.

How to Convince the IRS You Have an eBay Business	
Act like you're in business	Keeping good books and other records goes a long way to show that you carry on activities in a businesslike manner.
Acquire eBay expertise	Having expertise as an online auction seller shows you're serious. You can demonstrate this by attending eBay seminars and acquiring and reading material like this kit.
Work on eBay regularly	The IRS is looking for proof that you work regularly and continuously, not sporadically, on your eBay business. What's "regularly and continuously"? One court accepted 20 to 30 hours per week.
Establish a record	Having a record of success in other businesses in the past—whether or not they are related to your current business—creates the likelihood that your current activities constitute a business.
Earn some profits	Even if you can't satisfy the three-out-of-five-years profit test, earning a profit one year after years of losses helps show you are operating a business.

Does it help to incorporate? If you form a corporation, the IRS is likely to presume you are operating a business (and not apply the profit-and-loss test). But even with this presumption, the IRS can still pursue you if your business acts in an unbusiness like manner—for example, you fail to separate your corporate and personal funds. To form a corporation solely to overcome the hobby loss rule is not a financially prudent alternative.

Quicklist: Is eBay Your Hobby or Your Business?		
	Yes	No
Have you earned a profit from your eBay activity in any three of the last five years?	If yes, you're a business.	If no, consider the factors below.
For IRS purposes, businesses that satisfy the first three factors—you act like you're in business, demonstrate expertise, and expend time and effort—are routinely classified as businesses even if they don't expect to profit for years.		
Factor 1: Do you act like you're in business by keeping good books and carrying on activities in a businesslike manner?		
Factor 2: Have you acquired eBay expertise by attending eBay seminars and acquiring and reading material like this start-up kit?		
Factor 3: Can you prove that you work regularly and continuously (not sporadically) on your eBay business? What's "regularly and continuously"? One court accepted 20 to 30 hours per week.		
Factor 4: Have you established a record of success in other businesses in the past—whether or not they are related to your current business?		
Factor 5: Have you earned some profits on eBay? Even if you can't satisfy the three-out-of-five-years profit test, earning a profit one year after years of losses helps show you are operating a business.		

Use Depreciation to Show a Profit

Sometimes you have a choice about whether or not your business will show a profit on paper. For example, imagine that in the first year of your eBay business you incur $6,000 in expenses—most of it for computer equipment. If you deducted all of those expenses from your income, as you are entitled to do, you may show a loss. But you have a choice when it comes to these deductions. Instead of deducting the full amount of the equipment in one year, you can depreciate some or all of it over three or five years (depending on the equipment), which may allow you to show a profit in your first year. This would also provide deductions for the next year, when presumably your expenses would be lower and your income higher. Learn more about tax strategies in Chapter 22, *Paying Your Taxes,* and Chapter 23, *Tax Deductions,* or from your accountant or tax preparation expert.

Ask the IRS to Wait One Year

If the IRS challenges your classification and eBay business deductions during your early years, you can ask it to wait a year by filing IRS Form 5213, *Election to Postpone Determination As to Whether the Presumption Applies That an Activity Is Engaged In for Profit.* ●

What Will You Sell?

What Are People Buying on eBay? 34

Keep Track of Costs 39

Selling Strategies 39

F irst, the bottom line: When it comes to finding merchandise to sell on eBay, there's good news and not-so-good news.

The good news is that eBay has plenty of research data available so you can find out exactly what people are buying (and lots of other sales-related information). The not-so-good news is that everyone else can get that information, too, which sometimes makes it difficult to outsmart your fellow sellers.

If you're moving your brick-and-mortar retail store online, then you probably already have a supply of steady inventory to sell, and it's not an issue. But if you're starting fresh, your best strategy is to combine something you know or like with something that will sell. For example, if you're familiar with auto repair, then you may want to concentrate on selling hard-to-find Fiat parts or accessories. If things don't work out with your choice of merchandise, don't panic. You can change your approach with a few keystrokes, going from toys to office supplies to snow globes. Successful selling—whatever you choose to sell—requires monitoring, patience, and flexibility.

What Are People Buying on eBay?

Whether you know what you want to sell or you have no idea yet, you should start by checking out what people are buying at eBay. There are several ways to find out.

eBay Marketplace Research. You can get the most thorough eBay purchasing research by subscribing to the eBay Marketplace Research service. (You can find it on the left navigation bar on the eBay homepage.) This service compiles the previous 90 days of eBay auction sales data and provides detailed reports that can be viewed in various time increments. There are three levels of fees for the service: fast pass for two days ($2.99), monthly basic ($9.99), or monthly pro ($24.99). Try the fast pass and search by item type or name and then filter the results to find information such as the number of bids, completed sales, and average sale price.

As an example, we researched opening an audio book business. We learned (see chart below) that the average sale price for an audio book during the past two months was $11.32 and that approximately 25,000 audio books were sold. Further research indicated that one of the better-selling subcategories in audio books was children's audio books, particularly classic fairy tales. So, if we were to open an eBay audio book business, it would make sense to pay less than $7 or $8 per unit for audio book inventory, and it would be wise to stock children's classics such as Cinderella and Little Red Riding Hood.

eBay Marketplace Research Results Example

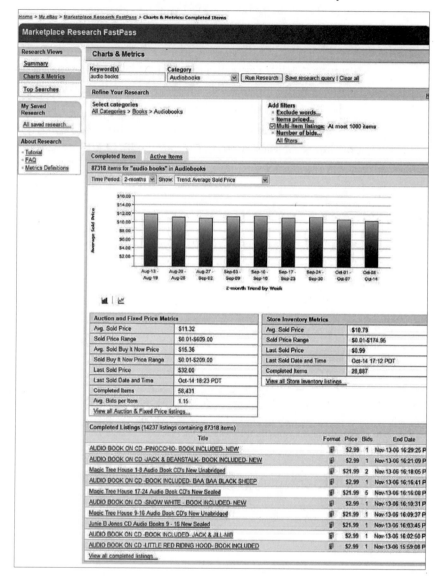

eBay Pulse. The free <u>eBay Pulse page</u> analyzes eBay member searches and compiles the data to give you an idea of what's hot on eBay. (You can find it on the left navigation bar on the <u>eBay</u>

home page.) eBay Pulse also shows you the most-watched items. By clicking on the drop-down menu (shown below), you can pick a category and see what's hot in that category.

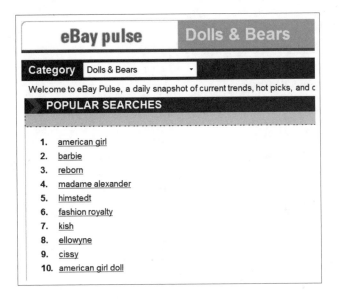

Popular keywords. Another way to analyze searching behavior is to check out the Popular keywords feature, where you can see what keyword terms eBay buyers are using to search for items. Of particular interest are the Top Category keywords.

Here, you can click on any of the categories on the left side of the page to find out what buyers are searching for in particular categories. For example, if you clicked on the China, Dinnerware subcategory of Pottery & Glass, you might see a screen like the one shown below. That would let you know what styles (art deco, chintz), what items (cookie jars, teapots), and what brands (Red Wing, Roseville, Wedgewood) are desired by buyers. You can click any of the keywords to see the items currently offered for sale to give you an idea of the bidding activity. You can also make a "Completed Listings Only" search using the same keyword to see what percentage of items sell and at what prices.

Popular Keywords

Top Categories

Categories

- Clothing, Shoes & Accessories
- Collectibles
- Jewelry & Watches
- Sports Mem, Cards & Fan Shop
- Home & Garden
- Toys & Hobbies
- Books
- Sporting Goods
- Music
- DVDs & Movies
- Computers & Networking
- Cell Phones & PDAs
- Health & Beauty
- Consumer Electronics
- Crafts
- Video Games
- Business & Industrial
- Coins & Paper Money
- Cameras & Photo
- Entertainment Memorabilia
- Pottery & Glass
    Pottery & China
    China, Dinnerware
    Art Pottery
    Wholesale Lots
- Art
- Antiques
- Stamps
- Musical Instruments
- Dolls & Bears
- Everything Else
- Baby
- Tickets
- Travel
- Gift Certificates
- Specialty Services
- Real Estate

- art deco
- chintz
- cookie jar
- czech
- dishes
- hull
- italy
- limoges
- mccoy
- nippon

- plates
- red wing
- roseville
- royal albert
- royal doulton
- tea set
- teapot
- vase
- wedgewood
- wedgwood

Popular Products page. eBay also maintains a <u>Popular Products</u> page. Check that out if you'd like to see the top ten selling items in various categories selected by eBay.

Other eBay sellers. You're unlikely to get merchandise leads from eBay sellers. eBay members are willing to share lots of information—you may get advice about fraudulent drop-shippers or bad manufacturers or distributors—but don't expect to get tips about where to buy merchandise. Supplier information is considered a trade secret.

Keep Track of Costs

Whatever you choose to sell, when buying (or making) merchandise, keep track of all your costs. Your "cost of goods" is not simply the item price you pay for goods. It's the total cost of acquiring the goods, including shipping, traveling, hotel (if you're attending regional trade shows), and related costs. You can't determine your business profits unless you realistically determine the cost of acquiring your items. The same is true for handmade items. You'll never know your profit margins unless you track the cost of yarn for that handmade crocheted scarf.

Selling Strategies

Choosing what products to sell may be the most challenging aspect of operating on eBay. Here, we briefly discuss some selling strategies.

- **Sell what you like.** It certainly is more enjoyable to sell something you like—for example, if you love antique dolls, why not put your expertise to use selling them to others who also appreciate them? Your enthusiasm and knowledge carry into your sales listings. You have a better chance of longevity as a seller if you enjoy dealing with the merchandise and you already know the common sources for acquiring goods.

- **Sell what you know.** If you've already spent retail time selling pet supplies, orthopedic shoes, or phone accessories, then you're familiar with these product lines and with the items that are most popular and profitable. Plus, you probably already have invaluable wholesale contacts.

- **Sell what you make.** Selling what you make—for example, wood carvings or quilts—means you have one-of-a-kind items, favored by some buyers. The trick is to find a niche and acquire repeat customers. If you're a photographer, for example, you may find a demand for pet photography, or if you create jewelry, you may find that astrological items are consistent sellers. Customers who buy handmade goods appreciate presentation, so you might consider putting those earrings in pretty gift boxes. Customers also enjoy contact with an artist—it adds to the work's history and allows the customer to say to others, "Oh, and the artist told me why he prefers using blue." So be generous with your emails.

- **Think collectively.** A strategy used by many eBay sellers is to buy several items and resell them as a group—for example, a gift basket of imported cookies or a unique collection of Frank Sinatra DVDs. The key to success here is in the choice of goods and in the presentation, particularly because these items are often purchased as gifts for others.

- **Follow trends and seasons.** Some sellers attempt to predict and ride out trends, looking for the timely items—for example, selling Halloween costumes, Coach purses, or Playstation games. This is a tough strategy to implement, because you will be competing with large eBay enterprises with the muscle to out-buy, under-price, and out-market you. It's a little bit like playing the stock market. The trick here is to try and guess at trends that others may not spot—for example, if you follow movies at the Internet Movie Database website, you may determine a year ahead of time when a Disney movie will be completed and buy lower-priced merchandise related to that film before others realize the potential of the release.

- **Move your retail outlet online.** Some sellers move portions of their brick-and-mortar retail business online, picking and choosing among existing inventory—for example, a comic book retailer may offer the most collectible comics at auction. Other retailers use online auctions to sell overstock, taking advantage of the national marketplace to liquidate items that are difficult to unload locally. Other retailers move only one aspect of their trade online—for example, a sports memorabilia shop may move all its team baseball caps online because they are easy to inventory, ship, and list.

- **Import creatively.** Some businesses focus on what they can buy cheaply from international wholesalers and manufacturers and then resell on eBay. The challenge here is getting to the sources before other eBay sellers find them. If you already have contacts in foreign markets through family, friends, or business, or if you travel to countries where consumer goods are manufactured—for example, India, China, Taiwan, Malaysia, or Hong Kong—then you have a head start. The key to successful importing is finding a local specialty—for example, jasmine incense, madras shirts, or rattan furniture—and creating a relationship with an exporter who will guarantee you a consistent source of goods.

- **Sell other people's stuff.** One way to increase sales is to sell items on behalf of others on consignment. eBay calls these types of sellers <u>trading assistants</u> and provides a trading assistants <u>directory</u>. Check out how to <u>get started as a trading assistant</u>, and then download the trading assistant toolkit. You can also find information at the <u>Trading Assistant Hub</u>.

Quicklist: What Will You Sell?

Answering the following questions may give you an insight into your eBay business:

	Yes	No
Is there an item or items you would enjoy selling?		
Do you have expertise regarding specific items?		
Have you had retail experience selling any items?		
Do you have wholesale contacts to buy any items?		
Do you make any items that could be sold on eBay?		
Can you provide any services that can be converted into products? (For example, a picture framer may have pre-made frames available.)		
Are there any items that you can group together for sale? (For example, a person who crochets washcloths may want to sell them with bars of soap.)		
Do you have special knowledge in a field that enables you to accurately predict trends?		
Do you have a retail business you can move online?		
Do you travel frequently to places where you could purchase items to resale?		
Do you have any contacts with people who can assist in importing items for resale?		

List an Item for Sale

I'm New to eBay 45

   Prohibited and Restricted Items List 45

Completing the Sell Your Item Form 48

The Fastest Way to List an Item for Sale 49

List an Item Using "Customize Your Listing" 54

Categories Matter 54

Using "Create Your Listing" (All Options) 56

Titles: The Rule of 55 56

What Condition Is Your Item In? 58

Getting It Picture Perfect 60

Tip: Photo Hosting Services 62

The Description: Use Words That Sell 63

Pricing 65

Choosing Your Price at eBay 65

Tech Tip: eBay Marketplace Research 66

Quantity 66

Timing and Duration 67

Keeping Track of Fees 68

Tech Tip: Fee Calculators 69

Additional Information (Terms and Conditions) 71

Shipping Costs..72

Payment 72

    Safety First 73

Review and Submit..73

Revising or Terminating an Auction 74

irst, the bottom line: When you list an item for sale on eBay, you need a good title, a truthful and appealing description, accurate photos, searchable keywords, and reasonable terms and conditions (for instance, no outrageous shipping and handling charges). By preparing these elements ahead of time you can effectively compete as an eBay business.

This chapter does not explain how to list items on eBay Motors. For information on these types of listings, see Chapter 10, *eBay Motors.*

I'm New to eBay

If you have never sold or bought anything on eBay, you'll need to become a registered user before you can list an item for sale. You'll also need to familiarize yourself with the various ways to sell items on eBay. We cover both of these topics in Chapter 2, *Getting Started.*

Make sure you can sell it. eBay prohibits sales of certain items and has restrictions for the sale of other items so before doing any listings, check out eBay's Prohibited and Restricted Items list. Don't assume you cannot sell something because it is listed below. In some cases, eBay has a broad ban—for example, you cannot sell alcohol, firearms, and lock-picking equipment—but you can sell some adult material, as well as many weeds and seeds. If in doubt, check the link on the online list for the item to read the eBay rules.

Prohibited and Restricted Items List

- Adult Material (see Mature Audiences)
- Alcohol (see also Wine)
- Animals and Wildlife Products—examples include live animals, mounted specimens, and ivory
- Art
- Artifacts—examples include Native American crafts, cave formations, and grave-related items

- Catalytic Converters and Test Pipes
- Cell Phone (Wireless) Service Contracts
- Charity or Fundraising Listings
- Clothing, Used
- Coins
- Contracts
- Cosmetics, Used
- Counterfeit Currency and Stamps
- Credit Cards
- Drugs & Drug Paraphernalia
- Drugs, Describing Drugs or Drug-like Substances
- Electronics Equipment—examples include cable TV descramblers, radar scanners, and traffic signal control devices
- Electronic Surveillance Equipment—examples include wiretapping devices and telephone bugging devices
- Embargoed Goods and Prohibited Countries—examples include items from Cuba
- Event Tickets
- Firearms, Weapons, and Knives—examples include pepper spray, replicas, and stun guns
- Food
- Gift Cards
- Government and Transit Documents
- Government and Transit Uniforms
- Government IDs and Licenses
- Hazardous, Restricted, and Perishable Items—examples include batteries, fireworks, and Freon
- Human Parts and Remains
- Importation of Goods into the United States—examples include CDs that were intended only for distribution in a certain country
- International Trading
- Items Encouraging Illegal Activity—examples include an eBook describing how to create methamphetamine

- Lockpicking Devices
- Lottery Tickets
- Mailing Lists and Personal Information
- Manufacturers' Coupons
- Mature Audiences
- Medical Devices—examples include contact lenses, pacemakers, and surgical instruments
- Multilevel Marketing, Pyramid and Matrix Programs
- Offensive Material—examples include ethnically or racially offensive material and Nazi memorabilia
- Pesticides
- Plants (see Weeds and Seeds)
- Police-Related Items
- Political Memorabilia
- Postage Meters
- Prescription Drugs
- Prohibited Services
- Real Estate
- Recalled Items
- Slot Machines
- Stamps
- Stocks and Other Securities
- Stolen Property and Property with Removed Serial Numbers
- Surveillance Equipment
- Teacher's Edition Textbooks
- Tobacco
- Transit- and Shipping-Related Items—examples include blueprints of transit facilities, airplane operations manuals, and flight attendants' uniforms
- Travel
- Weeds and Seeds
- Wine (see also Alcohol)

Completing the Sell Your Item Form

Once you have done the background work, you're ready to complete the online eBay "Sell Your Item" form—a series of questions with check boxes, drop-down menus, and fillable boxes. To find this form, click the "Sell" button on the eBay navigation bar that appears on every eBay page.

Listing an item for sale is a lot easier since eBay revamped its listing process in 2007. eBay created two ways to list an item: a new simplified short form with five sections ("Keep it simple with auction format and essentials like photos"), and a more advanced listing form with more choices ("Customize your listing with multiple selling formats, designs, and more"). As eBay notes on its site, the advanced form is really for experienced users. We recommend the newer shorter listing system.

Sell

List your item for sale
Enter 3-5 words about your item. For example: Nine West women's shoes

Star Tech Cute TV USB

⊙ **Keep it simple** with auction format and essentials like photos
○ **Customize your listing** with multiple selling formats, designs, and more

Start selling

Browse for categories

🚙 Sell a vehicle or auto part

The Fastest Way to List an Item for Sale

The fastest way to list an item for sale is to use the Keep It Simple choice in the Sell dialog box. Enter a few words to describe your item, check the button for Keep It Simple and click the "Start Selling" button. Next, you'll see a screen with five sections. We'll discuss each section below.

Step 1. Create a descriptive title for your item. Your title has to be "searchable"—easy for buyers to find.

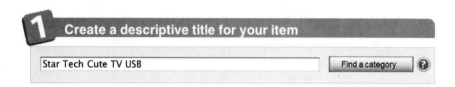

Step 2. Select the Category that best describes your item. eBay provides suggestions for the proper <u>category</u> for your item. You may list your item in more than one category, but keep in mind that you pay an additional listing fee for each category selected.

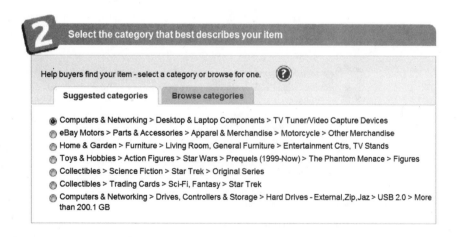

Step 3. Bring your item to life with pictures. Here you upload an image of your item. You'll need a digital photo (or a digital scan). If the item is damaged in any way, make sure the damage shows up clearly in the photo. If you need help, read more about <u>using and uploading images</u>.

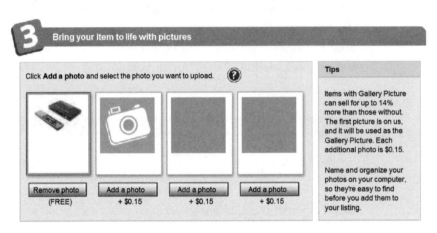

Step 4. Describe the item you're selling. The description must include all the information a buyer would want to know— for example, size, style, and model. See below for more on writing "sellable" titles and descriptions. If you need help, we provide some tips for <u>writing a great description</u>.

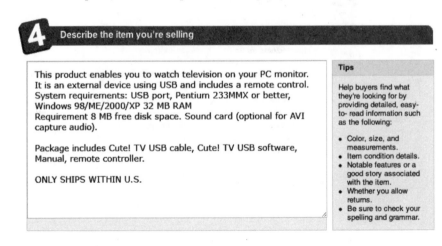

Step 5. Set a price and shipping details. Here you set the price for the item and list shipping costs. Use eBay's <u>Search</u> or <u>Advanced Search</u> feature (check the "Completed Listings only" box) to learn what buyers paid for similar merchandise. Sold items are listed in the search results in bold green; unsold items are listed in red. Also check active listings—those auctions that have not ended—to see what is currently listed. You can learn more about pricing in Chapter 6, *Buy an Item*. As for shipping costs, buyers are more likely to bid if they know (or can determine) the shipping charges. eBay provides easy-to-use <u>shipping calculators,</u> and buyers can calculate shipping costs based on the dimensions and weight you provide. Additional "handling" charges may be added, but keep it reasonable— buyers find exorbitant extra charges to be a turn-off. You can learn more about shipping in Chapter 17, *Shipping and Returns.*

5 Set a price and shipping details

Start auction bidding at $ 7.50   lasting for 3 Days (?)

☐ Add =*Buy It Now* to the listing $ ▮▮▮▮▮ ($0.05) (?)

Shipping destination Service   Shipping cost to buyer

(United States ‡) (US Postal Service Priority Mail   ‡) $ 4.60 (?)

⊕ Add other shipping destinations or services
⊙ Shipping Calculator

Step 6. Decide how you'd like to be paid. <u>PayPal</u> is the preferred choice for most buyers and sellers. For more information, see Chapter 8, *PayPal Basics*. You cannot accept a credit card directly through eBay—that is, without the aid of PayPal—unless you set up a merchant card account with a bank or other financial institution. Many companies offer merchant card services, and some sites also explain the <u>process for getting a merchant account</u>. If you don't have a PayPal account, now may be the time to get one. If you need help, read our section "Payment," below, and review Chapter 8, *PayPal Basics*.

6 Decide how you'd like to be paid

✓Accept payment with **PayPal** [   ] ?

☑ Block bids from buyers who might make transactions more difficult or expensive. ?

Quicklist: How to Prepare for an eBay Listing	
How will you sell?	☐ Auction ☐ Auction with BIN (Buy It Now) ☐ Fixed Price ☐ eBay Express ☐ eBay Store

What's the condition?	☐ New ☐ Used, choose one:
	        ☐ Mint ☐ Excellent ☐ Very good
	        ☐ Good ☐ Fair ☐ Poor

What's your category?	1st _____ 2nd _____
What's your title and description?	Title: _____ Description: _____ _____
Do you have a photograph of the item?	Name and location of photo file: _____ _____
For what prices have similar items sold?	$_____ on _____ $_____ on _____ $_____ on _____ $_____ on _____
What are your fees? Check the eB Calc online calculator.	Listing fees: $_____ Upgrade fees: $_____ Payment fees (PayPal or credit card fees): $_____
What are your shipping costs? eBay provides shipping calculators.	Weight: _____ Dimensions: _____ × _____ × _____ Estimated shipping costs within U.S.: $_____
How will you be paid? PayPal is the preferred method.	Choose as many options as you wish: ☐ PayPal ☐ Money order ☐ Personal check ☐ Credit card

List an Item Using "Customize Your Listing"

If you're a more experienced eBay seller or you have more time to place a listing, you may prefer to customize your listing. To proceed, fill in a three- to five-word description and check the button "Customize Your Listing," as shown below. If you choose this route, you will have more choices regarding the appearance, pricing, shipping and payment process.

Sell

List your item for sale
Enter 3-5 words about your item. For example: Nine West women's shoes

Star Tech Cute TV USB

○ **Keep it simple** with auction format and essentials like photos
⊙ **Customize your listing** with multiple selling formats, designs, and more

Start selling

Browse for categories

🚗 Sell a vehicle or auto part

Categories Matter

Categories where your listing will appear Get help

Category ⓐ
Computers & Networking > PC Components > For Desktops > Graphics, Video & TV Cards > Video Capture & Editing
Change category

First, you must choose a category. Although the vast majority of shoppers use eBay's search feature to comb the entire eBay auction marketplace, some buyers will go straight to a category that interests them and "window shop," thereby running across your item without specifically looking for it. In addition, using the category function provides you and other sellers an effective way to collect sales data for a category, allowing you to assess whether interest in a category is growing or declining and which categories are generating the most traffic.

The new version of eBay's Sell Your Item form suggests categories based on the other similar items in those categories. If you have used the same category previously, you can click on "Choose a previously used category." You can also enter keywords to search for a category on the Select Category page, which function will guide you through a hierarchy of category listings (see below). Choose "Browse Categories" on the Select Category page.

eBay's Select Category Page

Should you list in a second category? Probably not. Unless you are convinced that it will really double your exposure (for example, if you had wireless noise-canceling headphones and wanted to list them in the wireless headphones and noise-canceling headphones categories), there's probably not much logic in paying double the listing (or "insertion") fees.

Mature audiences. There are separate <u>rules</u> if you plan on selling anything in one of the Mature Audiences subcategories.

Using "Create Your Listing" (All Options)

SELL YOUR ITEM	1. SELECT A CATEGORY	**2. CREATE YOUR LISTING**	3. REVIEW YOUR LISTING

Create your listing

After choosing your category, you will see a page entitled, "Create Your Listing," containing nine sections. Below, we go into detail regarding each section.

Titles: The Rule of 55

Help buyers find your item with a great title Add or remove options | Get help

* Title ⓐ

Subtitle ($0.50) ⓐ

Since more than 90% of eBay buyers search by title, it is essential that your title contains the same terms (or "keywords") used by searching buyers. eBay allots 55 characters per title. For a $.50 additional charge, you can add a subtitle, thereby doubling the maximum number of characters (from 55 to 110). However, the subtitle won't show up when someone is doing a typical title search. Keep in mind the first four guidelines below for all listings:

- **Use common terms.** eBay's search feature only finds exact matches, not similar search terms. For example, a potential buyer who types in "headphones" will not find an item listed as "earphones" or "headset."
- **Use existing titles.** The best title is often the one that is used on the product packaging or advertising. If you are selling a juicer, for example, use the name of the product as it is listed on Amazon (such as the "Breville JE9000 Juice Fountain Professional Extractor").

- **Test out keywords.** You may find that listing your "clock" as a "vintage mantel clock" distinguishes it from hundreds of other "vintage clocks." eBay has made it easy for buyers and sellers to choose keywords by publishing popular <u>eBay keywords</u>.
- **Use adjectives carefully.** You will have plenty of opportunity to hype your item in the description so avoid using precious title characters for generic terms such as "stupendous," "super," and "incredible."

While the four title guidelines listed above apply to all listings, those below require a judgment call on your part:

- **Using eBay acronyms.** Most eBay experts advise maximizing your 55-character allowance by using familiar <u>acronyms</u>. But use them carefully; not everyone who searches uses acronyms. Serious cinema collectors may search for MPs, but occasional buyers will more likely search for "movie posters."
- **Repetition in titles.** Repeating information is generally considered a no-no because it wastes precious characters, but sometimes can work effectively. For instance you may choose to write out a number and repeat it in numerical form or use an acronym and spell it out. As an example, the title "1960 Ocean's 11 Eleven MP Movie Poster" would be picked up by several different searches.
- **Misspellings.** They can turn off some buyers. However, there are cases where buyers commonly have spelling problems— for example, they search for "Louis Vitton" or "Louis Vuiton" instead of "Louis Vuitton." If you are dealing in commonly misspelled goods, you may want to include a popular misspelling in order to snare more eyeballs. Curious about how many misspellings occur at eBay auctions? Check out <u>Typohound</u>.

What Condition Is Your Item In?

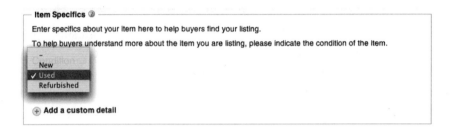

Grading an item's condition requires assessing that item's appearance, age, history, and/or functionality. This assessment will color the item's description (which must include any flaws or defects), help you complete the Sell Your Item form (a drop-down menu asks for your assessment), and determine how to photograph the item (the photograph should accurately reveal the item's condition). Here are some things to keep in mind when assessing an item's condition.

Condition affects value. Some sellers may think that Internet anonymity frees them from the consequences of misrepresenting their products, but the rules are the same as for any brick-and-mortar merchant—it is unethical and illegal to do so. You are legally obligated to represent the item accurately and to disclose defects. The eBay community has its own rules for dealing with disputes over how an item is presented. These are discussed in Chapter 9, *Rules, Disputes, and Feedback.*

New or used. Initially, you must indicate whether your item is "new" or "used." An item is new if (1) it is in the original condition from the manufacturer, distributor, or retailer; (2) it has not been refurbished or used for any purpose; and (3) it has no known defects or damages. You can also state that a handmade or custom-made item is new if it has never been used for any purpose.

Mint to poor condition. eBay sellers often grade their items using one of these terms: mint, near-mint, excellent, very good, good, fair, and poor. Mint indicates perfect or pristine condition, and poor means very damaged or heavily used. There are also variations on these terms, for example, Mint in Mint Package (MIMP) or Mint No Box (MNB).The use of these terms is subjective and experts generally advise that you rate your items critically, suggesting, when in doubt, to step down a grade rather than up. If you are looking for guidance, search through eBay's Reviews and Guides section, where many users post guides for authenticating merchandise and collectibles, or use Google to find the grading standards for your category. For example, two searches we made turned up grading suggestions for vinyl recordings and grading conditions for antique fishing lures.

> **⚠ CAUTION**
>
> In some item categories, particularly the collectible coin market, some shady grading services artificially pump up an item's value in order to unload similar items. Check eBay category chat rooms for warnings about such businesses. eBay is also in the process of creating a "wiki"—a user-edited, encyclopedic online resource to help users.

Professional appraisals. Buyers and sellers can also use eBay's Authentication and Grading Services. For a fee, an eBay-approved professional evaluator will evaluate an item for authenticity or physical condition. eBay's evaluators primarily deal with collectibles and gemstones. For other items, you can learn more from WhatsItWorthtoYou.com, or by locating a professional appraiser in your area using the Find an Appraiser service provided by the International Society of Appraisers.

Getting It Picture Perfect

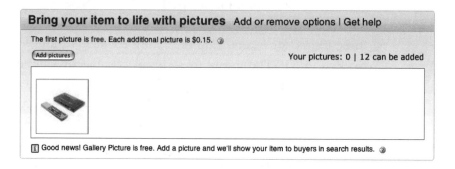

Whatever you sell, buyers rely on an image (and they may be suspicious if they don't see one). Unless you are planning on selling CDs or books (for which eBay provides the cover image, as explained below), you will need to master some photo tasks.

eBay provides a helpful photo tutorial, and you can find more tips in Marsha Collier's *eBay Business All-In-One Desk Reference for Dummies* (Wiley). If you are still using a film camera, now is the time to get a digital camera (you can buy it on eBay!), unless you are creating images of two-dimensional items only, in which case you may be able to create suitable images with a scanner. Listed below are some additional suggestions for creating eBay photos.

Get a mini studio. As any actor will tell you, lighting makes a difference in appearance. The best and easiest way to create professional lighting effects is with the aid of a portable enclosure—for example, a mini-photo studio, lighthouse, cloud dome, or light tent. Power sellers use these devices as shortcuts for creating consistently professional photos. These helpful devices (priced from $50 to $150 retail) are made of translucent material that diffuses light, allowing the photographer to illuminate an item from any angle without shadows. The cloud dome is ideal for small items like jewelry, stamps, documents, and gems. You can see examples of these various devices at the Pop Photo website.

Photo editing software. You can perform basic photo editing with programs like *Picasa* (free), *Adobe Photoshop Elements*, or Ulead's *PhotoImpact*. Photo editing programs like Pixby Software's *Fast Photos* and *FotoKiss* are created specifically for auction photography. In addition, some of the auction management tools discussed in Chapter 11, *Auction Management Tools* perform basic photo editing. Photo editing is helpful for removing extraneous background material, but do not use it to remove flaws in the item.

Photo specs. Your eBay photos should have a resolution of 72 pixels per inch (PPI). Image size should be no wider than 480 pixels. If you are unfamiliar with these terms, you can find both of them in your photo editing software's "image size" tool. Save your photo in JPG format (for maximum compression). If you take these steps, your photo files should be under 50 KB in size (ideal for posting at an auction). To determine a photo's file size, hold your mouse over the file or right-click on the file and click "Properties."

Cropping. Come in close to the item when photographing it. Use the crop tool in your software program to remove irrelevant background material.

Names and watermarks. To cut down on competitors using your photos to sell similar items, insert your business name into the image. This can typically be accomplished by a "text" tool feature in your photo editing software. eBay prohibits content and picture theft. Report any sellers who steal your photos or descriptions.

Images for books and CDs. You won't need to take photos if you are selling a book or compact disc that has an ISBN number (it's the number above the barcode). If you are selling one of these, a pop up window will appear (see the illustration below) as you are completing the Sell Your Item form. You only need to supply the ISBN. eBay provides the image as well as the name of the author or artist, the year of publication, the category (such as "business"), and the format (such as "paperback"). If the cover of your product is damaged, that is, it looks different from the image provided by eBay, include that information in the item's description.

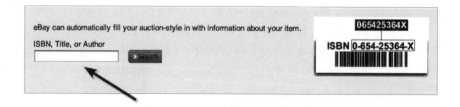

Loading photos onto eBay. eBay lets you post the first photo of an item for free. After that there's a charge of $0.15 cents per photo. Photos are easy to load onto eBay—you simply browse through your computer's files until you find the image and click on it to accept it. If you want a picture to be viewed in extra-large size, you must pay eBay for a <u>Picture Pack</u>, which lets you add up to twelve pictures and to supersize them (up to 800 pixels on the longest side).

Tip: Photo Hosting Services

Many power sellers use outside photo hosting services that store their photos at a website (this service may be offered with an auction management software program). These services can help organize your photos, making it easier to locate them. Additionally, your photos may load faster onto eBay, and the images may appear sharper. Most important for many sellers, you can load large images from a photo hosting service onto eBay without paying the supersize fee.

Learn more about photo hosting by reading this <u>AuctionBytes</u> article. eBay runs its own competitive subscription-based hosting called Picture Manager. If you would like to investigate other photo hosting services, you can find links to them by completing this <u>questionnaire</u>.

To link to a photo listed on another site. To link your photos from an online site, do one of the following:

- **Link picture.** While you are completing the Sell Your Item form, you will reach the Picture Details section. Click the tab for Web Hosting, which is under the Add Picture heading.

Then enter the Web address (URL) of the picture in the Picture Web address field.

- **Paste picture.** Use HTML code and paste the picture directly into your description. If you are not afraid of HTML code, get the address (URL) for the hosted image—for example, http://www.nolo.com/headphones1.jpg. Then copy that URL into the following code format:

    <img src= http://www.nolo.com/headphones1.jpg>.

    Next, paste that code into your description (make sure you have checked "HTML mode" above the text box). If you post multiple pictures using that code, place an HTML break (<BR>) or paragraph mark (<P>) between each line of code. If you are not used to HTML, this will take one or two tries before it's not intimidating.

The Description: Use Words That Sell

An item's description is the third key element in a successful listing, after its title and photo. An effective description will preemptively answer all questions a regular buyer would have about the item.

Answer everything you would ask if you were the buyer. For example, is the label still on the Juicy Couture hooded sweatshirt? Is there certification with the signed Oasis photograph? Does the Star Trek lunch box have a glossy or matte finish? If you are not sure what buyers want to know, read descriptions of similar items, particularly for sold items in completed auctions.

Go from general to specific. Good descriptions start with general information—for example, the brand and model of video camera you are planning to sell—and then become more specific, including details such as a scratch on the camera's handle and whether original packaging and manuals are included.

Use words that sell. Did you know that there are 62 ways to say "exciting" and 57 ways to say "reliable"? Richard Bayan's _Words That Sell_ (McGraw-Hill) is the best resource for jumpstarting your description or title. Check out all six sections of Bayan's book— Grabbers, Descriptions & Benefits, Clinchers, Terms & Offers, and Special Strategies.

Automate if you can. Auction management tools can help you create templates for commonly sold items. (See Chapter 11, _Auction Management Tools_ for more information.) Even without auction management software you can save commonly used item templates in your word processing file.

Appearance counts. Use an easy-to-read font, write short paragraphs, and make your description as concise as possible. If you really want to spice up a listing, check the box marked "HTML mode" and add HTML coding. It's not as hard as it may seem. eBay provides a basic HTML tutorial, and you can find more information at eBay-community style websites such as this one. For an additional $.10 you can use the eBay Listing Designer to enhance your description with a theme and picture layout (a patriotic motif is one choice). Check the box under the Description box and look at the preview.

Check it twice. Maintain high standards by first writing the description in a word processing program (using a spell-checker), and then copying and pasting it into the Description box. (There is also a spell-checker you can activate above the Description text-entry box.)

Pricing

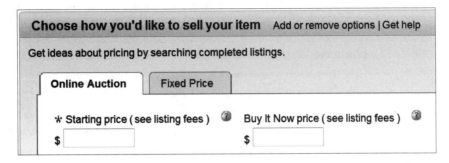

After you load your photos, eBay asks for pricing information. Keep in mind that your pricing decisions affect your <u>insertion fees</u> (as discussed in the section on fees, below).

Choosing Your Price at eBay

Starting price. The starting price is the amount at which you want bidding to begin. If you are using a reserve price, you should use a low starting price—for example, $.99.

Reserve price. The reserve price (optional) is the lowest price you are willing to accept for the item. If the bidding doesn't surpass your reserve, you don't have to sell the item (though you can offer the highest bidder a <u>second chance offer</u>). The reserve price is your secret; bidders don't see it unless you choose to disclose it in your description. The eBay fee for the reserve price is refunded if the item sells.

Pricing strategy. If you do some research and you are comfortable with the prices similar items sell for, a good strategy is to price the item at a low minimum bid and not use a reserve price, because many bidders stay away from auctions with reserves. (For this reason, you will often see sellers advertise "NR" or "no reserve" in their titles). If you are concerned you won't make your money back, you can also try a higher starting price. On the other hand, it's wise to use a reserve for high-ticket, one-of-a-kind items, because it guarantees you won't take a bath if the auction bidding doesn't proceed as expected.

Buy It Now (BIN) price. If you use this feature, a buyer can purchase your item immediately at your BIN price. You can use BIN in online auctions, or you can choose it for a fixed price sale or online store. When you use BIN in connection with an auction, the BIN feature stays on the site until the first bid is made, after which it is no longer available. If you want to use BIN without an auction, you must have a minimum feedback score of 10 or you must be ID Verified.

Tech Tip: eBay Marketplace Research

If you really want to research pricing, buying trends, and similar information, eBay offers a helpful subscription service entitled eBay Marketplace Research. This service compiles the previous 90 days of eBay auction sales data and provides detailed analysis, including top searches within a category or on the entire site, to see what buyers are searching for. There are three levels of fees for the service: fast pass for two days, monthly basic, or monthly pro.

Quantity

If you are selling multiple identical copies of an item, such as four copies of a movie poster, you can post either as a multiple item auction (also known as a Dutch auction) or as a fixed price listing. Dutch auctions have special rules, so be sure to review them before posting. If you are going to be doing multiple item auctions on a regular basis, try out Turbo Lister, a free eBay program designed to help mid-to-high volume sellers automate their listings.

Timing and Duration

```
* Quantity ⓘ
[ 1        ]   items

Duration ⓘ
[ 3 days   ▾ ]
  ◉ Start listing immediately
  ○ Schedule start time ($0.10)   [ -              ▾ ]   [ 1:00 AM ▾ ]
```

How long should an auction run? You can schedule your auction for one, three, five, seven, or ten days. The conventional wisdom is that unless you are selling a time-sensitive item, such as tickets to a baseball game, run the auction for at least seven days. There is an additional fee to run an auction for ten days.

When should an auction start? Consider when the auction will end and when buyers are most likely to bid. Your auction ends on the day you determine, during the same hour that you commence the auction. Most bidding occurs during the last hours of an auction and eBay has its highest traffic on weekends, particularly Sunday afternoons. During weekdays, eBay's traffic increases between 5:00 and 8:00 p.m. Pacific Standard Time (eBay operates on PST).

As an example, if you are posting items for a seven-day auction at 8:00 a.m. on a Tuesday, the final bidding will be between 2:00 and 3:00 a.m. Tuesday one week later—perhaps not an ideal time for buyers to seek out your crocheted baby hats (or maybe it is).

How is the schedule set? Use the dropdown menu in the Sell Your Item form to specify when you want the auction to commence.

Keeping Track of Fees

There are three types of fees to consider when posting your listing:

- **eBay fees.** You must pay <u>eBay fees</u> for posting and selling an item. These fees include <u>insertion fees</u> and <u>final value fees</u> (FVF). Insertion fees are based on your starting or reserve price, whether you use BIN pricing, and whether you use eBay enhancements like subtitles, bold lettering, borders, and so forth. Final value fees are based on the final sale price (see below). If the buyer backs out and doesn't buy the item, you can get a <u>final value credit</u>. There are miscellaneous eBay fees if you use eBay picture services or seller tools—for example, <u>fees for using Selling Manager, Blackthorne</u>, or other eBay software tools. In February, 2008, eBay overhauled its fee structure (to thunderous complaints and threats of boycotts). Sellers watched final value fees jump from 5.25% to 8.75% for items under $25. At the same time, eBay dropped its insertion fees by 25% to 50% for some categories, and began offering free gallery images and related offerings with the hope that the new pricing strategy would encourage more listings.

Final Value Fees	
Closing Price	**Final Value Fee**
No sale	No fee
$0.01–$25.00	8.75% of the closing value
$25.01–$1,000.00	8.75% of the initial $25.00 ($2.18), plus 3.50% of the remaining closing value balance ($25.01 to $1,000.00)
Equal to or over $1000.01	8.75% of the initial $25.00 ($2.18), plus 3.50% of the initial $25.00–$1,000.00, plus 1.50% of the remaining closing value balance ($1,000.01–closing value)

- **Payment services fees.** If you maintain a <u>Premier or Business</u> account with PayPal, you must pay fees in order to receive payments. Personal PayPal accounts are free but cannot receive credit card payments. These PayPal fees are charged to your PayPal account and not your eBay account. For more information, see Chapter 8, *PayPal Basics*.
- **Shipping fees.** Fees for shipping an item, such as UPS, USPS or FedEx charges, are typically passed on to the buyer and included within the final transaction fee. For more information, see Chapter 17, *Shipping and Returns.*

Tech Tip: Fee Calculators

Many eBay sellers use fee calculators, which are software programs that calculate eBay and related fees. You can find some good fee calculators online such as <u>eB Calc</u>, an eBay and PayPal calculator, shown below.

eB Calc Calculator Example

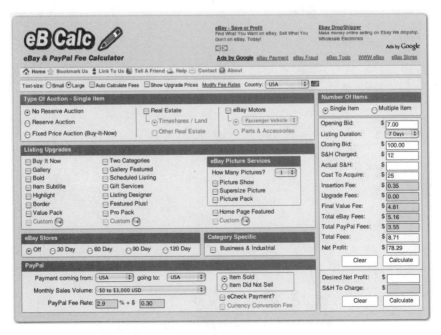

Other fee calculators are included within auction tools such as Hammertap's <u>FeeFinder</u> (shown below).

Hammertap's Fee Finder Calculator Example

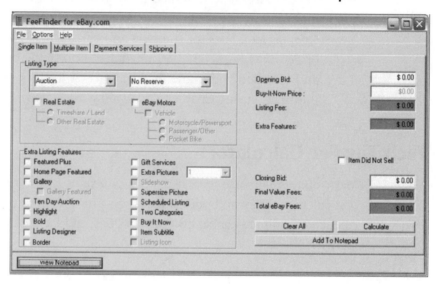

Additional Information (Terms and Conditions)

Other things you'd like buyers to know Add or remove options | Get help

Buyer requirements ⓘ
None: Allow all buyers
Add buyer requirements

Sales tax ⓘ

[- ⬍] [   ] %

☐ Also apply to shipping & handling costs

Return policy ⓘ

☑ Returns Accepted

Item must be returned within

[7 Days ⬍]

Refund will be given as

[Money Back ⬍]

Return policy details

Note: 500 character limit

Additional checkout instructions ⓘ

Note: 500 character limit

Near the end of the Create Your Listing form, you will be asked for information regarding sales tax and your return policy. If you're unsure how to complete these two items, we advise about sales tax rules in Chapter 22, *Paying Your Taxes*. If you don't have a return policy or are unsure whether you need one, you can review eBay's suggestions in Specifying Your Return Policy, or review Chapter 17, *Shipping and Returns*.

Shipping Costs

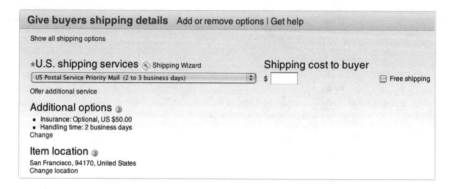

Keep in mind that eBay <u>rules</u> allow you to charge a reasonable shipping and handling (S&H) fee. Shipping and handling fees may not be listed as a percentage of the final sale price, and <u>excessive S&H charges</u> can result in suspension of your eBay account. If you offer insurance, you can charge the buyer only the actual fee charged to you.

Payment

Finally, you must choose a method of payment. PayPal is the most popular payment method, and it and other payment options are discussed in detail in Chapter 8, *PayPal Basics.*

☑ PayPal (fee varies) ⓐ

Accept credit card and bank payments online.

PayPal

MasterCard VISA AMERICAN EXPRESS DISCOVER BANK

Email address for receiving payment ⓐ

ebay@yahoo.com

Additional payment methods ⓐ

☐ Money order / Cashier's check

☐ Personal check

Safety First

There's one extra hitch when it comes to payments. In 2008, eBay began to require that some sellers offer "safe payments." What's a safe payment? It's one in which the seller offers either PayPal or a merchant credit card to customers. (PayPal buyer protection covers most qualified transactions up to $2,000.) Sellers are required to provide this option to customers when:

- the listing is in a "risky" category such as computers and cell phones
- the seller has 5% or more dissatisfied customers (as measured by the detailed seller rating (DSR)), or
- the seller has less than 100% Feedback.

Review and Submit

Once you have completed the form, click "Review" and check your listing for any errors. When you are satisfied with your form, click "Submit My Listing." You're auction is now "live" and buyers can place bids.

Revising or Terminating an Auction

You may revise your listing after it is posted, depending on what type of listing it is—auction, fixed-price, or store—and how much time has passed since it was originally listed. Check <u>eBay rules for revisions</u> before attempting any changes. eBay also has <u>rules for ending a listing prior to the scheduled end date</u>. You can end it in this manner if the item is no longer available for sale, there was an error in the starting price or reserve amount, there was an error in the listing, or the item was lost or broken. ●

Buy an Item

I'm New to eBay 76

Buying on eBay Motors 76

Tech Tools: The eBay Toolbar 76

Watch Before Bidding 77

Want It Now Listings 77

Tech Tip: eBay Marketplace Research 79

Quicklist: Before You Bid 79

Bidding 83

F irst, the bottom line: Research is the key to successful eBay buying. Doing your legwork (albeit on the Internet) helps you confirm an item's value, capture the best price, and avoid fraud or other unpleasant surprises.

I'm New to eBay

If you have never sold or bought anything on eBay, you'll need to become a registered user before you can bid on an item for sale. Read Chapter 2, *Getting Started*. eBay provides an <u>audio-visual demo about buying items</u>. (You must have Macromedia Flash to view it. You can <u>download a free Flash player</u>.) eBay also provides a <u>tutorial on bidding</u> for practicing "test bids" without obligation. Keep in mind that there are several ways to buy on eBay.

Buying on eBay Motors

Buying items such as automobiles, motorcycles, trucks, and related parts and accessories on <u>eBay Motors</u> involves a different process than what is included in this section. For more information, review Chapter 10, *eBay Motors*.

Tech Tools: The eBay Toolbar

If you will be using eBay regularly, you should install the <u>eBay toolbar</u> (shown above). Once installed, the toolbar appears as part of your Internet browser, allowing quick access to your My eBay page, the eBay home page, PayPal, and your favorite searches and sellers. Use the eBay search box to check what items are available on eBay no matter where you are on the Web. You can, for example, search by item title, description, or auction number. The toolbar may be customized in various ways—for example, you can add Bid Alert, Feedback, or Watch Alert features to your bar. Note that eBay's Account Guard feature offers protection from spoof eBay websites, fake sites that look like eBay and are created to elicit personal account information.

Watch Before Bidding

Once you bid on an item, you cannot retract it except in limited circumstances. Read about retracting a bid in "Bidding," below. Experienced bidders often watch an auction before bidding by clicking the "Watch this item" button on the listing page. eBay then puts the item in your Watch List. You can watch several auctions at once. Additional ways to keep track of an auction are described in more detail below.

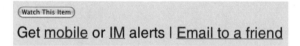

Want It Now Listings

<u>Want It Now</u> is a free want-ad service in which eBay buyers post notices for items. Sellers review these listings and respond. So, for example, if you're looking for an album by harpist Dorothy Ashby and cannot find it on eBay, you can post a Want It Now ad which might read as the example below:

I am searching for

Afro-Harping by Dorothy Ashby

Tip: Be specific. Think of words sellers might use to search for your post.
26 characters left.

Category

Music

Choose the <u>best category</u> to help sellers find your item.
If you prefer, you may <u>specify a category number</u> instead.

Describe it in more detail

I am searching for: Afro-Harping, an album by Dorothy Ashby.I'm looking for the compact disk in good condition. My price range is $10 to $15.

Tip: Be as detailed as possible; specify brand, condition, color, size, price range, etc.
356 characters left.

You can even post a picture of the item if you have one. Don't put your email address in the listing as eBay will connect any potential sellers with you via your eBay account.

Tech Tip: eBay Marketplace Research

Successful buying depends on successful research. One of the best tools for learning about pricing, buying trends, and similar information is eBay Marketplace Research, a service that compiles eBay auction sales data and analyzes buyers' searches and purchases. The different fees represent three levels of service:

- **Fast pass.** $2.99 for two days allows you to access 60 days of data and maintain 10 saved searches.
- **Monthly basic.** $9.99 per month allows you to access 60 days of data and maintain 10 saved searches.
- **Monthly pro.** $24.99 a month allows you to access 90 days of data and maintain 100 saved searches.

Quicklist: Before You Bid

If you are not a regular eBay buyer, the Quicklist of tasks, described more fully below, will help. Why is the background work necessary? When you make a bid, you are entering into a contract to buy the item if you are the highest bidder. Bidding before you have done your research might result in your paying too much for an item of questionable quality, so don't bid unless you are knowledgeable and ready to commit to the purchase. Actual bidding strategy is discussed later in this section.

> **CAUTION**
> You cannot retract a bid unless you meet the criteria described in the section on bidding later in this chapter.

Before You Bid	
What do similar items sell for?	Completed auctions: $_____ on _____ $_____ on _____ $_____ on _____ Other retail sources: $_____ @ _____ ☐ new ☐ used $_____ @ _____ ☐ new ☐ used $_____ @ _____ ☐ new ☐ used
What do you know about the seller?	Comments/Feedback: _____ _____ _____ Any seller guarantees? ☐ new ☐ used Refund policy: _____ _____ _____

Have you read the item description? What's the condition?	Notes: _____
	☐ new ☐ used
	     ☐ Mint ☐ Excellent ☐ Very Good
	     ☐ Good ☐ Fair ☐ Poor

Have similar items been subject to questions of authenticity or fraud?	_____ _____ _____
What are the shipping costs and does the seller ship to your area?	$_____
What is your maximum bid?	$_____

What do similar items sell for? Use eBay's <u>Search</u> feature to find similar items. These items may be currently listed for sale, in which case you can determine if they are attracting bids. Or the auction for the item may have closed (a "completed listing"). To find auctions that have closed and what price the items have sold for (or if they sold at all), check the "Completed listings only" box when you search. When reviewing search results for prices, sold items are bolded green; unsold are red. Check the price of new versions of the same product by searching on popular online shopping sites such as <u>Amazon</u>, <u>Froogle</u>, <u>Bizrate</u>, or <u>PriceGrabber</u>. (You may be surprised to find, for example, that bids on that used digital camera you are considering are surprisingly close to the price of a new camera with a manufacturer's warranty.)

Keep track of comparable items. If you find several items that match your search criteria, you can track these auctions using eBay's <u>comparison shopping feature</u>. eBay provides a <u>tutorial</u> to learn more about comparison shopping.

What do you know about the seller? Check out the seller's <u>feedback rating</u> (discussed more in Chapter 9, *Rules, Disputes, and Feedback*). Although not a perfect predictor of an eBay member's reliability, feedback can provide some insight about a seller's past dealings. Be sure to read the comments. You can also query the seller directly by clicking on "<u>Ask the Seller a Question</u>," a button located on the item listing page.

Look for seller guarantees. If you're concerned about fraud, look for sellers who participate in <u>PayPal's buyer protection plan</u> or, better yet, for sellers who are bonded through <u>BuySafe</u>, both of which are discussed in Chapter 9, *Rules, Disputes, and Feedback.*

Research other bidders. Although it may seem odd, one reason to do so is to determine your competitors' buying habits. For example, are there several bidders collecting the same die-cast farm vehicles as you? If so, you may decide to participate in a less-competitive auction. Checking on other bidders' histories can also help you avoid being a victim of bidding. A history of bid retractions may tip you off to this abusive tactic. To research who else is bidding on an item, click on the History link, which will reveal the list of bidders, but not the amounts of the bid (at least until the auction is over). To learn more about a particular bidder on the list, click the bidder's ID. You can also contact bidders directly via email (and by telephone if that information is available), although eBay prohibits any communication that interferes with the fairness of the auction—for example, you cannot make a side deal with another bidder.

Have you read the item description? What's the condition? It may seem obvious, but in the heat of an auction, buyers can miss crucial information such as the existence and terms of a refund and return policy. Keep in mind that you are not entitled to a refund if you misread the description, but you are if the seller made a misrepresentation that led you to buy the item.

Have similar items been subject to questions of authenticity or fraud? Unless you are already familiar with a particular product or item, you may need to research its authenticity, reliability, or desirability as a collectible. eBay members provide advice on hundreds of topics—from stamp collecting to engagement rings—in the Reviews and Guides section of the site. Non-eBay sites such as CNET or Amazon.com may also provide helpful user reviews of products offered on eBay.

What are the shipping costs and does the seller ship to your area? Get an accurate idea of shipping and handling costs, as these expenses may exceed the cost of the item. The shipping information is often posted in the item's description, or you can determine the expense using eBay's shipping calculators. If shipping costs cannot be determined based on the posted information, ask the seller directly.

Review the payment information. Most sellers and buyers use either PayPal or money orders, but some sellers also accept personal checks.

Bidding

Once you have registered on eBay and done your homework about an item you want, you are ready to bid.

What happens when you place a bid? As with any auction—whether online or off—placing a bid is the equivalent of entering into a legally binding contract by which you agree to buy the item if you are the highest bidder. Except for certain instances (see the discussion "Retracting a bid," below), you are not permitted to terminate the contract. For that reason, always be prepared to buy when you click the "Place Bid" button.

Retracting a bid. You cannot retract a bid unless one of the following is true:

- You made a typographical error and entered the wrong bid amount
- The description of an item changed significantly after you placed your bid, or
- You cannot contact the seller—the seller's phone doesn't work or your email comes back as undeliverable.

There is more to retraction rules (including time limits for making retractions), but the important point to remember is that retracting a bid is difficult. Also keep in mind that a member's retraction history is available to all eBay users. A buyer with a history of retractions may be suspected of participating in various fraudulent schemes, as discussed in Chapter 9, *Rules, Disputes, and Feedback.*

Placing a bid. Once you're prepared to bid, click "Place Bid" on the item's listing page. In the sample listing below, note that the item's history indicates no bids have been placed. In that case, your bid must match the amount the seller has for the starting bid (in this case, $2.99).

Bidding Box on Listing Page

Starting bid:	**US $2.99**
Your maximum bid:	**US $** [＿＿＿＿] **Place Bid >**
	(Enter US $2.99 or more)
End time:	**Jan-23-08 13:51:18 PST** (2 days)
Shipping costs:	**US $4.50**
	Standard Flat Rate Shipping Service
	Service to <u>United States</u>
	<u>(more services)</u>
Ships to:	Worldwide
Item location:	Houston, Texas, United States
History:	<u>0 bids</u>

On the Place Bid page (see an example below), enter your maximum bid—the highest price you will pay for an item. As you can see, the buyer's maximum bid must at least meet the starting price (in this case, $2.99). You can raise your maximum bid during the bidding process, but you cannot lower or retract it once it is confirmed.

Your maximum bid is kept confidential. Under a system known as proxy bidding, which is more fully described below, eBay compares your bid to other bidders in the auction, incrementally increasing it until reaching your maximum bid, when you will be notified that you have been outbid.

Placing a Bid

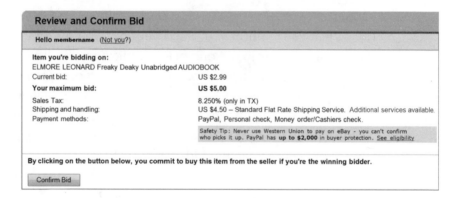

Place Bid

Hello hookywooky! (Not you?)

Item you're bidding on:
ELMORE LEONARD Freaky Deaky Unabridged AUDIOBOOK

Starting bid: US $2.99

Your maximum bid: US $ 5.00   (Enter US $2.99 or more)

Continue >

You'll review your maximum bid, shipping cost, and payment methods in the next step.

To avoid confusion, use the decimal point when entering your maximum bid—for example, $10.00, not $10 or $1000. After entering the amount, click "Continue."

Review and Confirm Bid

Hello membername (Not you?)

Item you're bidding on:
ELMORE LEONARD Freaky Deaky Unabridged AUDIOBOOK
Current bid: US $2.99
Your maximum bid: **US $5.00**

Sales Tax: 8.250% (only in TX)
Shipping and handling: US $4.50 – Standard Flat Rate Shipping Service. Additional services available.
Payment methods: PayPal, Personal check, Money order/Cashiers check.

Safety Tip: Never use Western Union to pay on eBay - you can't confirm who picks it up. PayPal has **up to $2,000** in buyer protection. See eligibility

By clicking on the button below, you commit to buy this item from the seller if you're the winning bidder.

Confirm Bid

On the Review and Confirm Bid page, you are given an opportunity to confirm your bidding information. Once you click the "Confirm Bid" button, you are officially "in the game"—you will see a confirmation screen and receive a confirmation email.

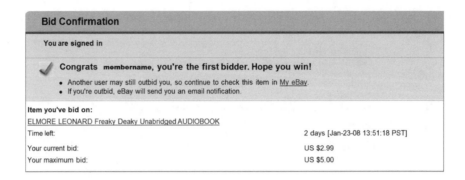

Information about the item and your bids will appear in the "Items I'm Bidding On" portion of your My eBay page.

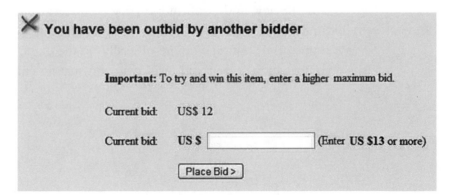

When you confirm your maximum bid, you may immediately see a page similar to the one below, indicating you have been outbid. How could that happen so quickly? Under the proxy bidding system, another bidder may have placed a higher maximum bid. If your maximum bid is lower than the other bidder's, you will automatically be outbid. However, you may stay in the game by increasing your maximum bid.

You've Been Outbid

You have been outbid by another bidder

Important: To try and win this item, enter a higher maximum bid.

Current bid: US$ 12

Current bid: US $ [   ] (Enter US $13 or more)

Place Bid >

Bidding on a reserve price auction. A reserve price is a confidential minimum price that the seller requires before selling the item. Bidders are aware there is a reserve (that fact is indicated on the item listing page), and bidders are aware whether the reserve has been met (also indicated), but the bidders do not know the amount of the reserve. If bidding on an item with a <u>reserve price</u>, you will not know whether you have reached the reserve until bidding surpasses it. Assuming the reserve price has been reached, the item is sold to the highest bidder as in any other auction. If the reserve is not met, the seller can choose whether or not to sell to the highest bidder.

Proxy bidding. Auction bidding is accomplished under a <u>proxy bidding</u> system. eBay automatically bids for you (up to your maximum bid) in a series of <u>bid increments</u>. In other words, after you place your maximum, eBay automates the bidding process, measuring your bid against competing bidders and incrementally raising the bids—something like an automated poker game. The incremental amount that each bid increases depends on the current price of the item and can range from $.05 (for items with a minimum price of under a dollar) to $100 for items with a minimum price of over $5,000. If you are outbid you will be notified by email.

Tracking your bids. You can track your bidding on your My eBay page. If you are outbid, you can re-enter the fray by clicking the "Bid" button on the item page. You can also receive bidding <u>alerts</u> via instant messaging (IM), text messaging, Skype, and telephone.

Sniping. Quite a few auctions (<u>approximately 15%</u>) are decided in the final minute of the auction time period. The process of waiting until the last few moments to place a winning bid (before anyone has time to outbid you) is known as "sniping." While it may seem like foul play, there is nothing illegal about the process. eBay even acknowledges that "<u>sniping is part of the eBay experience</u>," and many software products and services are available to enable the practice. (See a product <u>comparison</u> at the AuctionBytes website.) There are two approaches to sniping:

- online "hosted" services such as <u>eSnipe</u> that will handle the sniping for you and take a cut (for example, 1% out of each winning bid up to $10); you only need to supply your maximum bid, and
- standalone software products such as <u>Auction Sentry</u> that require users to monitor the auctions.

As the AuctionBytes comparison demonstrates, each approach—hosted or software—has its advantages and its fans. You can also read the eBay <u>Reviews and Guides</u> section where there are many articles on the topic (type "sniping" into the search box). ●

Open an eBay Store

What is an eBay Store? 90

What's It Cost to Create and Run a Store? 95

How to Open a Store..97

eBay Basic Store Information Intake 98

Just So You Know..100

ProStores: Beyond eBay Stores.. 101

F irst, the bottom line: Opening an eBay store doesn't mean that you will automatically generate more revenue. Or as eBay expert Marsha Collier notes, "Having an eBay store isn't a one-way ticket to easy street." Certain types of eBay businesses will be more likely to benefit from an eBay store than others. In general, you should consider opening an eBay store if all of the following are true:

- You are an experienced eBay seller—that is, you've completed over 50 eBay sales transactions.
- You have a steady stream of inventory to sell.
- There is some unifying aspect to the items you sell, just as in a typical retail store.
- You have a relationship with existing eBay customers or believe you can attract new customers to your store.
- You have the necessary time and energy (expect to spend several additional hours a day managing your eBay store).

eBay provides a set of <u>eBay store FAQs</u> to explain store basics.

You should probably not open an eBay store if any of the following are true:

- You are just starting out on eBay.
- You have limited merchandise to sell.
- You specialize in one-of-a-kind merchandise that requires custom listings for each item, thereby making it difficult to automate your listings.
- You are already strapped for time managing your usual eBay sales.

What is an eBay Store?

An eBay store is a series of Web pages on eBay. These pages showcase your inventory and cross-promote your auctions. Consolidating your eBay product offerings increases the likelihood of multiple item sales and gives customers an overall view of your business. Additionally, the About the Seller function of an eBay store enables you to describe your business in detail and to link to other websites.

Consolidate your online auction items and fixed-price items with an eBay store. Opening a store doesn't mean you should stop selling at auctions or offering fixed-price (Buy-It-Now) items. Most eBay store owners find it advantageous to continue using both methods, adding the eBay store logo to each of their listings. A buyer who clicks on the store logo at one of your auction listings or fixed-price listings is transported to your eBay store. Once there, the buyer sees all of your other ongoing auctions, as well as additional fixed-price items to purchase.

Store inventory sales. This special fixed-price format is available only to eBay store owners.

- **Advantages.** Store inventory sales offer a longer selling period (either 30 days or "Good 'Til Cancelled"), and the listing <u>fees</u> and final value fees for the sale of fixed-price eBay store items are generally lower than if they were sold at auction. The Good 'Til Cancelled feature is especially helpful, because you don't need to constantly re-list unsold items.

- **Disadvantages.** Store inventory sales will not (with a few exceptions) show up in a traditional eBay search (using the search box on the eBay home page). In order to find store inventory sales items within a store, members must use the search feature on the <u>eBay Stores home page</u>.

Check out some stores. The best way to get a sense of what eBay stores are like is to browse a few. Check out the <u>eBay Stores home page</u> (below). You can also see stores by clicking on the eBay Stores link on the eBay home page. Click on any of the store links to check out the operation and appearance of various types of stores.

eBay Stores Home Page

Most stores present items for sale in the style of a catalog. Take a look at the items being sold in the <u>Wisconsin Harley Davidson store</u> (below).

Wisconsin Harley Davidson eBay Store

Some eBay stores feature one or more lists of auctions. For example, <u>Distant Drums</u> (below) consolidates all of its auctions on one page in its eBay store.

Distant Drums eBay Store

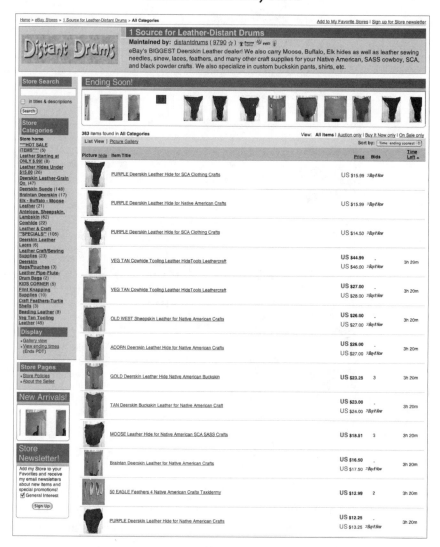

Many stores combine these approaches, listing auctions and items at fixed prices.

What's It Cost to Create and Run a Store?

Like selling at eBay auctions, an eBay store has its own set of fees, starting with a subscription fee for opening and maintaining the store, as well as inventory and transaction fees for the items listed and sold.

Subscription fees. If you decide to open an eBay store, you have a choice of three <u>subscription levels</u>:

- The Basic Store, with charges of $15.95 per month, is the most affordable store, and comes with five customizable web pages and a free subscription to <u>Selling Manager</u>, a solid sales management tool that lets you easily track your store sales; think of it as a seriously enhanced version of My eBay.

- The Premium Store, with charges of $49.95 per month, comes with 10 customizable web pages, a free subscription to Selling Manager Pro, and traffic and sales reports. A premium store's name sometimes appears in the Shop eBay Stores search results page at the U.S. and <u>Canadian</u> sites (instead of just the U.S. site), so increased exposure is an additional benefit of this subscription level.

- The Anchor Store, with charges of $299.95 per month, comes with 15 customizable Web pages, a free subscription to Selling Manager Pro, traffic and sales reports, and one gigabyte of free picture storage, and has the increased exposure of the Premium Store. This subscription level also includes access to 24-hour customer support.

Inventory fees. In addition to monthly subscription fees, you must also pay fees to eBay for your store inventory listings. These fees apply to all non-auction fixed-price listings at your eBay store under the store inventory system (described above) and are charged once for 30-day listings and every 30 days for Good 'Til Cancelled listings. For store listings, items priced at $25 or less are charged a $.03 insertion fee; items priced between $25 and $199 have an insertion fee of $.05 and anything over that has an insertion fee of $.10.

Fees on sales. If an item is sold at your eBay store, eBay collects a final value fee (FVF).

- **Items at or below $25.** The FVF equals 12% of the closing price and does not include shipping and handling charges.
- **Items over $25 to $100.** The FVF equals 12% of the first $25 plus 8% of the balance.
- **Items between $100 to $1,000.** The FVF equals 12% of the first $25, plus 8% of the next $75, plus 4% of the remaining balance.
- **Items over $1,000.** The FVF equals 12% of the first $25, plus 8% of the next $75, plus 4% of the next $900, plus 2% of the remaining balance.

Pay attention to store referral credits. Like every other site on the Internet, eBay is interested in expanding its audience. If your efforts bring a buyer from outside of eBay, you may be eligible to get back 75% of the FVF charged on an item from eBay. eBay has a set of FAQs explaining this store referral credit, but the three main requirements are:

- The purchase must be made by a buyer who came directly to your store from a location outside eBay—that is, from a website in which "eBay.com" is not part of the web address.
- The buyer came to your eBay store as a result of a promotion you posted outside of eBay—for example, by clicking on a link at another website.
- The buyer must purchase the item from your store during the same session in which it was entered—that is, the buyer cannot leave your store and return later to make the purchase.

How to Open a Store

Before opening a store, you must have a feedback rating of 20 or higher, and you must be registered as an eBay seller, which requires that you have a credit card on file with eBay. (For more on feedback and seller requirements, see Chapter 1, *Welcome to eBay*.) Additionally, although not a requirement, experienced eBay sellers would strongly recommend that you have a PayPal account that permits you to accept credit card payments. (For more on PayPal, see Chapter 8, *PayPal Basics*.)

When you are ready, setting up a store is fairly straightforward and can literally be done in minutes. One of the nicest features is that you can set it up in a few minutes but come back over and over to tweak the appearance, just like a real store.

Also, just like opening a real store, you can best prepare by thinking through your store concept or brand and organizing the items you want to sell. For example, if this were a brick-and-mortar store, what would you call it, how would you organize the items (think of your categories for shelving), and how would you price items?

Here are the steps to take:

- Go to the eBay home page, click "Stores," (under the search box), then click "Open a Store."
- Review and (assuming you agree with the terms) accept the user agreement.
- Choose the store subscription level: Basic ($15.95 per month); Premium ($49.95 per month), or Anchor Store ($299.95 per month). If in doubt, start with the Basic Store—you can always upgrade later.
- Enter your store name and give it a description. This information can be changed at any time. For advice on the legal aspects of naming your business, review this Nolo article.

eBay Basic Store Information Intake

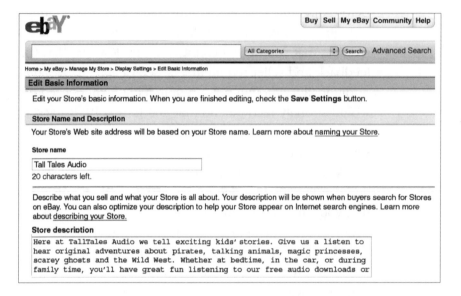

- Choose your theme and display layout; eBay offers various choices.
- Pick your photo, logo, and/or artwork; you can link to or upload your own artwork and imagery.
- Create store categories for your inventory. These categories don't need to match eBay categories; as eBay suggests, think of your store categories like aisles in a store and organize accordingly. Have fun with personalized categories such as "World's Friendliest Eye Glass Cases" or "Nearly Unbreakable Vases."
- Add your fixed-price inventory listings (keep in mind you have two choices—regular fixed-price (BIN) that appear as auctions and store inventory fixed-price items, as described above—and choose their duration.
- Use the eBay Store toolkit (see next page) for more help in building, promoting, and managing your store.

- Finally, review the eBay Store <u>Checklist for Success</u> for ideas on customizing display settings, building your brand, and highlighting items, among other tips.

eBay Store Toolkit

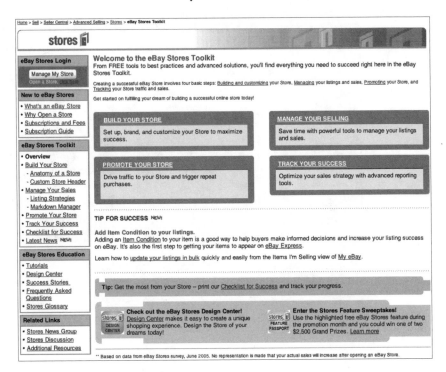

Keep in mind that it's always possible to customize your store's appearance in a manner that rivals the best retail Internet outlets—for example, consider <u>The Frenchy Bee</u>, an exceptional eBay store specializing in French products. But to do so, you may need to bring in help from web developers or learn the intricacies of HTML coding.

Frenchy Bee eBay Store

Just So You Know

eBay encourages you to operate a store (and over 300,000 eBay
members have done so), but eBay stockholders prefer that you
operate auctions and not fixed-price sales at stores. According to
former eBay President Meg Whitman, a recent increase in store
fees was an attempt to push more sales back to auctions—where

eBay earns more money. After the company announced it would raise store fees, eBay's stock jumped in value. Do the numbers to find out why: eBay store inventory represents about 83% of the listing volume on eBay's site but generates just 9% of the gross sales volume. That said, if an eBay store makes sense for you, go for it!

ProStores: Beyond eBay Stores

In 2005, eBay launched <u>ProStores</u>, a distinct level of online retail to complement eBay stores. Think of ProStores as separate web-based retail outlets, distinct from eBay (and the eBay logo) but capable of carrying the same merchandise as your eBay store. ProStores are more customizable than eBay stores, with many more design tools and wizards.

- **Advantages.** Your store and your merchandise are much more likely to show up in typical search engine results than an eBay store. You can utilize your existing PayPal account. You can easily create shopping cart functionality and modify your site. You can directly import your eBay store merchandise and you can integrate your store with QuickBooks. eBay store owners also get some <u>steep discounts</u> when opening a ProStore.

- **Disadvantages.** More fees, including a monthly subscription fee and a monthly transaction fee calculated as a percentage of the sales price of items sold on your store. Also, as of 2006, there is no direct way to move your images hosted by eBay's Picture Manager directly to your ProStores Web store. And you cannot refer to your ProStores items in your eBay Store listings. (Even though it is an eBay company, ProStores is considered "outside of eBay.")

Quicklist: Should you open an eBay store?

You should open a store if you answer 'yes' to *all* of these questions:	Yes	No
Are you an experienced eBay seller—that is, you've completed over 50 eBay sales transactions?	☐	☐
Do you have a steady stream of inventory to sell?	☐	☐
Is there some unifying aspect to the items you sell, as in a typical retail store?	☐	☐
Do you have a relationship with existing eBay customers or believe you can attract new customers to your store?	☐	☐
Do you have the necessary time and energy (expect to spend several additional hours a day managing your eBay store)?	☐	☐
You should probably not open a store if you answer 'yes' to *any* of these questions:		
Are you just starting out at eBay?	☐	☐
Do you have limited merchandise to sell?	☐	☐
Do you specialize in one-of-a-kind merchandise that requires custom listings for each item, thereby making it difficult to automate your listings?	☐	☐
Are you currently already strapped for time?	☐	☐

PayPal Basics

What Is PayPal? 104

Getting Started With PayPal 104

PayPal Fees 106

Billing With PayPal 107

PayPal Auction Tools and Integration 107

F irst, the bottom line: A PayPal account is essential to your eBay business. It helps in receiving payments but offers other functions as well: shipping and labeling services, dispute resolution assistance, refund facilitation, and sales reporting. PayPal is compatible with most popular auction management software. If you are a casual eBay seller, a personal PayPal account will work, but if you hope to receive more than $500 a month in revenue, you will need to upgrade to a premier or a business account.

What Is PayPal?

PayPal is an automated online payment system that enables anyone with an email address to make payments from across the country or around the world. Because the system works so well, it is the clearly preferred way to pay for items purchased at eBay auctions. Sending money via PayPal is free, but receiving money may be subject to a fee depending on the type of PayPal account you have.

Although developed and owned by eBay, PayPal is not just for use in eBay transactions. You can also use your account to accept payments via your website regardless of whether or not you have an eBay account. As part of its Merchant Services program, PayPal offers a free PayPal Shopping Cart system.

Getting Started With PayPal

Visit PayPal's signup page to open a PayPal account. Once there, you'll have three account types to choose from: personal, premier, or business.

Personal Account	Premier Account	Business Account
For Online Shoppers	**For Casual Online Sellers**	**For Business Owners**
Start Now	Start Now	Start Now
• Shop online and pay quickly. • Use your credit card without exposing your card number to merchants. • Speed through checkout without stopping to enter your card number or address. • Plus, it's free to send money to family and friends. Learn more about the PayPal Personal account	• Accept credit cards and other payment types for low fees • Ideal for casual sellers on eBay and all over the Internet Learn more about the PayPal Premier account	• Accept all payment types, including credit cards, for low fees • Ideal for businesses that need a merchant account • Do business under your company name Learn more about the PayPal Business account

If you plan to accept credit card payments or you expect to receive more than $500 per month in PayPal revenue, you will need a premier or business account. If not, start with the personal account (you can always upgrade later). Although there are no fees for sending or receiving money with a personal account, there is a monthly "receiving limit," (as of January 2008) of $500 for payments for the sale of goods and eBay items.

If you exceed your monthly limit, you will need to upgrade your account in order to receive additional payments of these types within that monthly period. Payments which exceed the monthly limit are placed in an "accept/deny" status, which means that if you do not accept or deny the payment, the buyer can cancel. Your receiving limit is reset monthly on the anniversary of your sign-up date. If you have a personal account, you can view your limit on the Account Overview page (click "View Limits" to see any limits that may apply to your account.) In summary, if you expect to earn more than $500 per month for eBay sales, a personal PayPal account is not the right choice.

Premier accounts are ideal for most eBay businesses and offer the same features as a business account. The only difference is that business accounts may be accessed by multiple users.

The chart below summarizes the primary features of the three types of accounts. For more detailed differences, see the description provided by PayPal in Account Basics.

PayPal allows members to have one personal account and one premier or business account. However, each PayPal account must contain unique email addresses and financial information. You may upgrade an account at any time.

Features	Personal	Premier	Business
Send money	✓	✓	✓
Accept credit, debit, and PayPal ATM cards		✓	✓
Merchant services	limited services	✓	✓
eBay software tools	limited software tools	✓	✓
Multiuser access			✓

PayPal Fees

For personal PayPal accounts, there are no fees to send, receive, or withdraw money from PayPal, so long as the money is sent to or from a U.S. bank account. There is also no charge to add money to your PayPal account. Currency conversion fees are the only PayPal transaction fees applicable to a personal account. Again, the primary limitation of a personal account is the limit placed on funds you can receive.

In addition to currency conversion fees, premier and business accounts incur fees for receiving money. The amount depends on your monthly PayPal receipts. For example, if you have average monthly receipts of $3,000 or less, your transaction fees will be 2.9% + $0.30. PayPal provides a breakdown of these transaction fees for domestic payments.

Even with these fees, PayPal is generally more cost-effective for accepting credit and ATM cards than typical merchant or credit card alternatives. In order to accept credit and debit cards outside of PayPal, you would need to open up a credit card account with a bank or other financial institution (often referred to as a merchant card account). In addition to per-transaction fees similar to PayPal's, a bank is likely to charge gateway fees (often $20 or more a month), additional monthly merchant card fees (sometimes as high as $90 monthly), and setup fees. PayPal provides a calculator to compare typical website transaction fees when using a standard bank credit card and PayPal.

Billing With PayPal

PayPal allows you to create invoices that enable your customers (even those who know nothing about PayPal) to use the system. You can create invoices in several ways:

- **Email.** Create an email invoice by filling out PayPal's online invoice form.
- **Request Money.** Use PayPal's Request Money page to send a customer an invoice directly from PayPal.
- **QuickBooks.** Use the Payment Request Wizard for *QuickBooks* which enables you to create an invoice from within your QuickBooks program.
- **Outlook.** Use the Payment Request Wizard for *Outlook* which enables you to create an invoice from within your Microsoft Outlook email program.

PayPal Auction Tools and Integration

PayPal is fully integrated with other popular auction management software, and its manual, the Website Payments Standard Integration Guide, explains all of the tools and methods by which you can incorporate PayPal into your auction experience. In addition to the invoicing wizards described above, these Auction Tools include:

- **Logo insertion.** Using PayPal's logo insertion system, the PayPal logo is automatically inserted in your eBay auction listing.
- **Seller protection.** PayPal's seller protection system includes anti-fraud protection and a dispute resolution process.
- **Buyer protection.** PayPal's buyer protection program prevents unauthorized payments from a PayPal account, provides a dispute resolution process, and offers up to $1,000 in buyer protection with sellers who participate in the buyer protection program. To qualify, sellers must meet certain qualifications, including at least a 98% positive feedback rating.
- **Reporting tools.** PayPal's extensive reporting tools enable you to download and keep track of your eBay transactions and payment history.
- **Refund tool.** PayPal's refund tool makes it fairly simple to provide refunds when necessary.
- **PayPal shipping services.** These services are described in more detail in Chapter 17, *Shipping and Returns.*

Rules, Disputes, and Feedback

eBay Rules... 110

Common eBay Frauds..113

Avoiding Auction Frauds.. 114

Resolving Common Disputes 115

Small Claims Court Usually Won't Work.. 119

Feedback 119

A Final Warning About Feedback.. 124

What's a Detailed Seller Rating?.. 124

F irst, the bottom line: eBay is a community with rules. Violators of these rules may find their listings canceled, account privileges limited or suspended, or PowerSeller status revoked. When disputes arise between buyers and sellers—typically over a winning bidder's failure to pay for an item, a seller's failure to deliver an item, or the state of an item when delivered—eBay and PayPal provide various means of resolving the disputes and providing compensation. Additionally, the eBay feedback system, although not perfect, allows buyers to rate sellers—although changes instituted in 2008 prevent sellers from leaving negative feedback about buyers.

eBay Rules

eBay's structure is built on the assumptions that people are basically trustworthy, and buyers and sellers will conduct business with fairness and cordiality. However, to ensure compliance with its community values, eBay has instituted rules. You may never need to refer to the eBay rule book, but you should be aware that just about every element of every eBay activity is governed by these rules. The most commonly referenced rules are listed alphabetically below with a brief description. The links provided on the left will take you directly to the full eBay rule.

eBay Community Rules and Guidelines	
Community content policy	When posting on eBay discussion and chat boards (or any other eBay sponsored posting site—for example, eBay's Wiki), you are not permitted to promote products or services outside of eBay or to violate any of the community values or other rules.
Discussion board usage policy	Users of eBay discussion boards must adhere to <u>eBay's Community Values</u> (which basically follow the principle "Do unto others as you would have done unto you.")
eBay groups guidelines	You can create your own eBay Group to communicate with other members about a shared interest, but you must follow eBay guidelines regarding formation and membership.
Email threats	You cannot use email or feedback to threaten another eBay member with physical harm.
Employee trading and community content policy	eBay employees must follow certain rules when participating in eBay auctions.
False contact information	eBay members cannot falsify or omit contact information.
Final value fee credit abuse	A seller cannot falsely report an unpaid item.
International selling	Members cannot violate the laws of any country in which they are buying or selling.
Invalid bid retraction	Only in rare instances can a buyer retract a bid.
Offers to buy or sell outside of eBay	You cannot bypass eBay fees by buying or selling listed items outside of eBay. This includes terminating an auction to sell to the highest bidder or offering duplicate merchandise to underbidders.
Previously suspended users	Suspension results in the loss of all eBay privileges.
Profanity	eBay does not permit profanity except when reproducing media titles that contain vulgar language.

eBay Community Rules and Guidelines (continued)	
Prohibited items	eBay prohibits the sale or purchase of a wide range of items including live animals, firearms, drugs, fireworks, alcohol, tobacco, lottery tickets, and potentially infringing merchandise. If you are in doubt about an item, check eBay's prohibited and restricted items list before proceeding.
Seller nonperformance	A seller must honor the auction contract—that is, fulfill the obligation and sell and ship the item to the winning bidder.
Shill bidding	Shill bidding—when a seller (or seller's accomplice) artificially increases the price or value of a listing, usually by bidding on it—is prohibited on eBay.
Site interference	You cannot mess with the eBay site or eBay-generated content unless permitted to do so by eBay.
Site outage policy	eBay has rules for protecting buyers and sellers if the eBay site goes down temporarily.
Tax policy	eBay members are responsible for all applicable taxes and fees associated with their sales or purchases.
Transaction interference	Generally, you cannot interfere with another person's transaction, either by contacting a buyer or seller or by offering to purchase a listed item outside of eBay.
Unpaid items	A buyer who wins an auction is legally obligated to buy the item. Sellers can file an unpaid item dispute.
Unsolicited email (spam)	eBay doesn't permit unsolicited commercial emailing.
Unsolicited idea submissions	eBay does not solicit new ideas for its site and if ideas are submitted without being solicited, the company will not guarantee that the information will be kept secret.
Unwelcome buying/ bidding	Buyers can't disrupt listings or bid on an item if they do not meet the listing criteria.
Using eBay intellectual property	Unless authorized to do so, you cannot freely use the eBay logo or other trademarks.

Common eBay Frauds

Occasionally, abusive behavior by at eBay members goes beyond rule-breaking and may include illegal activity or attempts to defraud or harm other members. Some common eBay frauds include:

- **Transaction interception.** This occurs when a perpetrator pretends to be the seller (or an eBay employee) and contacts the winner of an auction requesting payment or fees. (This fraud practice is much less common since PayPal became the payment standard).

- **Fraudulent bid retraction.** Bidders may fraudulently retract a bid, either as a means of learning another bidder's maximum bid or as part of a "bid shielding" enterprise in which the perpetrator retracts a ridiculously high bid at the last moment, thereby allowing an accomplice to buy the item at a much lower price.

- **Sales of <u>stolen</u> or <u>counterfeit</u> goods.** Unscrupulous sellers continue to offer these illegal items to unknowing buyers despite eBay's efforts to prohibit sales of stolen and counterfeit items.

- **Phishing or eBay or PayPal Spoofs.** Con artists often send fake emails to eBay members pretending to be from eBay or PayPal and requesting sensitive financial or personal information. The goal may be to obtain payment information or membership information (in order to impersonate the member for an unscrupulous purpose).

- **Feedback extortion.** This occurs when an eBay member threatens to post negative feedback unless unfair demands are met.

- **Shill bidding.** Shill bidding happens when a seller uses multiple identities (or has accomplices) to artificially jack up the price or value of an item.

Avoiding Auction Frauds

Various tools exist to protect eBay members, especially buyers, from fraud. The three tips below can help you protect yourself in your eBay transactions.

Review eBay guides. eBay provides a great deal of help and advice for common frauds within its help system. If you visit the eBay Reviews and Guides home page and enter "fraud" in the search box, you'll find over 600 guides on buying and selling items in almost every eBay category, including tips on avoiding fraud in that category. Other websites, including Auctionblacklist.com and AuctionBytes also offer help to members in avoiding auction misconduct and fraud.

Use Escrow.com. An escrow service sends a buyer's money to a seller only according to agreed-upon escrow instructions. Even though such services are not involved in dispute resolution, they often help to avoid disputes between buyer and seller when it comes to big-ticket (over $100) items. Beware of fraudulent escrow services, however. The only eBay-authorized service is escrow.com.

Buy from BuySafe sellers. BuySafe is a bonding service that guarantees a buyer will be reimbursed in the event of fraud or any other nondelivery issue with a seller. Buying from a BuySafe-bonded seller is a guarantee that you will not lose money on the transaction (at least up to $25,000). BuySafe's seal, and the accompanying statement "Bonded Seller, Protected Transaction Guaranteed to $25,000," can be used only by sellers who meet BuySafe's standards. BuySafe issues its surety bonds through a surety company, Liberty Mutual, and the qualification process for sellers is rigorous.

TIP

BuySafe urges buyers to click on the BuySafe seal to make sure that the merchant actually is bonded. When you verify a BuySafe seal by clicking on it in the item listing, you should see the URL http://www.buysafe.com/verifyseal.asp in your browser address bar.

Resolving Common Disputes

When members run into disputes with each other, eBay tries to help sort them out. Listed below are some common eBay transaction disputes and how eBay recommends they be resolved.

Unpaid item. Occasionally, a winning bidder may fail to pay for an item. In that event, the seller may, within 45 days after the end of the auction, file an <u>Unpaid Item Dispute</u> and receive a <u>Final Value Fee Credit</u> (a credit because a buyer backed out). You must be signed in to your eBay account in order to file. Normally, the seller must wait seven days to file the dispute form, but that delay is not required if the buyer is no longer registered with eBay or if the seller and buyer mutually withdraw from the transaction (even though there is no actual "dispute" in this case).

Item not received (or received but significantly not as described). eBay has a <u>procedure for resolving disputes</u> when the winning bidder fails to receive the item or the item received is "significantly not as described" (SNAD). If you are the winning bidder, you may first attempt to resolve the matter with a written demand on the seller. Although you should tailor the tone of any demand to fit the situation—sometimes there are extenuating circumstances for a seller—the sample auction demand letter <u>template</u>, shown below, may serve as the basis for your demand letter.

Online Auction Buyer Demand Letter

Date: _____

To: [*Name of seller*] _____

[*Address of seller*] _____

_____

I am writing to you regarding the dispute that has arisen over [*description of item purchased*] for which I was high bidder on the auction at [*name of auction site*] as Item No. [*number of item at auction site*].

A dispute has arisen because [*describe the reason you are dissatisfied with your purchase in as much detail as possible*] _____

_____

I would like to resolve the matter as follows:

[*Choose one*]

☐ I will return the item to you via [*describe the shipping method*] and request a refund from you in the amount of $_____ which includes the following costs [*list all costs for which you are seeking compensation, for example, shipping item to you, shipping item back to buyer, amount paid for item, etc.*]

☐ I will keep the item, but for the following reasons [*specify reasons for price reduction, for example, partial damage, not as advertised, and include proof such as photos of item*] I request a partial refund of $_____ .

☐ I seek a full refund of all monies paid as I never received the item.

Please make payment by [*specify the method by which payment shall be made to you; for example, if payment to seller was made by credit card, seek a charge back; if payment was made by money order, seek a money order, etc.*]

Online Auction Buyer Demand Letter (continued)

If you disagree with my request and would like to resolve the matter through a third party dispute resolution procedure, I am prepared to use online dispute resolution procedures at:

☐ SquareTrade (www.squaretrade.com)

☐ iCourthouse, (www.i-courthouse.com)

☐ clikNsettle (www.clicknsettle.com)

☐ other [*list online dispute resolution website*]

If I do not hear back from you by [*date*] _____ I shall presume that you do not wish to resolve the matter and I shall:

☐ seek a charge back on my credit card [*if payment was made by credit card*]

☐ file an online incident report at the National Fraud Information Center (www.fraud.org)

☐ post negative feedback at your online auction site

Signature: _____

Address: _____

_____

Email: _____

Assuming all attempts at resolution have failed—for example, you and the seller have already communicated without a satisfactory resolution—then eBay will step in, contact the seller, and seek to resolve the matter once you file an "Item Not Received or Significantly Not as Described" dispute. If you are given the choice to escalate this to an official eBay claim, eBay's Trust and Safety Team is alerted and your claim may result in the seller's account being closed.

For additional purchase protection, you may also consider eBay insurance. As a buyer, you may be entitled to a payment of up to $200 (minus a $25 processing fee) under eBay's free Standard Purchase Protection Plan for nondelivery or delivery of an unsatisfactory item. PayPal offers a similar program for payments made through PayPal. In addition, if the phrase "Free PayPal Buyer Protection" is displayed in the seller's listing, you may also request reimbursement from PayPal under PayPal's buyer protection plan.

Mutual feedback withdrawal. If members have a dispute over the content of feedback one or both write, they can mutually agree to withdraw it under eBay's mutual feedback withdrawal process. This differs from the process whereby eBay will remove the feedback if it violates the feedback abuse rules. You may also be able to get feedback removed if you invite the other party to participate in a SquareTrade mediation, described below, and the other party refuses. There are also special procedures for independent feedback review of eBay Motors transactions. There's more on feedback rules later in this chapter.

SquareTrade. SquareTrade is an independent online dispute resolution service that offers impartial mediation services for eBay users. The SquareTrade process requires the disputing parties' consent to the mediation. An impartial mediator guides the parties to a final resolution. The party requesting the mediation must pay a fee of approximately $30; there are no additional charges for participating in the mediation.

Small Claims Court Usually Won't Work

Can a defrauded eBay buyer take the matter to a local <u>small claims court</u>? The key is whether the court will have personal jurisdiction over the seller; that is, the legal right to pass judgment on the seller's action. If the seller is in the same state as the buyer (or has sufficient "commercial contacts" with that state), the small claims court may have jurisdiction and the buyer can file the matter in that state's small claims court.

Usually, that's not the case. For example, in a 2007 case, a New York judge ruled that New York did not have personal jurisdiction over a Missouri eBay seller. In that case, the Missouri seller had sold a defective Chevy 350 engine to a New York City resident. In order to have jurisdiction, the judge ruled, the seller would have had to have transacted business in New York City or had more than one transaction with a New York resident on eBay.

A buyer can always solve the personal jurisdiction problem by filing a suit in a small claims court in the seller's home state. The process of traveling to another state to file a claim, however, is often too expensive to merit the lawsuit. Even if a buyer wins a case in small claims court, the buyer may still have to go through the process of forcing the seller to pay the judgment, a time-consuming process known as <u>enforcing the judgment</u>. Except in the case of high-value items, pursuing a small claims action over an eBay transaction is probably too cumbersome for most buyers and sellers. You can read more about <u>personal jurisdiction</u> at the <u>Nolo</u> website.

Feedback

Feedback is an indication of how other eBay members have judged another member's handling of a transaction. For the first decade of eBay, sellers and buyers could leave positive or negative feedback for each other. But that all changed in 2008, when eBay revamped its feedback system to curb what the company referred to as "a disturbing trend of sellers using it to retaliate against buyers by giving them low ratings." eBay claimed that this discouraged buyers from leaving honest feedback and ultimately drove many of them away from eBay.

In May 2008 eBay instituted a new system: sellers can only leave positive feedback for buyers. In other words, a seller cannot leave negative feedback about a buyer. To counterbalance this change, eBay plans to continue and enhance some existing protections for sellers against inaccurate feedback from buyers, such as removing negative and neutral feedback when a buyer fails to respond to an "unpaid item" inquiry. In addition, eBay will remove all the negative and neutral feedback from buyers who are suspended.

Still, beware that unscrupulous buyers may abuse the feedback system by threatening to leave negative feedback about you if you complain about their handling of a transaction. If this occurs, refer to the feedback resolution and abuse procedures described above.

In addition to the "no negative feedback against buyers" rule, eBay instituted the following additional changes:

- Positive repeat customer feedback will count (up to 1 feedback from the same buyer per week.)
- Feedback more than 12-months old won't count towards a seller's feedback percentage.
- When a buyer doesn't respond to the unpaid item (UPI) process, the negative or neutral feedback they have left for that transaction will be removed.
- When a member is suspended, all their negative and neutral feedback will be removed.
- Buyers must wait 3 days before leaving negative or neutral feedback for sellers with an established track record, to encourage communication.

- All feedback must be left within 60 days (compared to 90 days previously) of listing end to encourage timely feedback and discourage abuse.
- Buyers will be held more accountable when sellers report an unpaid item or commit other policy violations.

Below is an example of how feedback is presented in an item's listing, with a summary score and detailed comments accessible to buyers through the link "See detailed feedback."

Buy safely

1. Check the seller's reputation
Score: 103 | 100% Positive
See detailed feedback

Entering feedback is fairly straightforward. You can do so by first clicking the My eBay tab and then clicking the Leave Feedback tab.

Feedback may also be entered on the item's auction page or the member's feedback page. Once on the page, choose whether your comment is positive, negative, or neutral; write in your thoughts and click "Leave Feedback."

While the process of writing comments is easy, what you say and when you say it may require more thought. Some tips to remember about feedback are listed below:

- **Have patience.** An eBay member may have suffered a personal setback and cannot complete the transaction right away. Always try to resolve misunderstandings before posting negative feedback. If you're really angry, always wait 24 hours before posting negative feedback.

- **Read what others are saying about a member before posting negative comments.** If your experience differs drastically from what others are saying, perhaps you should make another attempt at resolving the matter.
- **Be as specific as possible in your comments about what you liked (or did not like).** Generic statements such as "Great deal" or "A++ plus seller" (or any posting with an abundance of exclamation points) does not help others learn about the eBay member.
- **Keep it short.** If you had a problem, summarize it in two sentences. Do not exaggerate. Be professional. Do not make personal attacks.

You are not required to leave feedback. However, the eBay community expects it, as feedback helps other members and the effectiveness of the eBay process. The trick is to make your feedback suitable, succinct, and honest. Keep in mind one important rule: *It is extremely difficult to change feedback once it's posted.* While some feedback may be removed by eBay or by mutual agreement of members, generally, feedback that is posted on eBay, stays on eBay.

eBay assembles the feedback given for a particular member to create a <u>feedback</u> rating. That rating is visible by a member's name whenever that member posts or bids on items. Every positive rating is worth one point; for instance, the 93 shown above indicates that the member has had at least 93 positive ratings. A neutral rating earns zero points and a negative comment takes a point away. A user with a rating of minus four is terminated.

The star icon next to the feedback rating is a color-coded classification of your feedback rating; you get your first star (a yellow one) after achieving a rating of 10. As the number increases, the color of the star changes until you receive a rating over 100,000 (a red shooting star).

You can make your feedback profile private instead of public, but that will not endear you to buyers or sellers, who will be suspicious of your reasons for doing so.

To evaluate another member's reputation, click on the member's User ID or the number in parentheses next to it, which will bring up the member's feedback page. The page lists comments about the member over various time periods. For additional insight on the information, see eBay's guide for evaluating a member's reputation.

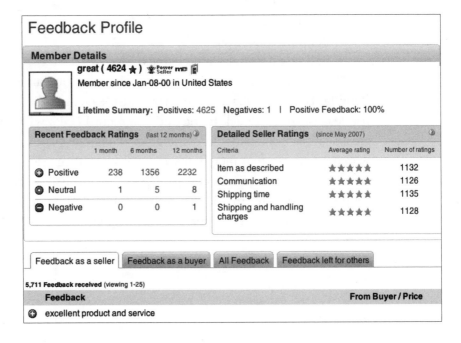

A Final Warning About Feedback

If you're a buyer and you fail to pay for an item, any feedback you leave about the seller—under feedback privilege rules—may be blocked from the seller's feedback score.

You may also lose feedback privileges—and much more—if you participate in feedback extortion—threatening to leave negative feedback about a seller unless that seller provides something not included in the original transaction.

What's a Detailed Seller Rating?

In addition to leaving feedback about a seller, a buyer can now also leave detailed seller ratings (DSRs) in four areas:

- item as described
- communication
- shipping time, and
- shipping and handling charges.

The system uses one- to five-star scale, and you can leave DSR from the Leave Feedback page. (You must leave it at the same time you leave your feedback rating and comment.) DSRs will have a greater impact on sellers in coming years as eBay plans to alter its search engine so that merchants with lower DSRs get less exposure on search results and sellers with higher buyer satisfaction ratings get better exposure. In addition, sellers who continue to score low DSR may be required to offer safe purchasing options.

eBay Motors

What Is eBay Motors? 126

Selling on eBay Motors 126

Buying a Car on eBay Motors 128

Quicklist: Selling a Car on eBay Motors 130

F irst, the bottom line: eBay Motors must be doing something right. Every minute a car is sold there—over $6 billion in revenue a year. eBay Motors operates like the typical eBay auction experience, with a few exceptions—for example, sellers of cars and other vehicles can lower their reserve price or offer a Buy-It-Now price after a listing has received bids.

What Is eBay Motors?

eBay Motors is the number-one automotive site on the Internet. It's estimated that 40% of the time consumers spend looking for cars online is spent at eBay Motors. There you will find every type of vehicle and automotive part, from sedans to jet skis to motorcycles to SUVs to RVs. Best of all, eBay Motors combines unique research features and protection plans with eBay's popular listing tools. (There's even a listing tool that can pre-fill features of vehicles on post-1981 vehicles.)

Selling on eBay Motors

Selling basics. eBay Motors does a great job preparing sellers. (There's even an <u>audio tour</u>.) You can find everything you need to know at the <u>How to Sell</u> page. No special registration is required other than the typical eBay member registration described in Chapter 2, *Getting Started*. You will need to complete the <u>Sell Your Vehicle checklist</u>, and you may also want to request a <u>vehicle history report</u> (for under $10).

Photos, photos, photos. One difference between listings at eBay Motors and typical eBay auction listings is the number of photographs. Expect to provide ten to 20 images. Buyers use the photographs to get a tour of the vehicle, including all views of the exterior and interior—for example, a close-up of the odometer.

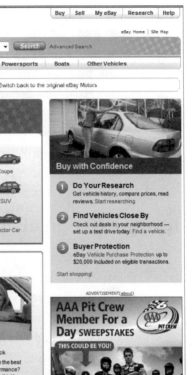

You can revise the price after you get bids. If you are selling a vehicle in the Cars & Trucks, Motorcycles, Other Vehicles, or Powersports categories, you can revise your item price after bidding begins. You can remove or revise your reserve price, or you can add a Buy-It-Now price.

If you're selling more than one vehicle. If you are selling several vehicles on eBay Motors, you may have to be licensed as a dealer or run the risk of violating your state's laws. For example, in Florida, anyone selling three or more vehicles within a 12-month period is presumed to be a dealer. You can find rules about most states dealership laws at DMV.org.

Moving a car dealership online. If you are a dealership planning to move online, eBay is eager to help. It provides a <u>special section where dealers can get started</u> and a <u>Dealer Center</u> for additional information and solutions.

Fixed fees. Sellers pay an <u>insertion fee</u> ($40 for passenger vehicles) and a transaction services fee ($40 for passenger vehicles, charged when the first bid is made on a listing without a reserve price or when your reserve price is met). There is no additional fee after the vehicle is sold.

Buying a Car on eBay Motors

Buying basics. You can pick up all the basics for buying on eBay Motors at the <u>How to Buy</u> page. Some good news for car buyers: eBay offers free <u>vehicle purchase protection</u> for up to $20,000 or the vehicle purchase price, whichever is lower. Check for <u>eligibility</u>.

Search and you will find. Searching for vehicles and auto parts is similar to searching at the regular eBay auction site, with a few variations. You can use the <u>advanced search</u> feature, in which you search using common keywords or brands such as "Chevrolet" or terms such as "Z4," or you may have better luck using the <u>eBay Motors Categories search page</u> (see below), in which you choose from a series of drop-down menus or enter information. If you want to find all the Honda minivans within 100 miles of your city, it's easy.

Paying for the purchase. Payment—at least a deposit, comprising a partial payment—is expected with 72 hours after the sale. Buyers can use PayPal for the deposit. Then buyer and seller must work out payment of the balance. Most sellers require a certified check, money order, or some type of financing. And wouldn't you know it? eBay offers financing through the <u>eBay Financing Center</u>. Once the purchase is completed, the seller transfers title to the buyer, who must pay all required taxes on the vehicle.

eBay Motors Category Search Page

Search: By eBay Motors Categories   Customize search options

Learn more about saving favorite searches.

Search

Items
· Find Items
· **By eBay Motors Categories**
· Items by Seller
· Items by Bidder
· By Item Number

Stores
· Items in Stores
· Find Stores

Members
· Find a Member
· Find Contact Information

💡 For more results try leaving some of the search options blank.

What are you looking for?

Cars & Trucks
Motorcycles
Parts & Access
Powersports

Vehicle make
Any

Vehicle model

Vehicle year
From: To:

Transmission type
Any

Enter keyword or item number

☐ Search title **and** description   ☐ Completed listings only   ☐ Save this search to My eBay

Items near me
☐ Items within [500] miles of

ZIP or Postal Code [94710]   or [Select a popular city...]

Sort by   **View results**   **Results per page**
[Time: ending soonest]   [All items]   [50]

(Search)   Clear search

Honk! Honk! Your car has arrived. Commonly, the buyer must make delivery arrangements and pay for picking up or shipping the vehicle. Some sellers provide estimates of shipping costs to various locations around the country. eBay also suggests a shipping service, Dependable Auto Shippers, which can provide an online quote for shipment.

Quicklist: Selling a Car on eBay Motors

The Quicklist, below, gives you an example of the information that is required when listing a vehicle on eBay Motors.

Selling a Car on eBay Motors	
VIN (your vehicle identification number, commonly 17-digits)	
Mileage	
Year	
Make	
Model	
Engine cylinders	(circle one) 3 | 4 | 5 | 6 | 8 | 10 | 12
Title type	(circle one) Clear | Salvage | Other
Transmission	(circle one) Manual | Automatic
Warranty	(circle one) Existing | None
Are you the original owner or do you know the ownership history?	☐ Yes ☐ No
Have you made any modifications to the car: accessories, wheels, etc.?	☐ Yes ☐ No
Do you have maintenance records on the vehicle?	☐ Yes ☐ No
Do you have a warranty?	☐ Yes ☐ No If yes, provide details about remaining coverage and transferability: _____ _____ _____
Do you have the title available?	☐ Yes ☐ No If no, specify timing and availability: _____ _____

Selling a Car on eBay Motors (continued)

Is there any condition not shown in your vehicle photos: mechanical, interior, exterior, cigarette odor?	☐ Yes ☐ No If yes, describe: _____ _____
Does your vehicle feature any unique customization or added accessories that you'd like to showcase?	☐ Yes ☐ No If yes, describe: _____ _____
Have you performed any recent maintenance on the vehicle, such as tire replacement or major service?	☐ Yes ☐ No If yes, describe: _____ _____
Are there any current mechanical or cosmetic issues or near-future needed maintenance (like tires)?	☐ Yes ☐ No If yes, describe: _____ _____
Do you have any of these?	☐ Anti Lock Brakes (ABS) ☐ Air Conditioning ☐ Cruise Control ☐ Dual Front Air Bags ☐ Dual Power Seats ☐ Leather Seats ☐ Moon Roof ☐ Multi Compact Disc ☐ Navigation System ☐ Power Door Locks ☐ Power Windows ☐ Premium Sound ☐ Tilt Wheel ☐ Traction Control
Any specific time frame for sale or any payment conditions?	☐ Yes ☐ No If yes, describe: _____ _____
Will you accept escrow payments?	☐ Yes ☐ No

Selling a Car on eBay Motors (continued)	
Any other paperwork required for a legal sale of a vehicle in your area (such as smog inspection)?	☐ Yes ☐ No If yes, describe: _____ _____
Starting price	$_____
Reserve price (the minimum you will accept)	$_____
Have you checked similar vehicles on eBay for pricing information?	$_____ $_____ $_____
Have you checked the Kelley Blue Book price?	$_____
Have you prepared a variety of photos that show the following views?	Exterior: ☐ left side ☐ right side ☐ front ☐ rear Interior: ☐ front seats ☐ back seats ☐ trunk ☐ dashboard Other: ☐ engine bay ☐ odometer close-up ☐ any customization ☐ wear/damage

Auction Management Tools

Desktop or Web-Based Tools.. 134

What Do Auction Management Tools Do?... 134

What Software Tools Do You Need?... 135

Quicklist: Software Tools... 135

Popular Auction Management Programs 138

eBay.. 138

Vendio 139

Auction Hawk... 139

Marketworks 140

Auctiva.. 140

InkFrog.. 140

More Information ... If You Want It... 140

Yes, There Are More eBay Tools.. 141

First, the bottom line: If you want to become a power seller—that is, generate at least $1,000 per month in eBay sales—you will likely need auction management tools, software that automates common eBay procedures such as adding listings, managing photos, responding to emails and feedback, shipping out merchandise, and managing inventory. If you're only intending to sell a few items a month, however, you probably won't need these aids.

Desktop or Web-Based Tools

There are two types of auction management tools: downloadable desktop applications and web-based applications. The advantage of a desktop application is that you do not need Internet access to manage your inventory or handle other tasks. Additionally, your data is stored on your computer, not online, which may offer you more peace of mind. The advantage of using a web-based program is that you can manage your eBay business and access your records anywhere, including at your local coffee shop or in an airport. Note, however, that there are software products, such as *GoToMyPC*, that allow you to access your desktop programs while away from home.

What Do Auction Management Tools Do?

Just as programs like *Quicken* and *Money* centralize all your financial information and tasks, auction management tools create a computer "headquarters" for all of your online auction activity. Think of these programs as a dashboard of your common eBay tasks. Using them, you can automate the process for listing items and you can post items in groups. You can even set the program so that it lists the items on eBay while you are at your day job.

You can modify photos and store them for easy access online. You can manage your inventory by accurately tracking what's sold and what isn't. You can calculate eBay fees before you post an item for auction. And you can integrate your inventory and sales information with financial software like *QuickBooks* or with spreadsheet software such as *Excel*.

What Software Tools Do You Need?

Auction management tools come in so many forms with so many features, zeroing in on what elements are really necessary for your eBay business may be difficult. If you need help figuring out which auction management features and tools you need for your eBay business, review the Quicklist, below.

Quicklist: Software Tools

The Quicklist, below, may help you narrow down the software tools you need. Check the items you feel could be important to you and then review the software tools listed in this chapter to see which are right for you. If you're not sure whether you need certain functionality, don't worry about it for now (you probably won't need it at this point). Just keep in mind the features that are of greatest importance.

Quicklist: Software Tools What eBay Functionality Do You Need?		
Do you want a desktop application (so you won't need to be connected to the Internet to manage your inventory and perform related tasks)?	☐ Yes	☐ No
Do you want a web-based application (so you can manage your auctions at any computer connected to the Internet)?	☐ Yes	☐ No
Will you be listing multiple versions of the same item for sale (that is, will you be doing bulk listings)?	☐ Yes	☐ No
Do you need support for multiple users (so employees or partners can also manage the site)?	☐ Yes	☐ No
Are you dealing with primarily one-of-a-kind items?	☐ Yes	☐ No
Do you need auction templates (preset artwork and layouts to make your listings more appealing)?	☐ Yes	☐ No
Would you like image hosting assistance? (This permits you to crop, resize and add photos more efficiently.)	☐ Yes	☐ No
Do you want the ability to create fixed-price listings?	☐ Yes	☐ No
Do you want the ability to preview listings before submitting them?	☐ Yes	☐ No
Do you need support for listings for multiple sites?	☐ Yes	☐ No
Do you want to import existing items from eBay (as well as your auction history)?	☐ Yes	☐ No
Do you want to be able to schedule when a listing will be submitted?	☐ Yes	☐ No
Do you want a WYSIWYG editor (that allows you to accurately view what you're doing as you work)?	☐ Yes	☐ No
Do you want to generate monthly profit and loss reports?	☐ Yes	☐ No
Do you want to export reports to *Excel*?	☐ Yes	☐ No
Do you want to manage your inventory?	☐ Yes	☐ No
Do you want to reschedule or cancel listings?	☐ Yes	☐ No

What eBay Functionality Do You Need? (continued)		
Do you want to be notified when sales end?	☐ Yes	☐ No
Do you want to track unsold items?	☐ Yes	☐ No
Do you want to provide bulk relisting of unsold items?	☐ Yes	☐ No
Do you want to manage customer information—for example, do you need customer contact card file software?	☐ Yes	☐ No
Do you want to track sales information (that is, do you need a program that alerts you as sales occur and that tracks sales numbers)?	☐ Yes	☐ No
Do you want customizable email templates (for example, commonly used statements about purchases or shipping)?	☐ Yes	☐ No
Do you want to communicate with buyers at various stages after completing the sale (for example, after being paid or after shipping)?	☐ Yes	☐ No
Do you want to send email in bulk?	☐ Yes	☐ No
Do you want to automatically send email notifications following payment or shipment?	☐ Yes	☐ No
Do you want to track and respond to non-paying bidders (NPBs)?	☐ Yes	☐ No
Do you want to maintain and use customized feedback messages?	☐ Yes	☐ No
Do you want to automatically generate feedback following payment?	☐ Yes	☐ No
Do you want to leave bulk feedback?	☐ Yes	☐ No
Do you want to track feedback?	☐ Yes	☐ No
Do you want to print shipping labels?	☐ Yes	☐ No
Do you want to print invoices?	☐ Yes	☐ No
Do you want to print invoices and labels in bulk?	☐ Yes	☐ No
Do you need automated help for NPBs or a request for a final value fee credit (FVF)?	☐ Yes	☐ No

What eBay Functionality Do You Need? (continued)	
Do you want automated reminders (for example, to track the next step in a sales transaction)?	☐ Yes ☐ No
Do you want to leave notes and comments (viewable only by you) regarding transactions?	☐ Yes ☐ No
If using a web-based tool, do you want your data stored for an unlimited period of time?	☐ Yes ☐ No ☐ N/A
Do you want snapshots (for example, a summary of pending, active, and sold listings)?	☐ Yes ☐ No
Do you want to customize how you view information (for example, to set the program to show you only specific categories)?	☐ Yes ☐ No

Popular Auction Management Programs

While dozens of auction management programs have been developed for eBay users, listed here are the companies that provide the most popular tools. Many of these are available on a trial or demo basis so you can test them out (and don't forget to read user reviews). Keep in mind that most of these programs require ongoing payments or subscription fees, and many include per-transaction fees.

eBay

eBay offers a variety of web-based and desktop management programs, such as Turbo Lister, which allows you to create listings in bulk; Selling Manager, which allows you to monitor listings, manage feedback and email, print invoices, and print labels; and Selling Manager Pro which does everything that Selling Manager does, plus manage inventory and provide profit and loss information.

In addition to these web-based tools, eBay offers desktop applications that accomplish similar tasks (*Blackthorne Basic, Blackthorne Pro,* and *Seller's Assistant Basic* and *Seller's Assistant Pro*). You can learn more about these Tools for Success at the eBay website, which also offers a comparison chart of eBay tools' features. eBay can help you sort through its software options with its tool recommendations wizard.

One eBay tool that's definitely worth highlighting is eBay's Turbo Lister, a program that enables you to schedule, preview, and post many listings at once. Not only is the program useful for mid- and high-volume sellers, it's free!

Vendio

Vendio offers web-based and desktop solutions, including *Sales Manager Inventory Edition,* for eBay sellers of multiple units of the same item (also known as "multiple quantity selling"), and *Sales Manager Merchandise Edition,* for sellers of unique items, such as one-of-a-kind collectibles. Vendio, which reportedly services $50 million in monthly eBay sales (and acquired the Andale software tools company), also has separate customer management tools (*Vendio Customer Manager*); image hosting services (*Vendio Image Hosting*); and revenue, profit and loss, tax, performance, cost, and customer reporting tools (*Vendio Reports*). Like some other software vendors, Vendio also offers web hosting and gallery services.

Auction Hawk

Auction Hawk is one of the few web-based tools offered at a flat fee. Services include the usual image hosting, templates (providing smart layouts and backgrounds for auction listings), email, a feedback scraper (that scours your listings and reports on buyers who are more likely to leave negative feedback), feedback management, gallery, inventory, and PayPal integration.

Marketworks

Marketworks offers a web-based, all-in-one management tool. Their services assist in listings, inventory management, email, feedback, and relistings and provide gallery and image hosting as well as counters to record the number of visitors.

Auctiva

If you plan on selling beyond eBay, for example, on Amazon and Yahoo, then check Auctiva's web-based and desktop tools. Auctiva's software can track listings on all of the sites as well as assist in creating postings for these sites. All of the expected functionality is here, including inventory management, scheduling, image hosting, and counters.

InkFrog

InkFrog was one of the first companies to offer a lower-priced web-based auction management system for a flat fee. The company offers, among other services, unlimited auction scheduling, image hosting, inventory, consignment, automatic relisting of items after an auction ends, and templates for winning bidder emails.

More Information ... If You Want It

While the number of software tools available for auctioneers (a quick search yielded over 60 products) is a tribute to eBay's success, how do you determine what products are right for you? Start at the Auction Software Review website, where you can learn about every type of auction software program and read user reviews. You must register to use the website, but it is free and members get discounts on some software. You can also find advice at the AuctionBytes website, which has a comparison chart of web-based auction management programs and services.

Other resources include <u>Solution Finder</u>, an interactive web application that helps you find the software you need based on your selling goals, and Debra and Brad Schepp's book, *eBay Power Seller Secrets* (McGraw-Hill/Osborne), which contains advice about auction management tools in Chapter 4.

Yes, There Are More eBay Tools

In addition to auction management programs, there are other applications and tools for eBay activities. Some of these tools augment tasks performed by auction management software, and some actually integrate with the software. For example, some auction programs can export information to an accounting program such as *QuickBooks*. These tools include:

- **Market research and analysis tools.** These products enable you to search and analyze information about completed auctions—for example, what items are selling and for how much. There's more discussion about these types of tools in Chapter 4, *What Will You Sell?*
- **Marketing software.** These tools help you promote your items to buyers by enhancing your listings, emailing certain buyers with information about your items, creating discount coupons, and helping you design and post eBay advertisements. There's more discussion about these tools in Chapter 12, *Become a PowerSeller.*
- **Buyers' tools/sniping.** These products make the buying process less complicated by enhancing searching ability and monitoring auctions. Sniping software enables buyers to bid during the very last moments of an auction. There's more discussion about these tools in Chapter 6, *Buy an Item.*
- **Miscellaneous tools.** Various utility tools help with specific eBay tasks. For example, you can use a free online fee calculator at <u>eB Calc</u>. The Hammertap company offers a free program, <u>BidderBlock</u>, which allows you to create a list of bidders to be blocked from your eBay auctions. ●

Become a PowerSeller

The Elite World of PowerSellers... 144

Ten Things PowerSellers Have in Common 145

Driving Traffic to Your eBay Store or Website..................................... 150

Borrowing Money to Grow.. 154

Warning: Don't Become a Power Debtor.. 156

F irst, the bottom line: eBay prides itself on its egalitarian community, but does have its own elite class: PowerSellers. Being designated a PowerSeller generally means that your business has a high level of sales and your customers have had good experiences with you. Benefits of the designation include special treatment by eBay and the fact that future buyers are more likely to trust your business. For your eBay business to be designated a PowerSeller, average sales must reach at least $1,000 per month and you must meet other performance standards. Once you hit these markers, you'll likely get an invitation from eBay to join the elite.

The Elite World of PowerSellers

When you see the PowerSeller logo in an eBay listing, you can be sure of five <u>criteria</u>:

- **Sales.** The seller averages a minimum of $1,000 in gross monthly sales for three consecutive months (or 100 items per month for three consecutive months); and a minimum of $12,000 (or 1,200 items) for the prior twelve months.
- **Feedback.** The seller has had at least 100 overall responses or feedback on its transactions, and 98% or more of those responses are positive.
- **Active membership.** The seller has been an active eBay member for at least 90 days.
- **Good financial standing.** The seller has an eBay account that eBay considers "in good financial standing."
- **4.5 DSR.** The seller has a rating of 4.5 or more on all <u>DSRs</u> (based on the last 12 months).

The PowerSeller world has its own hierarchy—from Bronze level (sellers who average $1,000 per month in gross revenue) to Titanium level (sellers who average $150,000 per month). eBay reviews its PowerSellers' accounts every month to ensure they continue to meet PowerSeller standards. eBay has posted some FAQs if you want to learn more about PowerSellers.

eBay rewards those who reach PowerSeller status with special benefits, including access to PowerSeller conferences, bulletin boards, PowerSeller letterhead and business cards, health insurance solutions, invitations to special eBay events, and, of course, the right to display the PowerSeller logo on their listings. The logo is an important marketing tool, as it communicates stability and reliability, both important factors in online buying decisions.

Besides these more concrete benefits, attaining PowerSeller status implies that you have successfully grown your eBay business. If that is your aim, your strategy will be no different from that for realizing success in any small business. To do so, you need great products or services, effective marketing, and reliable customer service.

Achieving PowerSeller status comes down to some personal soul-searching and number-crunching questions: How big do you want your business to be? How hard are you willing to work? How much inventory can you finance and manage? How big is the market, and how much sales volume can you handle in a way that will satisfy customers? In other words, PowerSeller status is really about setting personal goals and figuring out how to achieve them.

Ten Things PowerSellers Have in Common

Many people have no interest in PowerSeller status, simply enjoying eBay as a hobby. But if your goal is to increase your online business, you can learn a lot from those who have attained PowerSeller status.

RESOURCE

Four books with PowerSeller strategies. Much has been written about increasing online sales, and you can find out specific strategies from the four popular books below:

- *eBay Business All-in-One Desk Reference for Dummies*, by Marsha Collier (Wiley)
- *eBay PowerSeller Secrets: Insider Tips from eBay's Most Successful Sellers*, by Debra Schepp and Brad Schepp (McGraw-Hill)
- *eBay Strategies: 10 Proven Methods to Maximize Your eBay Business*, by Scot Wingo (Prentice Hall)
- *How to Buy, Sell, and Profit on eBay: Kick-Start Your Home-Based Business in Just 30 Days*, by Adam Ginsberg (Collins)

There seem to be some common characteristics among those eBay businesses that have achieved PowerSeller status:

PowerSellers run businesses that reflect their personal interests. Whether it's the fascinating world of collectibles at Collecticom, the wholesale sports cards sold by BlowoutCards, or the wide-ranging variety of antiques offered at Anderson Valley Antiques, it's evident that PowerSellers tend to have some personal connection to the products they sell and a passion for their business. The more you are interested in what you do, the more likely you are to gain knowledge about it and improve your skills. Of course, any gain in knowledge and skill increases your chance of success. As PowerSeller Brad Schepp (author of *eBay PowerSeller Secrets*) notes, "There is no such thing as a PowerSeller who is lukewarm about his business."

That makes sense. Long before eBay existed, business guru Michael Phillips came to an interesting conclusion after analyzing 650 San Francisco Bay Area businesses. Owners who loved their type of business had a failure rate 70% lower than business owners primarily motivated by profits. Phillips concluded that business owners motivated primarily by profits quickly become disenchanted. So, whether it's collectible beer cans or oil paintings of pets, your chances of achieving PowerSeller status increase with your interest in your eBay business.

PowerSellers maintain an eBay store or website. Running auctions is rarely enough to achieve PowerSeller status. Instead, PowerSellers need a second Internet location for centralizing their selling activity.

As PowerSeller Marsha Collier, the author of *eBay Business: All-in-One Desk Reference for Dummies*, explains, "An eBay store provides you with your own little corner of eBay where you can leverage your good relationships with your customers and sell directly to them." Considering that eBay stores have over 60 million unique visitors per month, it's no wonder that PowerSellers seek to expand their presence using these online outlets. For more on eBay stores, see Chapter 7, *Open an eBay Store*. For more on attracting customers, see "Driving Traffic to Your eBay Store or Website," below.

PowerSellers know the rules. PowerSeller Adam Ginsberg, in his book *How to Buy, Sell, and Profit on eBay*, describes his early days selling pool tables on eBay. Ginsberg watched in horror as—minutes before they were to close—his auctions disappeared from eBay, causing him to lose thousands of dollars and angering customers. Why? Ginsberg's listings had violated various rules that Ginsberg was unaware of, and eBay pulled the plug. Keep in mind that eBay does not police listings for violations, but instead relies on other eBay users to report them. Rule breakers may be reported by community-minded eBay members seeking to maintain the quality of the eBay experience, or by a competitor eager to see your listings disappear. In any case, PowerSellers like Ginsberg quickly learn that a key to success is mastering rules of the eBay game. For more on eBay rules, see Chapter 9, *Rules, Disputes, and Feedback*.

PowerSellers keep learning. PowerSellers take advantage of every service and knowledge base available within eBay, such as its Learning Center, as well as third-party resources such as the AuctionBytes website and Marsha Collier's Cool eBay Tools newsletter. All eBay sellers seem to agree that the best advice about eBay comes from other eBay sellers in eBay Groups, the Community Answer Center, the Community Discussion Boards, and eBay user-created Reviews and Guides.

PowerSellers make their products stand out. An accepted truism among eBayers is that whatever you're selling, somebody else is selling it, too. Studying the competition may help you learn what factors will help to distinguish your items and auctions from others.

Additionally, PowerSeller Scott Wingo (author of *eBay Strategies*) suggests that effective selling strategies will always take into account what he calls the "Five Ps." Analyzing these five factors will help would-be PowerSellers best distinguish their products and auctions.

- **Product.** Have you analyzed every aspect of your product—that is, everything from its profit margin to its likely customers?
- **Price.** What's the price that will allow you to make a profit while staying competitive?
- **Promotion.** How can you better promote and market your products?
- **Placement.** How can you best place the product, whether in a category, auction, website, or eBay store?
- **Performance.** How effective are your activities in increasing sales and profits? PowerSellers continually analyze what is and is not working in the other four categories, and make the adjustments necessary to improve their overall performance.

PowerSellers work really hard. There's no question that PowerSellers live a different lifestyle than casual eBay sellers. PowerSeller Brad Schepp (co-author of *eBay PowerSeller Secrets*) puts it this way, "If your goal is to become a PowerSeller, accept that you will live, breathe, eat, and sleep eBay every day." Adam Ginsberg likens PowerSeller status to a mild addiction. If spending endless hours in front of a computer screen doesn't appeal to you, it might be time to rethink those PowerSeller dreams.

PowerSellers are automated. Because PowerSellers must work so hard, they look for any technical means possible to automate their business. Shortcuts may include using systems for creating batch (groups of similar or related items) or multiple listings, managing inventory, tracking sales, or calculating and managing shipping and email responses. For more information on technical tools, read Chapter 11, *Auction Management Tools*.

PowerSellers know what to sell. As every eBay expert agrees, the biggest challenge in moving from casual eBay seller to PowerSeller is finding the right items to sell. For more information, review Chapter 4, *What Will You Sell?*

PowerSellers know their numbers. Knowing your numbers (or "vitals" as Scott Wingo describes them in *eBay Strategies*) is a crucial element for PowerSeller success. Wingo notes that successful PowerSellers closely track the numbers listed below in accounting software or spreadsheets and update them regularly:

- **Gross GMS.** GMS is your gross merchandise sales, or total revenue received per month.

- **NPB Rate.** An NPB is a nonpaying bidder, or someone who wins an auction for one of your items, then does not pay for it. Your NPB rate is determined by dividing the dollar amount not paid by NPBs by your Gross GMS. For example, if you had $1,000 in Gross GMS and your NPBs failed to pay $20, your NPB rate would be two percent.

- **Net GMS.** Subtract the amount that your NPBs failed to pay from your gross GMS and that's your net GMS. The smaller the difference between gross GMS and net GMS, the less time you are wasting on bidders that don't pay.

- **ASP.** Your ASP, or average sale price, is determined by dividing your net GMS by the number of items sold. If you sold 10 items and had a net GMS of $240, your ASP is $24. In general, the higher the ASP, the better. As your ASP increases, your sales become more efficient, that is, you are making more on each sale using the same amount of effort. (Remember that this is a measure not of profit, but of efficiency.)

- **AOV.** Your AOV (average order value) is determined by dividing the net GMS by the number of orders during that period. In general, and like the ASP, the higher the AOV is, the better. Each order requires processing, packing, and shipping, and the more you make per order, the less effort and perhaps cost you will expend.

- **CR.** One of the most important measurements is the CR (conversion rate). In a nutshell, CR refers to your success rate. Wingo determines it by dividing the number of items sold by the number items posted over the same time period. If you posted 1,000 items and sold 400, you would have a 40% conversion rate.

Becoming familiar with and monitoring these vital signs enables PowerSellers—and those who would like to be—to set and achieve goals. Understanding where your business stands with respect to these measurements can inspire strategies for improving your business without necessarily increasing costs. For example, one means of increasing GMS without investing in more inventory is to increase your conversion rate, or sell more of what you have. Similarly, if you seek to increase your AOV, you may try to get buyers to purchase more items with their order by offering "specials," such as a discount for multiple items in an order. Monitoring these measurements will let you know if your efforts are successful.

PowerSellers use their About Me page. As mentioned in our first chapter, using your About Me page is a great marketing tool, and according to PowerSeller Adam Ginsberg, it is an effective means of building and maintaining your brand. The About Me page is the only place on eBay where you may link to online locations outside of eBay, so it's the only place where buyers can click through to your store or website.

Driving Traffic to Your eBay Store or Website

As discussed above, PowerSellers often operate an eBay store or website. They know, however, that maintaining their status as PowerSellers requires more than having great stuff to sell and a site from which to sell it. As any retailer will tell you, there are no sales if you can't get the customers to the store. The same is true online. Below we provide some common approaches to increasing traffic to your eBay store or website.

Create great content and links. The most effective and low-cost method of driving traffic to any site is to create reliable and useful content that encourages other sites to link to it. For example, Glassine Surfer lists all ongoing eBay stamp auctions (not just its own auctions) at its site, making it a destination for many collectors. Any way that you can create content that makes others want to link to your site will increase your placement in Google searches (that is, your site will show up higher in listings as more sites link to your site). For example, Nolo, the publisher of this program, provides extensive free legal information at its website, making it one of the most linked-to legal sites on the Web.

Search engines and keywords. Most people find their desired Web destinations via search engines. Two types of listings appear in the results for any search: relevant and sponsored. Relevant listings are the primary search results that appear on the search page. Relevance (the order in which they are listed) is determined by the search engine algorithm (a mathematical formula that uses factors such as the content in a site), its domain name, material in its header (the headline that appears in the bar on top of your browser), information in its meta tags (information buried in the website code), and the number of sites that are linked to it. (By the way, if you are interested in seeing who is linked to your website, type "link:" followed by the address of your website, into the Google search engine; for example, "link:www.sitename.com.")

Sponsored links usually appear at the top and in the right margin of the search results pages. You can become a sponsored link by purchasing (or bidding on) keywords at a search company. For example, at the Google.com home page, you can click on the "Advertising Programs" link and buy keywords (Google calls them "Adwords") after you pay a small setup fee of approximately $5. Keyword are the words or terms that Web users type into a search engine to start their search. For example, if your business sold crocheted clothing items for infants, it might purchase the words "crochet" and "baby," and your ad would pop up when a user searched for crocheted baby hats.

In reality, keyword buying is more complex than it sounds. Your choice of keywords is crucial, because if you use terms that are not specific or appropriate, you will have wasted your money. Additionally, you often must bid for keywords against competitors. If you have the top bid, you will pay that amount every time someone clicks on your link when it appears in the search engine results.

There's strong sentiment in the online community for and against keyword buying. Some marketing people, especially those doing business in highly competitive and crowded fields, believe that keyword buying is an effective way to rise to the top of the heap. Others believe that it's useless trying to outbid competitors all of the time and that the only one who profits is the search engine. It is true that keyword prices have escalated in the past few years, making them a more expensive form of marketing.

In any case, everyone agrees that if you do buy keywords, you must closely monitor their effectiveness. If you are not getting any results from certain keywords, ditch those terms—fast. And, of course, if keywords in general are not generating sufficient returns, stop paying for them. For more information, type "Buy keywords" into your search engine.

Banner ads. As you probably know, banner ads are short advertising messages that appear at websites other than your own. Like billboards along a highway, your business can strategically place ads across the Web by purchasing this advertising space. Like any other form of advertising, the challenge is to get the viewer's attention and motivate her to take a closer look—in this case, to click on the banner ad, which will take the viewer to your site. It's a big challenge for a small ad. To get help in creating banners that get noticed, check out online sites such as WowBanners.

Once you have created an ad and decided where you want it, there are various ways to actually purchase and place the ad. You may buy ad space directly from a particular website by clicking on a sign seeking advertising ("Advertise on our site"), you may purchase ad space from a third-party agent—for example, Banner

Space—or you may be able to do a banner ad exchange (check one of the many free banner ad exchange sites). Unless you're using a free banner ad exchange, you pay for your ads either by impression (every time your banner appears), by click-through (every time someone clicks on your banner ad), or by sale (every time someone clicks on your ad and then buys your product). As with keywords, banner ads must be closely monitored for effectiveness. There are various ways to do this—for example, placing hidden code at your website that monitors click-throughs. If you're not getting responses or increased sales, promptly modify or pull the ad.

Affiliate programs. An affiliate program is any kind of arrangement whereby one website pays another for delivering sales or traffic. If you sell one-of-a-kind or niche products at your site, you can offer commissions (or other rewards) to third-party sites that drive customers to your site. For example, if your eBay store sells a specific brand of high-end audio equipment, you may wish to establish an affiliate system with audiophile websites; or if your eBay store sells safety helmets for young baseball players, affiliating with local Little League sites makes sense. Affiliate programs may be set up in various ways, but the key element is creating a method for tracking the referred shopper, usually done by attaching a "tracking code" to the URL (or link) that you give to the affiliate. You will likely need help from a programmer, software application, or online marketing assistant such as LinkShare or CommissionJunction. To find help, type "set up affiliate system" into your search engine.

Building a community. The key to eBay's success has been its ability to unite customers in a community atmosphere. You can do the same by creating a community among the visitors to your site. For example, if your eBay business sells soccer supplies, you may want to set aside a portion of your website for a chat room where customers can comment on soccer matches, create links for soccer enthusiasts, offer discounted tickets to soccer matches, or perhaps offer an interactive game in which players pick World Cup winners.

Borrowing Money to Grow

If your goal is to become a PowerSeller, keep in mind that you may need extra cash to acquire inventory, lease storage space, or pay for equipment or marketing. Listed below are a few sources and tips to consider when borrowing for your business.

Don't count on banks. It's unlikely that a bank will loan money to your eBay business unless you are willing to secure the loan with real estate, personal property, or other business assets—for example, the inventory of a brick-and-mortar retail shop. Banks and other financial institutions are looking for a guaranteed return on their loans, and eBay businesses are usually considered too speculative. Nevertheless, if your business has been around for several years and has a solid profit and loss statement (and perhaps a brick-and-mortar component) you may be able to convince a loan officer or the Small Business Administration to grant a loan. For additional information from Nolo, see the Lowdown on Business Loans.

Borrowing from family and friends. If you're borrowing from people close to you, make sure you sign a promissory note, calculate interest and principal, set up a payment schedule, and most important, respect the people loaning you money. If you don't, you may find yourself embroiled in money disputes over Thanksgiving dinner.

You can easily draft your own promissory note. Included here is a sample promissory note to use in your word processing program, along with explanatory notes. (If you have any problems accessing the form from your browser, all of the forms are included in a separate folder on this disk.) You can calculate interest and payments for use in the promissory note using this loan calculator.

VirginMoney.com. If you would like to borrow money for your business from people you know but do not feel comfortable creating the official documents yourself, consider using the services of VirginMoney.com. Virgin Money does not lend money but helps facilitate loans between other people. A Virgin Money loan specialist examines the terms of a loan that two parties have agreed to, helps to prepare a legally binding agreement (with secured collateral, if required) that includes those terms, and then creates a payment schedule for the borrower. The company also sends payment reminders to the borrower and manages the payment process through automatic electronic debits and credits to the borrower's and lender's accounts.

The added advantage of using services such as those offered by Virgin Money is that your loan may be structured in a way that corresponds to your business plans. For instance, if you believe that you could repay half of the loan within two years, you may set up the loan terms so that half the loan is repaid with a balloon payment after that period of time, with the remainder (and interest) paid off over the following three years.

Borrowing with credit cards. Many people finance their businesses with their credit cards, with all the attendant risks: Credit card interest rates are typically higher than any other type of loan, and extraordinary penalties apply if you exceed a credit limit or make a late payment. If you miss a payment on one card, all of your cards can raise their interest rates. When you take a cash advance on a card, there are more unbearable fees and usually no grace period, which means you pay interest from the day you take the advance, even if you pay off your balance within a month. Obviously, credit cards users can quickly get in over their heads. There are some ways to protect yourself, if you are reconciled to reading some fine print. When shopping for a card, be wary of teaser rates (low introductory rates that jump after a few months) and check the grace period (the period of time from the end of the billing cycle that you can pay your balance in full without being subjected to an interest charge). Many companies have been shortening their grace periods for purchases from 30 to 20 days. Shop around for perks such as airline miles, travel discounts, or other purchasing credits, but be aware that most cards that offer some type of "bonus" charge an annual fee for the privilege and limit the use of the bonus in some way. Always compare the periodic rate that will be used to calculate the finance charge.

Signature loans. The term "signature loan" refers to the fact that your signature is all that is needed to make it binding. Typically, these loans offers arrive in the mail from a bank, credit card, or other finance company; are based on your credit rating and history; and are in the amount of $5,000 or less. The terms of signature loans are typically the same as the terms of a cash advance on a credit card—high interest rates on monthly payments along with an assortment of fees. If your credit history is good or you own a home, you can likely borrow a few thousand dollars using a signature loan without pledging collateral. Signature loans can offer an easy way to get some fast cash, but they can also be risky if you do not understand the terms of the loan. As with credit cards, read the fine print!

Warning: Don't Become a Power Debtor

eBay buying and selling is fun; out-of-control debt is definitely not fun. If your credit card balances are greater than 80% of your credit limits; you've already got a credit card problem and you should avoid using your card(s) to finance your eBay business. Additionally, bankruptcy laws make it much harder to get rid of credit card debts even if you file for bankruptcy—particularly if your income is greater than the median income for your state. Nolo offers more information on credit issues and credit repair. ●

Should You Quit Your Day Job?

Two Tips If You Decide to Quit 159

Avoid Problems With Your Current Employer 159

First, the bottom line: The time may come when you are convinced that quitting your day job is absolutely necessary. If you are not obligated to support anyone, indifferent to your career, flush with cash, and in love with your eBay business, you are an ideal candidate for doing so. Unfortunately, few of us match this description. Before taking that big step, make sure there's firm financial footing beneath your feet. You'll need to consider the following.

What's the financial effect? To know what effect quitting your job will have, you will need to do some financial forecasting, for both your business and you personally. (The basic principles of projecting income and expenses for your business are described in Chapter 16, *Recordkeeping*.) After forecasting your eBay business income, estimate your personal living expenses for a year by making a budget based on the past year's expenditures (or average the past two years' expenditures, if possible). Include in your budget those costs that are now paid by your employer, such as health insurance. Based on that budget, will you have enough income from your business to pay your expenses? Even if the answer to that question is "yes," many financial planners recommend that you also have savings to cover all expenses for nine months, in the event that the business projections were too optimistic.

Beyond day-to-day expenses, also consider your retirement. How close are you to retirement age, and how will leaving your job affect your retirement? There are no bright lines for determining the right financial mix, but when you weigh these factors you should feel comfortable that you could weather a worst-case scenario, as in the eBay business not being the success you hoped.

Do you have a spreadsheet program? If you have *Microsoft Excel* (or a program that can read *Excel* spreadsheets, you can create a budget using the blank Personal Financial Statement included on the disc. A printed version is included at the end of this chapter

What's the psychological effect? How much of your identity is embedded in your current day job? Do you have friends there? Many departing employees are surprised how much they miss the social life provided by a regular job. How does your family feel? Will they support your decision and get behind your eBay business? Are people counting on you to take care of them? Again, there are no simple yes or no answers. You need to examine all of these personal factors before making your decision. Experts use self-actualization techniques to help you make these decisions. You can see how these techniques work in Barbara Sher's book, _I Could Do Anything If I Only Knew What It Was: How to Discover What You Really Want and How to Get It_ (Dell).

Two Tips If You Decide to Quit

Don't burn bridges. You may want the job back. Keep in touch with your boss and coworkers—there may be an opportunity for you in the future.

Get your teeth cleaned. Before you leave your job, get in those doctor and dental appointments you have been avoiding. Health insurance coverage for self-employed people leaves a lot to be desired.

Avoid Problems With Your Current Employer

Your employer is more likely to support your eBay business goals if your dual role is not perceived as interfering with your productivity or competing in some way with the business. Here are some "don'ts" for moonlighting employees and ways to avoid them.

Don't steal office supplies. If you want to avoid problems with your employer, don't stock your new business with supplies from your day job. In _The Scorecard at Work_, author Greg Gutfeld says stealing office supplies is one of the five fastest ways to get fired. Historically, employees rationalize this theft saying "The company can afford it." Because office supplies account for a fairly large chunk of the $67 billion lost to employee theft each year, employers apparently don't think they can afford it—and are now more than ever on the lookout for disappearing staplers.

Don't use computer time at work to run your eBay business. Your employer will view your use of company computer time for your eBay business as akin to stealing office supplies—that is, you are using company equipment and services for private purposes. You can rationalize all you want about your right to conduct auctions at the office, but your employer will have employment laws on his side.

Don't compete. It may seem logical if your day job is at an auto-parts company to start a competing eBay business. After all, you know how to obtain the products and you know the prices. Not a good idea. For obvious reasons, employers don't like it when employees compete. It may also violate a noncompete or trade secrecy agreement you signed on the job. Think instead whether there is a problem that you could solve for your current employer with your eBay business. Is there damaged or excess inventory your employer cannot get rid of? It may be worth offering to sell it on your own time, earning yourself a commission while earning some additional income for your employer. The risk, of course, is that if you are too successful, your employer may want to take the whole operation in house!

Personal Financial Statement

Assets

Cash and Cash Equivalents

Institution Name	Account Type and #	Current Balance

Total Checking and Savings Accounts _____

Time Deposit Accounts (Include Certificates of Deposit)

Institution Name	Account #	Maturity Date	Current Balance

Total Time Deposit Accounts _____

Cash on Hand/Miscellaneous Cash (Drawers, Safety Deposit Box, Etc.)

Location	Amount

Total Miscellaneous Cash _____

Total Cash And Cash Equivalents _____

Marketable Securities (Include Mutual Funds)

No. of Shares/Face Value of Bonds	Name of Stock/Bond	Exchange Listed	Current Market Value

Total Value of Marketable Securities _____

Cash Value of Life Insurance

Policy Description and Company	Cash Surrender Value

Total Life Insurance Cash Value _____

Accounts and Notes Receivable

Note/Account Description	Current Balance

Total Accounts And Notes Receivable _____

Trust Deeds and Mortgages

Note Description	Current Balance

Total Trust Deeds/Mortgages _____

Real Estate

Description _____ Market Value

_____ _____

_____ _____

_____ _____

_____ _____

_____ _____

Total Value of Real Estate _____

Personal Property

Description _____ Current Value

_____ _____

_____ _____

_____ _____

_____ _____

_____ _____

_____ _____

_____ _____

Total Value Personal Property _____

Other Assets (Include Interests In Partnerships and Privately-Held Stock)

Description _____ Current Value

_____ _____

_____ _____

_____ _____

_____ _____

Total Other Assets _____

Total Assets _____

Personal Financial Statement

Liabilities & Net Worth

Credit Cards and Revolving Credit Accounts

Name of Creditor   Amount Owed

_____   _____

_____   _____

_____   _____

_____   _____

_____   _____

_____   _____

_____   _____

Total Credit Cards And Revolving Credit Accounts   _____

Unsecured Loans

Bank (or Other Lender)   Terms   Amount Owed

_____   _____   _____

_____   _____   _____

_____   _____   _____

Total Unsecured Loans   _____

Loans Secured By Real Estate

Bank (or Other Lender)   Terms   Amount Owed

_____   _____   _____

_____   _____   _____

_____   _____   _____

Total Real Estate Loans   _____

Loans Secured by Personal Property

Bank (or Other Lender)	Terms	Amount Owed

Total Personal Property Loans _____

Loans Against Life Insurance Policies

Insurance Company	Terms	Amount Owed

Total Insurance Policy Loans _____

Other Liabilities

Name of Creditor	Terms	Amount Owed

Total Other Liabilities _____

Total Liabilities ━━━━━━━━━━━

Net Worth (Total Assets Minus Total Liabilities) ━━━━━━━━━━━

Personal Financial Statement

Annual Income

Gross Salary and Wages

Source	Annual Amount

Total Gross Salary and Wages _____

Income From Receivables and Loan Repayments

Person Owing	Terms	Annual Amount

Total Receivable and Loan Repayment Income _____

Rental Property Income

Source	Annual Amount

Total Rental Property Income _____

Dividends and Interest

Source	Annual Amount

Total Dividends and Interest _____

Income From Business or Profession

Description   Annual Amount

_____   _____

_____   _____

_____   _____

                          Total Income From Business or Profession   _____

Other Income

Description   Annual Amount

_____   _____

_____   _____

_____   _____

_____   _____

                                              Total Other Income   _____

Total Annual Income   _____

Personal Financial Statement

Annual Expenses

Real Estate Loan Payments or Rent

Mortgage Holder/Landlord	Rent or Own?	Annual Payment

Total Real Estate Loan Payments or Rent _____

Property Taxes and Assessments

Property Taxes/Assessments	Annual Payment

Total Property Taxes and Assessments _____

Federal and State Income Taxes

Description	Annual Payment

Total Income Taxes _____

Other Loan Payments

Creditor	Annual Payment

Total Other Loan Payments _____

Insurance Premiums

Insurance Company	Type of Policy	Annual Payment

Total Insurance Premiums _____

Living Expenses

Description	Annual Expenses

Total Living Expenses _____

Other Expenses

Description	Annual Expenses

Total Other Expenses _____

Total Annual Expenses

_____

Date: _____ _____

Business Entities: What Kind of Business Should Your eBay Business Be?

How Do You Know What Kind of Business Entity You Have? 172

What Is Limited Liability? 172

LLC or Corporation? 173

How to Create an LLC 175

Converting to an LLC 175

Why Choose a Corporation Instead of an LLC? 176

If Your eBay Business Is a Partnership 178

Odd Ducks: Limited Partnerships and S Corporations 180

Ways to Organize Your Business 180

F irst, the bottom line: Many people start their eBay business as a sole proprietorship or, if there is more than one owner, as a partnership. If you are concerned, however, that your eBay business will create lawsuits, debts, or other liabilities that could affect your personal assets, you should consider forming a limited liability company (LLC) or corporation. You should also consider doing so if your accountant or tax preparer believes there are tax benefits from it.

How Do You Know What Kind of Business Entity You Have?

If you are operating an eBay business by yourself and have not taken the steps to form a corporation or an LLC, then you are considered to have a sole proprietorship. If you are operating an eBay business with other owners and you and your fellow owners have not taken steps to form a corporation or an LLC, then you are considered to have a general partnership. These classifications will determine how the business will be treated tax-wise, and whether liabilities that arise from the business are limited to business assets or extend to your personal assets.

What Is Limited Liability?

One of the main reasons to form an LLC or corporation is to have "limited liability," that is, to limit your personal liability for business debts. Creditors of your business must go after the business, not you personally. If you form one of these entities, business creditors cannot take your home or car or attach your wages. But forming an LLC or corporation will not always shield all of your personal assets. Even if you operate your eBay business as a corporation or LLC, a creditor can still go after your personal assets in the following circumstances.

You personally guarantee a loan or lease. If your eBay business borrows money or if you lease space, chances are that the lender or landlord will condition the loan or lease upon the business owner's personal guarantee. Both the business and you as the owner would have to file bankruptcy in order to escape these debts.

You owe federal or state taxes. If your eBay business fails to pay income, payroll, or other taxes, the IRS or state tax agency can try to recover the unpaid taxes personally from you or any other directors, officers, or owners of your LLC or corporation.

You act negligently. If your eBay business does something that could subject you to potential negligence claims—for example, you manufacture and sell defective products—you can be personally liable for the damage. In these cases, buying insurance may offer more protection than forming a corporation or LLC.

You fail to abide by corporate rules. If you don't take corporate responsibilities seriously, for example, you mix corporate and personal funds and don't keep records of meetings of shareholders, a judge may strip away the asset protection feature of the corporation or LLC.

Keep in mind that in seven states (Hawaii, Illinois, Montana, South Carolina, South Dakota, Vermont, and West Virginia), it may be possible for a personal creditor of an LLC owner to ask a court to dissolve the LLC. You can learn more about debts, personal liability, and bankruptcy by reading the Nolo article, "When You Can't Pay Your Business Debts: Personal Liability and Bankruptcy Options."

LLC or Corporation?

If forming an LLC or corporation seems like the best plan, you will need to choose which type is best for your eBay business. Their primary characteristics are described below.

Comparisons Between LLCs and Corporations	
What do they have in common?	LLCs and corporations both shield owners from personal liability.
What's the difference?	The LLC does not pay income tax. It is a "pass-through" tax entity, meaning that profits and losses pass through the business to the owners. If a business is an LLC, the income, loss, credits, and deductions from it are reported on the individual income tax returns of the LLC owners. Sole proprietorships and partnerships are also pass-through entities. An LLC with several owners is taxed like a partnership; a one-owner LLC is taxed like a sole proprietorship.* A corporation** is different. It is a legal entity separate from its shareholders. The corporation files its own tax return (IRS Form 1120) and pays its own income taxes on the profits kept in the company.
Which is best for your eBay business?	If you're primarily concerned about limiting your liability, you're generally better off forming an LLC. If you're seeking tax benefits, your accountant may advise forming a corporation.

* The IRS permits LLC owners to elect alternative tax treatment, for example, they may choose to be taxed like a corporation. Ask your tax adviser for more information.

** When we refer to a corporation, we're speaking of the regular or "C" Corporation. Another type of corporation, the "S" Corporation, is discussed below.

How to Create an LLC

Many people who decide to create a formal business entity (such as a corporation or LLC) choose the LLC, because it provides limited liability without having to file a separate return and pay taxes on behalf of the business entity. Each state's requirements are different, but to form an LLC, you need to take the following steps.

- **Name it.** Choose an available business name that complies with your state's LLC rules.
- **File articles.** File formal paperwork, usually called articles of organization, and pay the filing fee (ranging from about $100 to $800, depending on your state's rules).
- **Create operating agreement.** Create an LLC operating agreement, which sets out the rights and responsibilities of the LLC owners (referred to as "members").
- **Publish notice.** Publish a notice of your intent to form an LLC (required in only a few states).

Converting to an LLC

If you are operating your eBay business as a sole proprietorship or partnership, you can convert to an LLC with no change to your income tax treatment and filing requirements. In other words, the owner (or owners) of an LLC files taxes in the same way as a sole proprietorship or partnership.

If your eBay business is a partnership, you and your partners must agree in writing to terminate the partnership and convert to an LLC. You may have to complete additional paperwork to legally terminate your partnership when you convert it to an LLC—for example, publish a notice of dissolution in a newspaper. Check with your secretary of state. Since your new LLC assumes the debts of your prior partnership, you should seek the advice of your accountant or tax consultant before making the conversion.

Three Ways to Handle LLC Formation	
Least expensive ($20 to $70 plus filing fees*)	Do it yourself. You can learn more about LLC formation procedures and fees for your state by visiting your state's business filing office website (usually your secretary of state's website). Start by finding your state's home page (at www.statelocalgov.net), then look for links to either your secretary of state or business resources. You can also find step-by-step instructions on forming an LLC in the book *Form Your Limited Liability Company*, by Anthony Mancuso (Nolo), or by using the software program *LLC Maker*.
More expensive ($200 to $300 plus filing fees*)	Hire an incorporation service. Companies such as The Company Corporation (www.corporate.com) will incorporate your business or form an LLC on your behalf. To locate one of these services, type "incorporation service" into your Internet search engine.
Most expensive ($500 to $1,000 plus filing fees*)	Hire an attorney. An attorney can help form a corporation or an LLC, usually for a fixed fee.
* LLC filing fees in the majority of states are under $100. However, in some states the filing fees (or fees and annual LLC taxes) are as high as $900. For more information, see LLC Basics.	

Why Choose a Corporation Instead of an LLC?

Since forming either a corporation or an LLC reduces an owner's liability, why would someone choose a corporate form rather than an LLC? The most common reason is tax savings. A corporation is a legal entity separate from its shareholders. The corporation files its own tax return (IRS Form 1120) and pays its own income taxes on its profits. Although reporting and paying taxes on a separate corporate tax return can be time-consuming, there are some benefits to having a separate level of taxation. A tax expert can provide you with a complete explanation of the pros and cons of corporate taxation. Keep in mind that only the largest eBay businesses are likely to enjoy the tax benefits of corporate form. Further, there can be real disadvantages for a corporation that experiences losses or may soon be sold. Here is more about how corporations are taxed.

To form a corporation, you must file "articles of incorporation" with the corporations division (usually part of the secretary of state's office) of your state government. Filing fees are typically around $100 to $800.

For most small corporations, articles of incorporation are relatively short and easy to prepare. Most states provide a simple form for you to fill out, which usually asks for little more than the name of your corporation, its address, and the contact information for one person involved with the corporation (often called a "registered agent"). Some states also require you to list the names of the directors of your corporation. In addition to filing articles of incorporation, you must create corporate bylaws. While bylaws do not have to be filed with the state, they are important because they set out the basic rules that govern the ongoing formalities and decisions of corporate life, such as how and when to hold regular and special meetings of directors and shareholders and the number of votes that are necessary to approve corporate decisions.

Finally, you must issue stock certificates to the initial owners (shareholders) of the corporation and record who owns the ownership interests (shares or stock) in the business.

In summary, here is what you must do to form a corporation:

- **Name it.** Choose an available business name that complies with your state's corporation rules.
- **Appoint directors.** Appoint the initial directors of your corporation.
- **File articles.** File formal paperwork, usually called "articles of incorporation," and pay a filing fee that ranges from $100 to $800, depending on the state where you incorporate.

- **Create bylaws.** Create corporate bylaws, which lay out the operating rules for your corporation.
- **Meet.** Hold the first meeting of the board of directors.
- **Issue stock.** Issue stock certificates to the initial owners (shareholders) of the corporation.

To learn more about how to form your corporation, read *Incorporate Your Business: A Legal Guide to Forming a Corporation in Your State*, by Anthony Mancuso (Nolo).

If Your eBay Business Is a Partnership

If you own your eBay business with others and have not incorporated or formed an LLC, then legally and tax-wise, your business is automatically considered to be a general partnership. If you are a partner in a general partnership, you should know the following.

If your eBay business partner defrauds a buyer or runs up a debt, can the buyer or creditor go after you for the money? Yes, each partner is personally liable for any other partner's business debts and legal claims regardless of each partner's ownership interest. In addition, any partner may bind the entire partnership (in other words, the partners) to a contract or business deal.

Does a partnership have to file a separate tax return? Yes. Even though a partnership does not pay its own taxes, it must file an "informational" tax return, IRS Schedule K-1 (Form 1065). In addition, the partnership must give each partner a completed copy of this form showing the proportionate share of profits or losses that each partner must report on an individual 1040 tax return. A partner pays taxes on his entire share of eBay profits, even if the partnership chooses to reinvest the profits in the eBay business rather than distributing them to the partners. See IRS tax requirements for partnerships for more information.

What type of paperwork do you need to form a general partnership?
You don't have to pay any fees or prepare any paperwork to form
a general partnership; you can start it with a handshake. It makes
far more sense, however, to prepare a partnership agreement.
Without an agreement, the one-size-fits-all rules of each state's
general partnership laws will apply to your partnership. These
rules usually say that profits and losses of the business should be
divided equally among the partners (or according to the partner's
capital contributions, in some states), and they impose a long list of
other rules. You'll undoubtedly prefer to make your own rules. Your
agreement should cover issues such as division of profits and losses,
partnership "draws" (payments in lieu of salary), and the procedure
for selling a partnership interest back to the partnership or to an
outsider. _Form a Partnership_, by Denis Clifford and Ralph Warner
(Nolo), explains how to form a partnership and create a partnership
agreement. If you are not comfortable preparing your own
agreement, an attorney should be able to prepare one for between
$500 and $1,000. Here's more about partnerships and partnership
agreements.

Are you and your spouse a partnership? According to official
rules posted on the IRS website, if spouses co-own and run a
business in a community property state (Arizona, California, Idaho,
Nevada, New Mexico, Texas, Washington, and Wisconsin), they can
operate as a sole proprietorship and report their business income
as part of the joint return. That makes for a much easier income tax
filing. Some tax experts maintain that the rules are the same for non-
community property states as well. That is, if spouses co-own the
business and file a joint return, the IRS will not question it if they file
as a sole proprietorship. Officially, however, if spouses co-own and
run a business in a non-community property state, they are supposed
to operate as a partnership and file a K-1 partnership return. In all
states, if one spouse owns the business and the other works for it,
the business is a sole proprietorship, and the owner will have to
declare the spouse as an employee or independent contractor. For
more rules on employees, see Chapter 19, _Hiring Help_.

Odd Ducks: Limited Partnerships and S Corporations

As you consider what type of business entity is right for your business, you may hear or read about two other types: the limited partnership and the S Corporation. Both are older forms of business entities, and neither offer the small business owner the advantages or flexibility of the relatively new LLC form. They are listed here for your information, but they are probably not right for your eBay business.

Limited partnership. A limited partnership has two types of partners: general partners who manage the business and limited partners—typically investors—who contribute capital to the business but are not involved in day-to-day management. With the introduction of the LLC, which offers liability protection to all owners, the limited partnership has lost favor with small business owners.

S Corporation. S corporations still exist, but like limited partnerships, they have for the most part been replaced by LLCs. The S corporation's shareholders receive the same basic pass-through tax treatment afforded sole proprietorships, partnerships, and LLC owners. S corporation shareholders have limited personal liability for the debts and other liabilities of the corporation. To form an S corporation, you must first form a regular C corporation, and then convert it to an S corporation by filing an S corporation tax election with the IRS. The S corporation form does not offer the flexibility of the LLC entity. Among other restrictions, an S corporation can have only a certain number and types of shareholders (no non-U.S. citizens, for example).

Ways to Organize Your Business

Thoroughly confused? The chart below lists the pros and cons of corporations, LLCs, partnerships, sole proprietorships, and more.

Types of Business Entities		
Type of Entity	**Main Advantages**	**Main Drawbacks**
Sole Proprietorship	• Simple and inexpensive to create and operate • Owner reports profit or loss on his personal tax return	• Owner personally liable for business debts
General Partnership	• Simple and inexpensive to create and operate • Owners (partners) report their share of profit or loss on their personal tax returns	• Owners (partners) personally liable for business debts
Limited Liability Company	• Owners have limited personal liability for business debts even if they participate in management • Profit and loss can be allocated differently than ownership interests • IRS rules now allow LLCs to choose between being taxed as partnership or corporation	• More expensive to create than partnership or sole proprietorship • State laws for creating LLCs may not reflect latest federal tax changes
Regular (or C) Corporation	• Owners have limited personal liability for business debts • Fringe benefits can be deducted as business expense • Owners can split corporate profit among owners and corporation, paying lower overall tax rate	• More expensive to create than partnership or sole proprietorship • Paperwork can seem burdensome to some owners • Separate taxable entity

Types of Business Entities

Type of Entity	Main Advantages	Main Drawbacks
S Corporation	• Owners have limited personal liability for business debts • Owners report their share of corporate profit or loss on their personal tax returns • Owners can use corporate loss to offset income from other sources	• More expensive to create than partnership or sole proprietorship • More paperwork than for a limited liability company, which offers similar advantages • Income must be allocated to owners according to their ownership interests • Fringe benefits limited for owners who own more than 2% of shares
Limited Partnership	• Limited partners have limited personal liability for business debts as long as they don't participate in management • General partners can raise cash without involving outside investors in management of business	• General partners personally liable for business debts • More expensive to create than general partnership • Suitable mainly for companies that invest in real estate

For more information on business forms and business formations, check out the free Nolo resources on <u>ownership structures</u>.

Insurance

Basic Insurance Terminology 184

Basic Coverage 185

Coverage Through Your Homeowners' Policy 188

If Your Business Needs More Coverage 189

Lower Your eBay Insurance Costs 189

F irst, the bottom line: Insurance can lower your business risk and reduce your personal liability, but it is also expensive, and many types may be unnecessary for smaller eBay businesses. For instance, you may need property insurance; you are less likely to need liability insurance. In certain circumstances, for example, leasing commercial space or borrowing from a commercial lender, the landlord or lender may have insurance requirements that you must fulfill in order to enter into the contract.

Basic Insurance Terminology

Listed below are a few key terms to know before discussing insurance. If you have had a lot of experience dealing with insurance in other contexts, these will likely be familiar to you.

- **The policy.** The written document or contract between you or your company and the insurance company.
- **Premium.** The periodic payment paid to the insurance company for the benefits provided under the policy.
- **Rider.** A special provision, sometimes referred to as an endorsement, attached to a policy that either expands or restricts the policy.
- **Claim.** Notification to an insurance company that you believe a payment is due to you or your company under the terms of the policy.
- **Commission.** A fee or percentage of the premium paid to an insurance broker or agent.
- **Deductible.** The amount of out-of-pocket expenses that you or your business must pay before the payment is made by an insurer. For example, if the deductible for business equipment loss is $1,000 per year and you suffer $1,000 in damage in one year, there will be no payment under the policy.
- **Exclusions.** Losses an insurance policy will not cover.
- **Underwriter.** The person or company that evaluates your business and determines if it qualifies for insurance coverage.

Basic Coverage

No matter what kind of business you have, you'll want to insure it against hazards common to the type of business you have. In general, virtually every eBay business can benefit from some form of property insurance. However, most eBay business probably don't need liability insurance. Listed below are descriptions of various types of insurance, and factors to consider when deciding what types you need.

Property insurance. Business property insurance compensates you for damage or loss of your property, both the physical space where you work (your eBay home office, for example) and the equipment and inventory of your eBay business. If you lease commercial space—for example, to store inventory and ship products— your lease may require that you carry a specified amount of property insurance.

A "named peril" policy protects against only the types of damage listed in the policy—typically, fire, lightning, vandalism, storms, smoke, and sprinkler leaks. A "special form" policy offers broader coverage, usually insuring against all but a few specifically excluded risks (floods and earthquakes are typically excluded), and is more expensive. A good insurance professional can help you decide which choice makes more sense for your business. (Choosing and working with an insurance broker or agent is covered below.)

If you operate a home office, like most eBay businesses, your property insurance needs may be met through an inexpensive rider/ endorsement to your homeowners' policy. But don't assume that this will cover all eBay business losses—most homeowner policies offer very limited coverage for business property (see below).

When buying property insurance, your choice is between a cash value policy, which pays whatever your damaged property is actually worth on the day it is damaged, or a replacement cost policy, which pays to replace your property at current prices. A replacement cost policy is always more expensive but is worth the extra money. Business equipment like computers, fax machines, and digital cameras lose their value quickly, and cash value proceeds generally will not come close to purchasing replacement equipment in the event of a loss. If you're like most new eBay business owners, you're probably using some equipment that's already out of date. If you suffer a loss, you'll need to replace this equipment quickly so you can get back to work.

Liability insurance. Liability insurance covers damage to other people or their property for which you are legally responsible. This includes, for example, injuries to a UPS delivery person who trips on your son's skateboard on the way to your eBay office and damage caused by any products you manufacture and sell (called product liability coverage). Liability insurance policies typically pay an injured person's medical bills and other out-of-pocket losses, any amount you are ordered to pay in a lawsuit for a covered claim, and often the cost of defending you in such a lawsuit. If you are a home-based eBay business that is seldom visited by outsiders, you will probably be able to get a relatively inexpensive liability rider/ endorsement to your homeowners' policy.

Car insurance. If you have a car, you probably already have insurance that covers your personal use. However, your personal insurance policy may not cover business use of your car—for example, driving to and from trade shows, or picking up large deliveries of inventory. If your policy doesn't cover business use, you'll want to get business coverage to protect against lawsuits for damage you cause to others or their vehicles while using your car for business. If you don't do much business driving—and particularly if you don't often have business passengers, such as clients or customers—then you can probably get coverage simply by informing your insurance company of your planned business use (and paying a slightly higher premium). Many insurance companies simply factor in occasional business use of a vehicle, along with commuting miles, driver experience, and many other factors, in setting your insurance premium. If you use a commercial vehicle such as a van or put most of the miles on your car while doing business, consult with your agent to determine if your business liability policy will cover this use (and whether it will cover employee use of the vehicle, as well). If not, you will probably have to get a separate business vehicle insurance policy.

Business interruption coverage. A business interruption policy replaces the income you won't be able to earn if you must close your eBay business due to a covered event such as a fire or storm. These policies typically provide money to both replace lost profits, based on your eBay business's earnings history (as shown by its financial records), and pay any operating expenses still due even though you can't do business. Business interruption policies are not typically sold as standalone products; instead, they're added to property insurance policies or sold as part of a business insurance package (see below). If you can't afford any type of interruption in your flow of eBay income, consider acquiring some form of interruption coverage. When you're shopping for this type of insurance (or any other, for that matter), always check the exclusions and coverage. For example, some policies may provide an "extended period of indemnity," which kicks in after you reopen, to cover your continuing losses until you are fully back on your feet. If your customers don't immediately return after a temporary shutdown, your policy will pay for the business you're still missing during this transition period.

Web insurance. Some insurance companies offer Web insurance policies, which protect business with websites against a variety of risks, including theft, copyright infringement, and interruptions of service. Today, you can get insurance for a simple site for anywhere from $500 to $3,000 a year. An insurance professional can help you decide whether your cyber-risks are great enough to justify this expense.

Insurance specific to eBay transactions. In addition to more general types of business insurance protection, there are policies which protect particular aspects of an eBay transaction. eBay offers insurance to buyers against nondelivery and misrepresentation, which is discussed in Chapter 9, *Rules, Disputes, and Feedback*.

Shipping insurance, as offered by the various carriers, is discussed in Chapter 17, *Shipping and Returns*. Additionally, some third-party insurers such as BuySafe reimburse buyers in the event of a rip-off, fraud, or other nondelivery issue with the seller, also discussed further in Chapter 9, *Rules, Disputes, and Feedback*.

Mandatory insurance for employees. This chapter does not cover workers' compensation or employee-related insurance requirements, but you can read about them in Chapter 19, *Hiring Help*.

Employee benefits. Similarly, this chapter does not discuss the myriad employee benefit programs you may offer employees or provide for yourself, such as health insurance, life insurance, or long-term disability coverage. If you're interested in these types of insurance, a good place to start gathering information is the National Association for the Self-Employed website.

Coverage Through Your Homeowners' Policy

According to one study, 60% of home-based businesses don't have business insurance coverage because the owners assumed they were covered by their homeowners' insurance. That's not always the case. If your eBay business is based in your home, make sure you understand your coverage by checking your homeowners' policy and confirming your understanding with your agent.

If your business is home-based, you may be able to get fairly inexpensive coverage with an in-home business policy. These policies typically cover business property and liability, and some also provide business interruption protection. According to the Insurance Information Institute, an in-home business policy will cost something in the range of $250 to $400 a year for about $10,000 of coverage. However, your business will have to meet the insurance company's requirements for coverage, which may include having very few employees, bringing few business visitors to your home, or purchasing your homeowners' insurance from the same company.

If Your Business Needs More Coverage

If your eBay home business cannot meet the requirements of an in-home business policy, or if your business is outside your home, look into a business owners' policy (BOP). BOP packages typically include business property insurance, liability protection, and some business interruption protection.

Lower Your eBay Insurance Costs

When shopping for insurance, the better you know your business, the better consumer you will be. Keeping the following tips in mind will help you get the most appropriate coverage for your business at the best price.

- **Determine what insurance is required.** You may be legally required to carry certain types of insurance, such as workers' compensation if you hire employees. See Chapter 19, *Hiring Help*. If your eBay business is carried on outside your home, your commercial lease may obligate you to carry a certain amount of property insurance. You will need proof of these types of coverage to get your business off the ground.

- **Assess and prioritize your true risks.** Once you've dealt with required coverage, spend your money where you need it the most—protecting you and your business from the most probable risks. Wherever potential losses are greatest is where your insurance dollars should go. How much business property do you own? Do you make or sell products that may cause someone injury? Will you carry a large inventory of completed products or valuable raw materials? Will you have employees, and if so, how many? Your answers to questions like these will help you and your insurance professional figure out what your priorities should be and the type of coverage you really need.

- **Reduce your risk.** Risk management will minimize your insurance claims and bring your premiums down. Depending on your business, there may be things you can do to reduce your likelihood of suffering a costly loss, or to transfer risk to others, either through insurance or by other means. The federal Small Business Administration offers a <u>free primer</u> on business risk and ways to transfer it, as well as a detailed checklist to help identify the coverage you need.

- **Consider higher deductibles.** Increasing the deductible on a policy will result in lower premiums—a financial lifesaver for a business struggling to get off the ground. The downside, however, is that, in the event of a loss, you will have to pay more money out of pocket before the insurance company pays anything.

- **Ask your insurance pro about discounts.** Many companies offer lower premiums or discounts to policyholders who take certain safety precautions. Find out whether any of these discounts are available through the companies you're considering—then take the necessary steps to lower your insurance bills.

- **Don't duplicate coverage.** Carefully review all of your policies. For instance, your homeowners' or renters' insurance policy may or may not cover a few relatively inexpensive pieces of business equipment.

- **Consider a rider/endorsement to your existing policy.** Home-based eBay businesses that have few business-related visitors can purchase a relatively inexpensive liability endorsement to a homeowners' policy. An endorsement may also be available to extend property coverage to business equipment. If you use your personal car for eBay business and your existing auto insurance policy doesn't cover business use, you may be able to get the coverage you need through an endorsement. However, if you use a car solely for business, you will have to buy a separate business/commercial auto policy.

- **Always read the fine print.** Before you write your premium check, make sure you understand exactly what you're getting for your money. Insurance policies are notoriously difficult to read, so your insurance professional should help you with this. Know exactly what is covered and what is not (exclusions), and the limits of coverage. Many insurance companies place a limit on how much you can collect per item, per incident, per person, or per year—and may further break these limits down depending on what caused the loss, what type of property was damaged, or other factors.

- **Take the time to prepare for a claim.** Make sure you can collect if necessary. If you need to submit an insurance claim, you will have to prove the extent of your loss. For property coverage, you should photograph your eBay business equipment and inventory and keep records of what you paid for it or other indicators of its value. If you buy and sell very valuable items, such as fine art or antiques, consider having them valued by an independent appraiser. Keep all such records in a different location, such as a safety deposit box.

- **Keep your coverage up to date.** Most experts suggest reviewing your coverage annually. Have you or your business purchased property, grown substantially, gotten another vehicle, expanded into a different line of business? These are all factors to discuss with your insurance provider in investigating whether to increase your coverage or otherwise change your existing policies.

Recordkeeping

What Records Should You Keep?.. 194

eBay Accounting Software... 197

Accounting Resources 199

Choose an Accounting Method.. 199

Keep Your Business and Personal Finances Separate...........................200

What Records Do You Need If You're Audited?....................................... 201

How Long Should You Keep Records?... 203

First, the bottom line: Every retail business must track finances (income, expenses, and taxes) and inventory. For novice businesspeople, the idea of keeping these records may seem challenging, but don't fear. Popular software programs—particularly *QuickBooks*—make it possible for you to manage inventory, income, expenses, and taxes with a relatively small learning curve (usually one or two days). In fact, if you want to skip this chapter entirely, buy *QuickBooks Pro* and find a one-day course in your area that explains how to use the program, if necessary. We should also note that as we were preparing this start-up kit, Microsoft had released a new version of its *Office Accounting* program that includes some eBay features, too (and Microsoft was also offering free downloads of its program *Accounting Express* as well; see below).

What Records Should You Keep?

To run an efficient, profitable eBay business, you will need to manage some or all of the following information.

Income. Income is the money you get from eBay sales. You will need to transfer the sales information in your eBay and PayPal accounts into your business recordkeeping.

- **How to record income.** Some eBay businesses manually enter the information in their accounting software or books. Other eBay businesses and eBay stores automatically download this information into their accounting software or spreadsheet program using auction management tools.

- **How income affects taxes.** It's important to accurately track eBay sales income. If you get audited by the IRS, unreported income is often the first thing the auditors look for. They will be very suspicious if you have significant bank deposits beyond the income you claimed on your return, even if those deposits are to your personal account. (If you have significant nontaxable income, make sure to keep the records you'll need to prove where it came from.)

Expenses. Expenses are what you spend on your eBay business—for example, for inventory, wages, rent, telephone, insurance, office equipment, and travel. You can see a spreadsheet with typical expenses on the <u>Profit and Loss Forecast</u> that's included with the disc. (You will need a program that can read Microsoft Excel spreadsheets).

- **How to record expenses.** If you are charging your expenses to a credit card or paying them with a bank account with online access, you can download this information to a financial software program or spreadsheet. Expenses that are part of your eBay account, such as auction fees, shipping through PayPal, inventory purchases made on eBay, or subscription fees, can also be downloaded to your accounting software (as discussed below). Otherwise, you will have to enter your expenses manually.

- **How expenses affect taxes.** Keeping track of expenses lets you identify every tax deduction you're entitled to take and is crucial to determining profits. But don't expect the IRS to allow your tax deductions if you don't keep records to back them up. If you have no records at all, your deductions will be disallowed in an audit, and you might face penalties as well. If you can prove that you had some business-related expenses of a type that makes sense for your line of work, the IRS may still allow a deduction, but it will be much smaller than what you claimed. Under the Cohan rule (named for a tax suit against entertainer George Cohan), if you can show some proof that you incurred deductible expenses, the IRS can estimate those expenses and allow a deduction for that amount. But, as you might expect, the IRS's estimates will be low. And this rule doesn't apply to expenses for travel, vehicles, gifts, and meals and entertainment. The IRS requires more detailed records for these types of deductions.

Sales and inventory. As you buy inventory, you must deduct the expense. And every time you sell an item, you must deduct the item from your inventory—otherwise you won't know what you have available to sell. (Note: inventory is treated differently from other expenses for tax purposes; review Chapter 23, *Tax Deductions.*) Also keep in mind, even though it's not a tax issue, that sloppy tracking and reporting wastes time and costs money. Efficient recordkeeping enables you to better forecast the future.

- **How to record sales and inventory.** You will need either a spreadsheet or software that can manage both inventory and sales. Review Chapter 11, *Auction Management Tools,* for an idea of your choices. Most of the tools provided can manage inventory. You can learn more about eBay's <u>Tools for Success</u> at the eBay website, which also offers a <u>comparison chart of eBay tools</u>' features. eBay can help you sort through its software options with its <u>tool recommendations wizard</u>. Keep in mind that inventory management software is not the same as accounting software. If you are using financial software, it should integrate with your inventory program. *QuickBooks* is one of the few accounting programs that provides integration and can provide sales reports summarizing your sales.

- **How sales and inventory affect taxes.** Obviously, sales reflect income, and accurate income reporting is essential for taxes. As a retail business, you will also need to generate an accurate inventory report, detailing inventory value at the beginning and ending of the year. Programs such as *TurboTax* can incorporate your inventory information to determine your tax bill.

Sales tax. As discussed in Chapter 22, *Paying Your Taxes*, you may have a responsibility for assessing and paying sales tax. If sales tax is an issue for you, make sure that the accounting or auction management tool you use can calculate the correct sales tax (it can vary from county to county) and provide sales tax reports. Again, programs such as *QuickBooks* can provide reports of taxable and nontaxable sales.

Payroll. If you have one or two employees, you may be able to calculate, track, and record payroll taxes (and the resulting deductions). If you don't want the hassle, consider an online payroll service such as Paychex or *QuickBooks* Payroll Services.

Money owed to your business. Known as "accounts receivable," this is money that others owe to your eBay business. For most eBay businesses, accounts receivable are the money that customers owe you for completed transactions. You track this in your accounting program—for example, you enter when the sale is completed, then enter when the payment is received and becomes income.

Money you owe to others. Known as "accounts payable," this is money that you owe—for example, subscription fees, loans, or uncompleted payments for inventory. Once paid, these amounts become part of your business expenses.

Income taxes. Accurate accounting of inventory, income, and expenses is essential for preparing your taxes.

Most eBay business owners use tax preparation software that integrates with their accounting software. *TurboTax* provides a special edition for eBay businesses.

eBay Accounting Software

Most small eBay businesses get by with a very basic set of books, at least at the beginning. Many of them track only a few things: what they earn (income), what they spend (expenses), money they owe (accounts payable), and money they are owed (accounts receivable). Usually this can be done with a spreadsheet program such as *Microsoft Excel*.

But if you're handling more than 20 or 30 eBay transactions a month, and you're unfamiliar with spreadsheets, you should consider software that's designed for accounting novices. There are several products for small business owners, the most popular of which are *QuickBooks, Peachtree, Microsoft Office Accounting,* and *MYOB*.

For eBay businesses, one good choice is *QuickBooks*. If you use *QuickBooks* with eBay's *Accounting Assistant*, you can download your eBay sales information and PayPal transaction history directly to *QuickBooks*—no need to manually enter the information. Not only does the *QuickBooks/Accounting Assistant* integration increase accuracy, it's a tremendous time-saver if you're handling many transactions. In addition to *Accounting Assistant*, many of the software tools mentioned in <u>Auction Management Tools</u> also integrate with *QuickBooks*. And keep in mind that *QuickBooks* also integrates with *TurboTax*.

eBay's *Accounting Assistant* will <u>work with most post-2002 versions of *QuickBooks* Pro, Premier, or Enterprise editions</u>. These products cost from about $200 (Pro) to $300 (Premier) to $3,000 for the Enterprise edition. (*Accounting Assistant* also is supposed to work with *QuickBooks* Simple Start, but some users report problems integrating *Accounting Assistant* with this *QuickBooks* version, the most basic of the *QuickBooks* programs.) On the <u>*QuickBooks* home page</u>, you can take an online interview to determine the best version of *QuickBooks* for your eBay business.

Rather than *QuickBooks*, you may want to try *Microsoft Office Accounting*. This software debuted in 2006, and in 2007 it was <u>customized specifically for eBay users</u>. Using *Office Accounting* you can download information about eBay items you have sold and calculate how much you've earned (as well as sales tax and related information). The program also allows you to list items and triggers *Outlook* so that you can email invoices. (And, as of December, 2007, Microsoft was providing <u>free</u> downloads of *Office Accounting* Express.)

eBay *Accounting Assistant*. You get *Accounting Assistant* for free when you subscribe to eBay Stores, Selling Manager, Selling Manager Pro, or eBay Blackthorne products. You must have <u>one of these subscriptions</u> in order to take advantage of the download capability.

Accounting Resources

There are lots of good books and websites that explain how to keep your books on paper or on a computer spreadsheet. Some of our favorites are:

- *Minding Her Own Business: The Self-Employed Woman's Guide to Taxes and Recordkeeping*, by Jan Zobel (Sourcebooks). A good basic introduction to bookkeeping, including detailed examples of income and expense sheets (and it's not just for women).
- *The Complete Idiot's Guide to Accounting,* by Lita Epstein and Shelly Moore (Alpha). Greater detail, for those who plan to keep more complex records and are comfortable with basic accounting concepts (and it's not just for idiots).
- IRS Publication 583, *Starting a Business and Keeping Records*, free at www.irs.gov. A clearly written and very handy guide to basic bookkeeping.
- www.toolkit.cch.com. The Business Owner's Toolkit site offers plenty of helpful free information. Click "Managing Your Business Finances" for a crash course in basic accounting principles.

Choose an Accounting Method

The two basic ways to account for your income and expenses are the cash method and the accrual method. Most eBay businesses use the cash method, which is simple and commonsensical.

The cash method. With this method, you count income when you actually receive it and expenses when you actually pay them. For example, if you complete a sale in December but don't get paid until January, you record the income in January. Similarly, if you buy a digital camera for your eBay business on credit, you record the expense not when you charge the camera and take it home, but when you pay the bill. (The IRS won't let you manipulate your income by, for example, not depositing a seller's check until the next year; you must report income when it becomes available to you, not when you actually decide to deal with it.)

The accrual method. Under the accrual method, you record income as you earn it and expenses as you incur them. For example, if you complete a sale in December, that's when you record the income you expect to receive from it, no matter when the buyer actually gets around to paying you. (If the seller never pays, you can eventually deduct the money as a bad debt.) And if you charge some office furniture, you record the expense on the day of purchase, not when you pay the bill.

As you can see, the cash method is much easier to use; most of us deal with our personal finances this way, so it's a system we're familiar with. It also gives you a clear picture of your actual cash on hand at any point in time.

As long as your eBay business makes less than $1 million a year, you may choose whichever method seems right for your business. (If your eBay business made more than $1 million in any of the last three years, you might have to use the accrual method—but if your business is pulling in a million dollars, we hope you're getting some professional tax and accounting advice.) For more information, check out IRS Publication 334, *Tax Guide for Small Business*, and IRS Publication 538, *Accounting Periods and Methods.*

Keep Your Business and Personal Finances Separate

If you plan on making eBay efforts a tax-deductible business, one of the wisest things you should do is to separate your eBay business income and expenses from your personal accounts. Don't pay business expenses with a personal check or credit card, and don't deposit business income into your household checking account along with a spouse's salary, tax refunds, client reimbursements, inheritances, lottery winnings, and heaven knows what else. Here is why it matters:

- If you have a joint account with anyone other than a co-owner in your eBay business, that person could be dragged into a business audit.
- If you have a joint account with anyone other than a co-owner in your eBay business, that person will also have access to all of your business funds. That could be a problem if, for example, you have to pay a large bill for new inventory on the same day that your joint account holder decides to make a major purchase for your household.
- If you run your eBay business under a name other than your own legal name, you might not be able to deposit payments made out to your business in your personal account.
- You'll have a much harder time figuring your business deductions for interest, banking fees, and so on, because you'll have to separate out the costs attributable to personal purchases.

Even if you have to pay a bit extra to open more accounts, having separate business accounts will simplify your bookkeeping life greatly. At the very least, open a business checking account. And if you can't find a no-fee business credit card, simply use one of your personal credit cards just for business—that way, you'll have no trouble calculating your interest deduction.

What Records Do You Need If You're Audited?

If you face an audit, the IRS is not going to take your word for anything. You'll have to come up with receipts, cancelled checks, bank statements, and other records to support both the amount of income you claimed and any business deductions you took. You really can throw it all in a shoebox if you want, but most business owners find it easier to use a set of file folders or an accordion file. You can buy one that's already labeled with common business expense categories at an office supply store.

Here's a brief rundown on what you need to keep as proof of income and expenses:

- **Income.** Keep copies of your bank statements, copies of checks you've deposited, copies of any 1099s you received, and, if you have nontaxable income, copies of documents showing the source of that income (for example, from an inheritance). Remember, the IRS is less interested in the business income you reported than in the income it thinks you failed to report. This means your job is not really to prove the amount of income your business earned, but to prove that any income you didn't report came from a nontaxable source.

- **Business expenses.** Keep records showing what you bought, whom you bought it from, how much you paid, and the date of the purchase. In most cases, you can prove this with your receipt and a cancelled check or credit card statement (which proves that the receipt is really yours).

- **Vehicle expenses.** Keep records of the dates of all business trips, your destination, the business purpose of your trip (for example, to meet with a client or scout a retail location), and your mileage.

- **Meals and entertainment.** Keep records of where you were, what you paid for, how much you paid, the date of purchase, whom you were with, and the business purpose of your meeting. The first four facts are often included on a receipt; write the remaining two in a datebook or calendar.

- **Use of property.** Keep records of how much time you spent using it for business and using it for other purposes. This rule applies to "listed property," items that the IRS believes people often use for personal purposes, including computers and cameras. (There really is a list of listed property, and you can find it in IRS Publication 946, *How to Depreciate Property*.) You might also want to keep track of the time you spend in your home office, to prove that you used it regularly. You can keep these records in a log or journal.

How Long Should You Keep Records?

In most situations, the IRS has up to three years to audit you from the date you file a tax return (or from the date when the return was due, if you filed early). However, if the IRS claims that you have unreported income exceeding 25% of the income you did report, it has six years to audit you. And if you didn't file a return or the IRS claims that your return was fraudulent, there is no audit deadline; you're always fair game.

Based on these rules, some experts advise that you simply give up and keep all of your tax records forever. There's no harm in keeping all of your actual tax returns forever; they don't take up much space and can help you track the financial life of your business over time. You can generally get rid of supporting documents six years after you file your tax returns. They are only required if there is evidence you filed a fraudulent return. ●

Shipping and Returns

Shipping Tips...206

Shipping Solutions...208

Stay Away From Drop-Shipping..210

Shipping and Delays: The Legal Rules...211

Returns and Refunds...212

Terms and Conditions...213

irst, the bottom line: Your shipping policies—how fast you ship and whether you offer free or reasonably priced shipping and handling—are really part of your marketing effort on eBay. If you handle shipping well, customers will come back, and they'll recommend you to their friends. Your choice of shipping system and your ability to ship quickly will also affect your eBay business's efficiency and, ultimately, your bottom line. A fair and responsive refund policy is part of your marketing too, and can increase your traffic and encourage repeat customers.

Shipping Tips

Here are few suggestions for your shipping practices.

Buy supplies on eBay. Buy your shipping supplies on eBay, where hundreds of etailers are ready to cater to your most specific shipping needs—from vinyl record shipping mailers to forklifts. Prices are competitive, if not better than many box stores. Also keep in mind that if you do prefer the big box stores, many, like Office Depot, offer free shipping for orders over $50.

Get a label printer and a good postage scale. For $200 to $300, you can buy a thermal label printer on eBay or other online retailers. If you ship more than 30 or 40 items a month, you will find this an invaluable time-saver because it gives you precut, ready-to-stick labels. As for postage scales, there are also plenty of excellent deals on eBay. Expect to pay $50 to $100 for a good digital scale.

Pack and weigh your item before you list it. We mentioned this before, but it bears repeating. Once you've photographed the item you should pack and weigh it. Once you have the accurate weight and dimensions you can enter the calculated shipping costs in the Sell Your Item form. Then, shipping costs are automatically calculated for the buyer based on zip code, saving you considerable email correspondence with potential buyers. You can also calculate shipping insurance rates for UPS and USPS shipments at eBay.

Use USPS Priority boxes. If you're shipping via USPS Priority Mail, there's no need to buy boxes—the USPS will provide them for free. (See below for a few examples.) At the <u>USPS website</u>, search for "priority boxes."

USPS Priority Mail Packaging

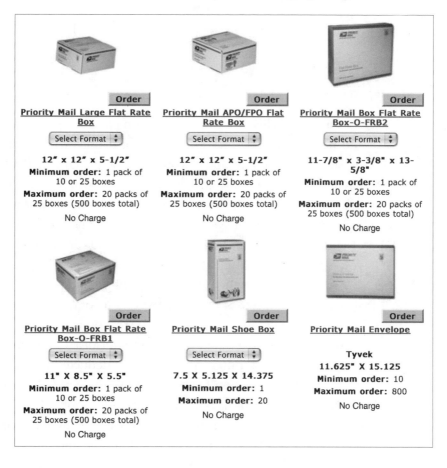

Shipping Solutions

Here are the most popular methods for eBay shipping:

PayPal. ThePayPal Shipping Center offers a handy method of shipping via either UPS or USPS. When you complete a sale on eBay, you will see a button labeled "Print shipping label" in your PayPal Overview.

Once you click the button, you can choose a shipping carrier and fill out the necessary package information. When you're satisfied with the rate quote, you print the postage-paid label and pay for it through your PayPal account. You can also use the system to ship internationally; PayPal provides preprinted customs forms as well. With the PayPal system, you can track and confirm the arrival of your shipments, and you can get a refund for misprinted labels if you cancel them within 24 hours.

You can download your shipping information to other software such as *QuickBooks*. Some eBay experts recommend withdrawing your eBay sale money from PayPal before processing the shipping. That way, if you download data to another program such as *QuickBooks*, the shipping costs won't be deducted from the sale, creating some confusion for your bookkeeping.

USPS. You can print USPS Express and Priority Mail shipping labels and postage using the USPS Click-N-Ship system. Click-N-Ship allows you to store up to 3,000 domestic and international addresses, provides email ship notification, stores your shipping history for six months, and prints up to ten domestic labels with a single credit card transaction. It will also find zip codes and permit you to buy insurance up to $500.

UPS. Using <u>My UPS</u> online services, you create UPS shipments, prepare and print labels, compare various shipping options, and pay for your UPS shipments with a credit card. The system stores addresses, allows you to void shipments, provides email notifications and shipping history, and offers detailed tracking information.

FedEx. Although it is not as popular among eBay users as some of the other srevices, FedEx offers many of the same options as UPS and USPS. Using <u>My FedEx</u> online services, you create FedEx shipments, prepare and print labels, and pay for everything with a credit card. The FedEx system, like UPS, stores addresses, allows you to void shipments, provides email notifications and shipping history, and also enables you to provide detailed tracking information.

Stamps.com. <u>Stamps.com</u> (along with Endicia, below) is an online service that lets you print USPS postage and pay for it with your credit card. There is a monthly subscription fee of $21.99. Why pay for postage when you can get it from the USPS without the monthly fee? Because Stamps.com is like a postage meter for your home. It's easier for bulk shipments and it integrates with many common programs such as *Microsoft Outlook* and *Word*, and *Quicken*. The site commonly has free trial offers so you can give it a spin to see if it will work for you. Stamps.com has most of the typical bells and whistles: tracking, email notifications, and shipping history. It also offers free delivery confirmation on Priority Mail and provides downloadable shipping reports.

Endicia. <u>Endicia</u> is also a postage-meter-on-a-website, like Stamps.com, and, like Stamps.com, it offers a free trial. Endicia has a few features and a pricing system that sets it apart from competitors. Most notably, it incorporates *Dazzle* software, which allows you to include company logos on your postage. You also get free delivery confirmation on USPS Priority Mail and can print postage for all USPS services from first class through Media Mail. It's available in several <u>pricing plans</u>, including $9.95 (Endicia Standard), $15.95 month (Endicia Premium), and $34.95 (Endicia Professional).

Stay Away From Drop-Shipping

If you're like most eBay businesses, you maintain an inventory of products and ship when you get orders. With this arrangement you have complete control of the order until you hand it off to the USPS, UPS, or FedEx.

Drop-shipping is a process in which you sell items you don't keep in stock. Instead, you collect the money and forward the order to a distributor or manufacturer, who ships to the customer, usually using your packaging. The drop-shipper bills you for the sale.

Drop-shipping sounds appealing because you can offer a wide variety of merchandise without maintaining an inventory. And for many web-based stores, it works well. But there are many disadvantages of using drop-shipping at eBay, including:

- You may be required to pay expensive setup fees—always avoid any drop-shipper who requests this.
- You may have to make monthly minimum orders regardless of your sales—watch out for this requirement.
- If the drop-shipper screws up, it may be difficult—since you're the one in the middle—to obtain a refund from the drop-shipper for the customer. That means you're the one making the refund or you're the one stuck with the negative feedback.
- You will have little control over an item's price. The drop-shipper may suddenly mark up an item, cutting into your profits.
- Drop-shippers are often in long lines of distribution, so that if any step along the way has a problem—manufacturer, wholesaler, middleman—you will suffer.
- You will likely not get any warning before the drop-shipper runs out of stock—again, more negative feedback.
- Drop-shipper lists are often sold on eBay, which means that companies often flood the eBay market with similar merchandise.

Shipping and Delays: The Legal Rules

If your products are late getting to customers, not only will it cause you a loss of goodwill, it may also violate federal law.

FTC rules. The Federal Trade Commission's <u>mail or telephone order merchandise rule</u>, also known as the "30-day rule," imposes basic shipping and refund rules on businesses.

When you advertise merchandise on eBay and don't say anything about when you plan to ship, you're expected to ship within 30 days from the date you receive the payment and all the information needed to fill the order. If your listing does state when you will ship the merchandise—for example, within two days of payment—you must have a reasonable basis for believing you can meet this shipping deadline.

If there's a delay—that is, it will take longer than 30 days for you to ship—you have two choices:

- You can ask for the customer's consent. If you can't get consent to the delay, you must, without being asked, refund the money the customer paid you for the unshipped merchandise.
- You can simply cancel the order, notify the customer, and refund the payment.

Keep a record of how you notified the customer about the delay, whether by email, phone, fax, or regular mail; when you gave the notice; and how the customer responded.

Drop-shipping. In cases of drop-shipped orders, you (the person taking the order), not the shipper, is responsible for complying with the rule.

Because you're responsible for a drop-shipper's screw-ups, find out the distributor/drop-shipper's return policy and post it at your point of sale or in your catalogue, or, if that's not possible, include it with the order. If the customer complains about the merchandise— for example, it arrives damaged or has a factory defect—the distributor has to correct the error. But because the customer made the purchase with you, not the distributor/drop-shipper, you'll have to stay on top of the transaction—for example, get the RMA (return merchandise authorization) number from the distributor, and email it to the customer. The RMA allows you and the distributor/drop-shipper to accurately track and process the returned merchandise.

Returns and Refunds

Your return policy can be a marketing tool. What could be better than a money-back guarantee? Millions of consumers confidently patronize certain online businesses—for example, Amazon, Land's End, or REI—because these companies have customer-friendly, simple-to-use return policies. On the other hand, every consumer remembers an unpleasant experience trying to return something and probably stopped shopping at that business afterwards.

Not every business needs an unlimited return policy, but we do recommend that you establish a customer-friendly policy of some sort and that you communicate it to your customers.

Before you draft that policy, keep in mind the legal rules. You don't have to give a refund unless either of the following is true:

- You broke the sales contract—for example, your goods were defective.
- You have a policy that allows a refund for returns.

If you want to provide refunds and impose conditions on when merchandise can be returned, post your return and refund policy prominently with your listing or at your store.

A typical policy might require the customer to return the merchandise within 30 days for a refund.

State rules on refunds. A few states have laws regarding refunds. It's not always clear whether these laws apply to online retailers doing business with residents of these states. California's law seems to apply to Internet transactions, because it applies to "other sellers of goods at retail, and mail order sellers which sell goods at retail in California …". New York's law is silent on the issue. So far, there have been no cases enforcing this issue, but if you prefer to err on the conservative side, then when dealing with residents of these states consider abiding by the retail rules as follows:

- **California.** You must post your refund policy unless you offer a full cash refund or credit refund within seven days of purchase. If you don't post your policy as required, the customer is entitled to return the goods for a full refund within 30 days of purchase.
- **Florida.** If you do not offer refunds, that fact must be posted. If the statement isn't posted, the customer can return unopened, unused goods within seven days of purchase.
- **New York.** If you offer cash refunds, that policy must be posted, and you must give the refund within 20 days of purchase.
- **Virginia.** If you don't offer a full cash refund or credit within 20 days of purchase, you must post your policy.

Terms and Conditions

Many websites post "terms and conditions" that define the rules for using a website. Do you need terms and conditions at your eBay listings, your eBay store, or at your Web store, too? Maybe.

- **Disclaimers.** You may want to include disclaimers—statements that inform customers that you won't be liable for certain kinds of losses they might incur. For example, you may disclaim responsibility for losses that result if pottery breaks when a customer ships it back for a return.
- **If you are gathering information from your customers,** including credit card information, you should post a privacy policy detailing how this information will be used or not used. Yahoo!'s privacy policy is a good example of a broad, easy-to-understand policy. Whatever policy you adopt, be consistent, and if you are going to change it, make an effort to notify your customers of the change.

- **If your website provides space for chats or postings from the Web-surfing public,** you'll want to limit your liability for offensive or libelous postings or similar chat room comments. There are three things you can do. First, regularly monitor all postings and promptly take down those you think are offensive or <u>libelous</u>. Second, if a third party asks you to remove a posting, remove it while you investigate. If you determine—after speaking with an attorney—that you are entitled to keep the post, then you can put it back up. Third, include a disclaimer on your site that explains that you don't endorse and aren't responsible for the accuracy or reliability of statements made by third parties. This won't shield you from claims, but it may minimize your financial damages if you're involved in a lawsuit over the posting.
- **Include notices regarding copyright and trademark**—for example, "Copyright © 2006 <u>ndasforfree.com</u>" or "Cyzuki is a trademark of Cynthia Lloyd."
- **If you are catering to an audience under 13 years old, special rules apply.** You should learn more about dealing with children at the <u>Federal Trade Commission's website</u>.

Working from Home

Zoning, Lease, and Homeowners' Association Restrictions 216

Warning: Don't Let Your eBay Home Business Disturb the Neighbors 217

Can You Get the Insurance You Need? 217

Can You Separate Your Work From Your Home Life? 218

Tips for Maximum Home Office Efficiency 218

Leasing Space 221

Welcome Home 223

F irst, the bottom line: While working from home sounds appealing, there are some things to consider. Before devoting the spare bedroom, the basement, or the extra closet to your eBay business, consider neighborhood restrictions, insurance limitations, your personal comfort about working at home, and the alternative to the home office and storeroom: leasing separate space.

Zoning, Lease, and Homeowners' Association Restrictions

Depending on where you live, zoning laws, lease restrictions, or subdivision or condominium rules ("covenants, conditions, and restrictions," or CC&Rs) may affect your ability to run your eBay business from your home. For example, zoning laws may limit or prohibit employees working in your home (other than domestic help), limit noise levels (typically by imposing "quiet hours" in the evening and early morning), or prohibit any enterprise that would increase traffic or competition for scarce parking spaces. You can find the zoning laws that apply to your neighborhood by checking with your local zoning office, usually located at city hall or your county government offices. Some towns have zoning maps and zoning ordinances online (and also in local libraries).

If you are renting your living space and have never read your lease, now would be the time. If you are a member of a condominium or subdivision association, review your CC&Rs before converting your living space to a commercial enterprise. Finally, if you are leasing from someone and the property is subject to CC&Rs, you will need to read both the lease and the CC&Rs.

If prohibitions apply, you might be able to get around them by applying for a variance (an exception), although you will need to get your neighbors to buy into this idea. For a zoning variance, you will likely have to go through a public process involving your community's planning commission, which can be a lengthy and expensive process. If the restrictions are limited in a lease, get your landlord to sign off. With the CC&Rs, you'll likely need to get approval of the condominium or homeowners' association that governs the property. Be prepared to offer something up for the agreement of your neighbors—for example, creating more parking in the area or limiting your work hours.

Warning: Don't Let Your eBay Home Business Disturb the Neighbors

As a practical matter, the only way you are likely to get caught for violating zoning or other restrictions is if your neighbors report you to local authorities, your landlord, or the homeowners' association. Unless you have particularly mean-spirited neighbors, they are likely to take action only if your business causes problems for them—for example, if you make noise late at night, your employees park in front of their driveways, or the constant comings and goings of delivery trucks make the street feel like a Wal-Mart parking lot.

Can You Get the Insurance You Need?

Home eBay businesses should be insured against common hazards and events. Even if you already have homeowners' or renters' insurance, however, most policies either don't cover home businesses or provide only about $2,500 worth of protection for losses to business property. Because just one uninsured loss could easily put you out of business, you should protect yourself.

If your existing policy doesn't offer enough (or any) protection, you can probably get some basic protection from a home-business rider to your homeowners' or renters' policy. Talk to your insurance agent and see Chapter 15, *Insurance* for more information.

Can You Separate Your Work From Your Home Life?

To operate an eBay business from home—particularly if you want to become a PowerSeller—requires self-discipline and will power. At a separate workplace, the only distractions might be walking to the water cooler or playing solitaire on the computer. At home, however, it's a different story: We all have things we should be doing (folding the laundry or washing the dishes) and things we'd like to be doing (watching television or reading the paper). Unless you can knuckle down and accomplish your eBay goals despite distractions like these—and more compelling ones, such as your children or other loved ones—your eBay business may never get off the ground.

If you do decide to work from home, setting up your home workspace in a separate room or building can help minimize distractions by keeping you out of household traffic patterns (and giving you a door you can close). If you live with others, consider writing down your work schedule and posting it on the refrigerator or your workplace door, and asking the people you live with not to disturb you during your posted work times.

If you have children, you can find a lot of great information about avoiding distractions and other tips for work-at-home parents on the Web. Among the more popular sites are <u>WebMomz</u>, <u>WAHM</u> (Work at Home Moms), and <u>BizyMoms</u>.

Tips for Maximum Home Office Efficiency

If you've concluded that you want to keep your business at home, you'll want to do all you can to make that business productive and efficient. Taking a few simple steps will help you make the most of your home business space.

Spend some money on decent furniture. Most of us who work at home spend plenty of time sitting down, often in a chair that was previously banished to the attic because it lacked comfort, style, or both. Although this seating solution is cheap, it's also a sure road to physical problems. Additionally, if you're not comfortable in your eBay home office, you won't be able to put in the necessary hours to make your business a success. For ergonomics and comfort, a good office chair is a must. You should expect to pay several hundred dollars for a decent chair. Among the features to look for are adjustable height and tilt, lumbar support, and padded, adjustable armrests. For help, read this <u>article</u> explaining the various features available and what they do. You can also find plenty of information on office ergonomics at the <u>UCLA Ergonomics Program</u> website.

Your desk or work surface needs to be the proper height as well. For optimum efficiency, your work surface should be generous. Working on a too small space is inefficient—you'll have to scatter your equipment and other materials around the room instead of having them all within easy reach.

You don't have to break the bank to outfit your home office. If you're an experienced eBay seller, then you're probably fairly good at tracking down good deals. Apply those skills to find decent used home office furniture, whether at garage sales, on eBay, or on <u>Craigslist</u>.

Another resource is the <u>HomeFurnish</u> website, where you can find an extensive list of links to office furniture companies and other home office equipment suppliers.

Get the right connections. Most eBay business owners agree that a high-speed Internet connection (also known as "broadband") is essential for running an eBay business. Prices are dropping in many areas—some DSL providers offer service starting at $25 to $30 per month. In addition to increasing your eBay efficiency, broadband is essential if you operate a separate website and plan to modify it.

There are, however, many types of broadband to choose from, including DSL, cable, satellite, and wireless. Speeds vary depending on the provider and the plan. Cable is currently considered the fastest medium and may be the ideal choice for online businesses, although a baseline DSL hookup is probably sufficient for most eBay business owners.

Ideally, you should look for speeds of at least 384Kbps/128Kbps. The first number is the speed at which you download files; the second is your upload speed, when you transfer files or place them at a website. The folks at <u>CNET</u> (www.cnet.com) offer lots of helpful advice for choosing a provider. They also recommend that home business users look for additional features such as free dial-up access (just in case the broadband fails or you're on the road), multiple email in-boxes with at least 10MB storage for each, and personal firewall and antivirus software.

Get organized. Remember the old saying, "A place for everything, and everything in its place"? In an eBay home business, space is often at a premium. Storage of inventory and maintenance of records can be a challenge. Use file folders, desk dividers, bookshelves, and other storage systems to organize your paperwork and project materials. If you're working in a small spot, use vertical space—put shelves, folder racks, or other organizing tools above your workspace. If organizing your home is the biggest challenge for your eBay business, you should check out <u>LifeOrganizers</u>, where you'll find helpful tips on organizing your eBay home office. Another resource is the <u>OnlineOrganizing</u> website, which has lots of helpful articles, links to websites on a variety of organizational topics, a referral service for finding a professional organizer in your area, an online product catalogue, and a long list of tip sheets and checklists that will help you get organized and make the best use of your time.

Hire experts for one-time projects. Don't reinvent the wheel. If you're facing a one-time task that you don't know how to handle—like designing your store website, remodeling a room to serve as a home office or storage space, or developing an eBay store logo—it's much more efficient to pay for a few hours of an expert's time and get the job done right than to try to learn how to do it yourself. Used sparingly, expert help can really save time and money.

Prioritize and automate your work. Some business efficiency experts recommend a triage system for tasks and paperwork—in other words, you classify tasks and the related paperwork into categories such as "urgent," "to do soon," "wait," and "forget it," then prioritize your time accordingly.

Others suggest a grading system: On your to-do list, you give each task a grade, with "A" tasks having the highest priority. Then, you don't allow yourself to move on to a single "B" or "C" task until you've completed your A-list.

If you're having trouble figuring out where your time is going, keep a log of your eBay hours for a couple of weeks, recording what you work on and how long you spend on it. You may be surprised at what you find. For lots of good advice on managing your work time, check out any of the excellent time management books by Julie Morgenstern or David Allen. In addition, consider investing in any of the helpful auction automation tools discussed in Chapter 11, *Auction Management Tools*.

Leasing Space

Even if they start out at home, eBay business owners often outgrow their garages and need additional space to store inventory, serve as a shipping station, or use as their office headquarters. In these cases, the only alternative—other than leasing your neighbor's garage, too—is leasing commercial space. When you are ready to take that step, consider the following to get started.

What's the difference between a commercial and a residential lease? On the negative side, commercial leases usually last five or more years, much longer than the typical residential lease. More important, commercial tenants do not have the consumer protections—for example, strict laws regarding the return of security deposits—that apply when you rent a house or apartment. Finally, commercial leases are usually harder and more expensive to break than residential leases. On the plus side and unlike residential leases, commercial leases are usually negotiable. If there is a lot of available commercial rental space, you may be able to get a great space for low rent or a shorter-term commitment.

Finding commercial space. Start with local newspaper listings and Craigslist (under "Housing," click "Office/Commercial"). Craigslist usually posts the square footage, rent, available amenities, location, and photos of the space. Beyond Craigslist, there are two companies that dominate commercial leasing: LoopNet (www. loopnet.com) and CoStar Group. Both sites have extensive national listings and can refer you to a broker in your area who can assist you in finding and leasing space.

Check out local restrictions. You want to be sure that any space you're considering is okay for your business in terms of local land-use rules. Most communities have different classes of zoning for different types of business, such as retail, manufacturing, or business offices. If you're in doubt about zoning, find the applicable rules through your local planning department (check your local government website).

When you talk about the rent. Commercial leasing usually comes in two flavors: gross lease and net lease. In a gross lease, you pay a basic rent, usually based on square footage. The landlord pays for all property expenses such as utilities, taxes, and maintenance. With a net lease you pay a fixed rental charge plus a portion of the building's property taxes, insurance, and maintenance costs.

Things to consider when you negotiate your lease. Below are some things you should consider when negotiating your lease. For more help, read *Negotiating the Best Lease for Your Business,* by Fred Steingold and Janet Portman (Nolo).

- **Your personal liability for rent.** You'll be personally liable for any amounts due if you operate your eBay business as a sole proprietor or a general partner. If you operate your eBay business as a corporation or LLC, the landlord can reach only the assets of your eBay business, and your personal assets are not at risk unless you signed a personal guarantee. A personal guarantee is a promise that you will pay any debts arising from a breach of the lease. In certain real estate markets favoring the tenant, the landlord may waive the guarantee, limit it to the first year or two of the lease, or ask for a larger security deposit instead. If you're uncomfortable with a personal guarantee, keep the lease short, perhaps limited to a one-year term.

- **How long are you tied to the property?** If things go bad and you can't continue to pay rent, you may be sued for the remaining value of the lease. For that reason, you may prefer a lease of one year or less or a month-to-month tenancy.

- **What happens if you fail to pay rent?** Most leases give you 30 days to "cure" your first failure to pay rent, which means you have 30 days to pay before the landlord can terminate the lease and begin eviction proceedings. The landlord also may take some "self-help" measures such as deducting the money from your security deposit (which you will then have to replace). The landlord is legally entitled to all of your rent through the end of the lease term, even if you vacate the premises. However, in most states, the landlord must take reasonable steps to rerent the space and credit the new rent money against your debt (that obligation is called "mitigation of damages").

Welcome Home

Even though we've framed the work-at-home experience in terms of challenges—distractions, zoning, unhappy neighbors, and insurance—there's little doubt you'll find it a vast improvement over commuting and the artificiality of office environments—and of course, it's the only place where you can work in your pajamas and slippers, if you want! ●

Hiring Help

What's the Difference Between an Employee and an
Independent Contractor?..226

Misclassifying Workers..228

How Does the IRS Decide Who Is an IC?...228

Before You Hire a Friend or Family Member for Your eBay Business..........229

Finding the Right Person for the Job 230

Employment Resources 231

Legal and Paperwork Requirements: ICs 232

Getting Started as an Employer 233

Legal and Paperwork Requirements: Employees 235

Set Up a Payroll System 236

F irst, the bottom line: When you're hiring someone to work for your eBay business, you have two options. You can hire an independent contractor, sometimes known as a consultant or freelancer, or you can hire a full-fledged employee. This decision affects your tax and legal obligations, the way you run your business, and your profitability. Once you've decided which type of worker fits the position you hope to fill, your next task involves choosing the right person, then dealing with tax forms and other reporting and paperwork requirements.

What's the Difference Between an Employee and an Independent Contractor?

In general, an independent contractor (IC) is someone who provides specialized services on a per-project basis for a number of businesses or clients. Services that an IC provides usually require a certain level of skill, experience, and sometimes licensing—for example, bookkeepers and attorneys are often ICs. You can hire an IC on an ongoing basis—for example, to maintain your eBay store—or on a periodic basis, for example, to do your taxes each year. ICs also work by the job—for example, to remodel a home office or help an eBay business launch a product. In comparison, an employee follows the rules you set and meets the standards you require, often at your workplace. As an employer, you exercise a lot more control over an employee than over an IC, from setting work hours to dictating exactly how the employee does every aspect of the job. Although you may hire an employee on a short-term basis (such as helping you during the hot eBay selling seasons), employees are more commonly hired on an open-ended basis, such as until the work runs out, or she quits or is fired.

Sometimes it may be tough to tell how a worker should be classified, but it is usually straightforward: If you're hiring someone who runs his own business and you are a customer of that business, you're probably hiring an IC. If you're hiring someone to work for your business, subject to your control and your standards, you're probably hiring an employee.

For typical eBay tasks, you're likely to hire workers on the following basis:

- **Setting up your website or eBay store.** You are probably better off hiring an IC to set up your site—a task that is fairly well-defined, complicated, and short-term. You will need someone who has had a lot of experience accomplishing this one task, and that is more likely to be an IC who makes a living doing so. Also, because most ICs are paid by the project (unlike employees, who generally are paid for their time), ICs have a stronger incentive to finish the work quickly. The sooner you are up and running, the better!

- **Day-to-day eBay business.** Employees are usually a better choice for doing work that is an integral and ongoing part of your eBay business, such as listing items, shipping orders, and dealing with customers. If you hire employees to do this work, you'll have more control over their training and the quality of their output, and you will have someone helping you who understands your way of doing business and provides consistent service to customers—all essential factors in establishing your company's reputation. You are also likely to satisfy the IRS if it checks the classification of your helpers in an audit. If your workers are doing the tasks typical for an eBay business, the IRS is much more likely to classify them as employees, not ICs. Misclassifying workers can get you in big trouble, as described below.

- **Accounting and inventory.** Accounting, inventory, and other types of data management of your eBay business may be handled by ICs or employees, depending on the size of your business and the frequency at which these tasks are performed. For example, large eBay businesses may hire employees for part-time or full-time inventory management, while a startup company may hire an IC for a short time to manage an annual physical inventory or to set up its bookkeeping system.

Misclassifying Workers

Business owners are eager to classify a worker as an IC because there is much less paperwork and expense. However, both the IRS and your state taxing authority or employment board may impose significant penalties if you misclassify an employee as an IC, and there are plenty of ways to get caught. For example, if someone you hired as an IC applies for unemployment, your state's unemployment insurance agency might decide that the worker was really an employee—and is entitled to unemployment compensation. Something similar might happen with your state's workers' compensation board or tax agency.

However, the agency you need to be most concerned about is the IRS—both because it imposes hefty penalties for misclassification and because it will have more contact with your business (and more opportunities to look closely at how you classify your workers). The IRS test considers workers employees if the company they work for has the right to direct and control the way they work—including the details of when, where, and how the job is accomplished. In contrast, the IRS considers workers independent contractors if the company they work for does not manage how they work, except to accept or reject their final work product.

How Does the IRS Decide Who Is an IC?

The IRS looks at a number of factors when determining whether a worker is an employee or an independent contractor. The agency is more likely to classify as an independent contractor a worker who:

- can earn a profit or suffer a loss from the activity
- furnishes the tools and materials needed to do the work
- is paid by the job
- works for more than one firm at a time
- invests in equipment and facilities
- pays her own business and traveling expenses
- hires and pays assistants, and
- sets her own working hours.

On the other hand, the IRS is more likely to classify as an employee a worker who:

- can be fired at any time by the hiring firm
- is paid by the hour
- receives instructions from the hiring firm
- receives training from the hiring firm
- works full time for the hiring firm
- receives employee benefits
- has the right to quit without incurring liability, and
- provides services that are an integral part of the hiring firm's day-to-day operations.

Before You Hire a Friend or Family Member for Your eBay Business

Many eBay businesses employ family or friends. But when you are trying to find the right person for the job, take it slow when hiring friends or family members.

Many business owners have a sad tale to tell about hiring a friend or family member only to find that their new worker—while pleasant enough in a social context—was never going to be a serious competitor for employee of the month. Here are some questions to think about before asking a friend or family member to join your eBay business:

- **Is the person qualified?** Relatives and friends are easy to hire and hard to fire. Consider asking friends or family members to work on a specific project or for a defined period of time to avoid painful terminations if things don't pan out.

- **How will it affect family finances?** Don't bring in a spouse or other relative until you project the short- and long-term impact on your family balance sheet. If your spouse leaves a day job to work for your eBay business, it may cast a shadow over the family's financial picture—credit rating, tax deductions, and benefits—and negatively affect your personal relationship.

- **Does the friend or family member share your vision?** You can't expect your friends and family to be as driven as you about your eBay business, but it helps if the person working with you believes in what you're doing. A shared vision can promote your business and strengthen your relationship; a lack of interest can cause resentment. Keep in mind that fair compensation of family and friends is important, or they will resent your success.

Finding the Right Person for the Job

Unless you are lucky enough to meet a qualified candidate through someone you trust, you will have to write a help-wanted ad and place it. Your success will depend not only on what is in the ad, but also where you post it. Once you figure out what kind of people you want to attract, think about what they read, where they hang out, and where they look for work. Then you'll know where to post your job. Here are some examples:

- **Colleges and universities.** If you're looking for some basic help with graphic design, marketing, research, or anything else someone might learn in a degree-granting program, post your job at a local college or university. Students are eager to do a good job—after all, they want experience and solid job references for the future. At their schools, they probably also have access to useful equipment, technology, and experts.

- **Online job listings.** When we asked business owners where they look for qualified workers, many of them gave us the same answer: Craigslist. This website (or "online community," as its founder calls it) offers local bulletin boards for about 70 U.S. communities. Here people can post jobs, items for sale, personal ads, housing listings, and input to discussion forums. To look for workers, you can either search listings by people who want work, or for $75, post your own help-wanted ad. Craigslist offers 25 categories of jobs, from accounting to writing and editing. And because it's such a popular site, you can count on getting plenty of responses to your ad.

- **Temporary agencies.** Depending on the type of help you need, you might find qualified people through a temp agency. These days, many agencies specialize in particular fields, such as graphics and art design and website maintenance.

Once you have some ideas about where to post your ad, put your job description in writing. The best help-wanted postings are short and sweet. Start by listing what you want the worker to do, focusing on specific tasks and duties. Specify whether the worker must have particular experience—for example, using a certain software program or working with specific machinery or customers. Don't forget to tell applicants how to contact you and what to send, such as a résumé, work sample, or references.

Employment Resources

For help in hiring, check out Nolo's <u>Business and Human Resources</u> website and Commerce Clearing House's <u>Business Owner's Toolkit</u>. Other helpful resources include *The Employer's Legal Handbook*, by Fred Steingold (Nolo).

Legal and Paperwork Requirements: ICs

There are only a couple of legal requirements you need to meet when hiring an IC.

Get the IC's taxpayer identification number. The IRS knows that many ICs are paid "under the table,"—that is, in cash—and that they either don't report or underreport those earnings to the IRS. To put a stop to this, the IRS requires those who hire ICs to get a copy of their taxpayer ID—their employer identification or Social Security number that they use on their tax returns. If an IC won't give you an ID number or the IRS informs you that the number the IC gave you is incorrect, you have to withhold taxes from the IC's pay and remit that money to the IRS. (The IRS calls this "backup withholding.") Obviously, you want to avoid this extra chore—and you can, by requiring the IC to fill out <u>IRS Form W-9</u>, *Request for Taxpayer Identification Number.* If the IC doesn't have an ID number yet, you don't have to start withholding until 60 days after he applies for one.

Write down your agreement with an IC. Do not hire an IC for more than a very minor project without signing an agreement. You are not legally required to do so, but creating an IC agreement helps you and the IC clarify the terms of your deal, creates a written record of exactly what you agreed upon, and can help convince the IRS and other agencies that you and the IC did not intend to create an employer-employee relationship. Projects that involve the creation of written or design materials, as in designing a website, especially require a written agreement, as the law presumes that the person who creates it continues to own the copyright in it, unless there is a written agreement that states otherwise. At the very least, an IC agreement would include a statement of the services to be performed, the fees, the time period for completion, a statement regarding the working relationship (for example, that the worker is an independent contractor, not an employee), and a process for resolving disputes. For help creating a written IC agreement, take a look at *Consultant & Independent Contractor Agreements*, by Stephen Fishman (Nolo).

Complete and file IRS Form 1099-MISC, *Miscellaneous Income*. Form 1099 is very straightforward, and you only have to complete and file it if you pay an IC $600 or more in the tax year. You simply enter identifying information about your business and the IC, then enter the amount you paid the IC in the box marked "Nonemployee compensation." You must provide copies of the form to the IC no later than January 31 of the year after you made the payment, which gives the IC an opportunity to correct any mistakes in his identifying information. You also have to file copies of the form with the IRS and possibly your state taxing authority (you have to file with the IRS by February 28 of the year after you made the payment; check with your state tax agency to find out its filing deadline). When you file the 1099 with the IRS, you must send along IRS Form 1096, *Annual Summary and Transmission of U.S. Information Returns*. Form 1096 is essentially a cover letter for Form 1099, on which you state how many 1099s are being submitted with it. If you are transmitting Form 1099-Misc to the IRS electronically, then a Form 1096 is not required.

Finding the forms. You can download both Form 1099 and Form 1096 from the IRS website, where you can also find additional details on filing.

Getting Started as an Employer

Before hiring an employee, you must do some work to legally establish yourself as an employer. These tasks essentially let the government know that you are hiring people and trigger some ongoing filing and other requirements.

Get an employer identification number (EIN) from the IRS. You've probably obtained an EIN, but if you haven't, apply for one before hiring. You will need it when completing various government forms, reports, and returns required of employers.

Don't forget workers' compensation insurance. Many states require all of their employers to have workers' compensation coverage, obtained either through paying into a state fund or buying a separate policy. Some states exempt employers with no more than two or three employees from this rule, but it might make sense to purchase coverage anyway. Beyond the legal requirements, having workers' compensation coverage can save you a bundle if one of your employees is hurt on the job.

Register with your state's labor department. Once you hire an employee, you are obligated to pay state unemployment taxes. These payments go to your state's unemployment compensation fund, which provides short-term relief to workers who lose their jobs. Typically, you must complete some initial registration paperwork, then pay money into the fund periodically. Unemployment compensation is a form of insurance, so the amount you pay in will depend, in part, on how many of your former employees file for unemployment (just as your insurance premiums depend, in part, on how many claims you file against the policy).

Finding the forms. Start at the federal Department of Labor map, which provides a link to each state's unemployment agency. Once you get to your state agency's website, look for a tab or link on unemployment or find the material for employers or businesses. Many states provide downloadable forms and online information about your responsibilities.

Hang up required posters. Even the smallest businesses are legally required to post certain notices letting employees know their rights under a variety of workplace laws. The federal government wants you to put up a handful of notices; many states have additional posting requirements.

Finding the posters. The federal Department of Labor's website has a special page detailing poster compliance requirements; it also provides downloadable posters. Your state's labor department probably also has any required posters on its website. If you're having trouble figuring out which requirements apply to you (or you don't want to post a dozen different notices), you can usually purchase an all-in-one poster that combines all required state and federal notices from your local or state chamber of commerce.

Legal and Paperwork Requirements: Employees

Once you are legally ready as an employer, you can hire your first employee, and ... fill out more forms. Hiring an employee requires more paperwork than hiring an IC. Fortunately, most of the paperwork is fairly simple, and you can find the forms online. When you hire an employee, you must do all of the following:

Have the employee complete IRS Form W-4, *Employee's Withholding Allowance Certificate.* On this form, the employee provides basic identifying information and the number of exemptions to use when you calculate how much tax to withhold from each paycheck. You must have this form in your files, but you don't have to send it to the IRS.

Finding the forms. You can download Form W-4 from the IRS website, or get it by contacting your local IRS office (you can find a list of offices at the IRS website) or by calling 800-TAX-FORM.

Complete USCIS Form I-9, *Employment Eligibility Verification.* This form confirms that the employee is eligible to work in the United States. The employee must complete a portion of the form and then show you documentation that proves her eligibility. The form tells you what kinds of documents are considered acceptable. A U.S.

passport, or a driver's license and birth certificate or Social Security card, are the typical forms of proof provided by U.S. citizens. You don't have to file Form I-9 with an agency, but you must keep it on hand for the later of three years from hiring the employee or one year after the employee quits or is fired.

Finding the forms. You can download <u>Form I-9</u> from the website of the <u>United States Citizenship and Immigration Services</u> (USCIS, formerly the Immigration and Naturalization Service, or INS).

Report the employee to your state's new hire reporting agency. Employers must submit basic information on new employees to the state, which uses that information to track down parents who owe child support. At a minimum, you must submit your employee's name, address, and Social Security number, and some states require additional information, such as the employee's date of birth or first day of work.

Finding the forms. To get the information and forms you need, start at the <u>Employer Services</u> website of the Administration for Children and Families, a subdivision of the federal Department of Health and Human Services. Click the tab for <u>New Hire Reporting</u>, to learn more about your state reporting requirements.

Set Up a Payroll System

Once you become an employer, you'll be responsible for with-holding and paying a variety of taxes on behalf of your workers. For example, you'll have to withhold federal income tax, Social Security tax, and Medicare tax from your employees' paychecks and periodically pay that money (along with your own contribution for the employee's Social Security and Medicare) to the IRS. In most states, you'll also have to withhold and periodically pay state income tax. A handful of states also require you to withhold and pay taxes for state-run disability insurance programs (and, in

California, for paid leave to care for a sick family member). And you'll have to generate end-of-the-year paperwork, such as IRS Form W-2, showing your workers how much they earned and how much they paid in taxes.

As you might imagine, it would be somewhat difficult to do all of this math yourself—and generate an itemized pay stub detailing all of the withholding for your employees. Fortunately, there are plenty of options for small business owners, including relatively inexpensive software and Web-based payroll services that do the work for you. A couple of the most highly recommended are the *QuickBooks* series (from Intuit), which offers a range of payroll options starting at just $17 a month, and Paycycle, an online payroll service that costs about $10 a month. Other payroll services are available from banks or other financial institutions or companies such as PayChex, but these services are generally more expensive. The advantage of using a *QuickBooks* product is that it can integrate with your Intuit accounting and tax software. Several software auction management programs will export data to *QuickBooks*, as well. Another good choice may be *Microsoft Office Accounting* which has extensive eBay integration. ●

Financial Forecasting

Break-Even Analysis 240

Profit and Loss Forecast 242

Cash Flow Projection 246

F irst, the bottom line: Financial forecasting is a matter of making educated guesses as to how much money you'll take in and how much you'll need to spend—and then using these estimates to calculate whether your business will be profitable.

Financial projections simply predict the amount of sales revenue you can expect from your eBay business; the expenses you will incur, including the cost of the products you are selling; and the profit you can anticipate. If your eBay business is not already off the ground, your projections will help determine how much you'll need to invest or borrow to get it started. Forecasting is always easier if you've been in business for a little while, because you have months (or years) of actual revenue and expenses upon which to base your forecasts. If you do not have any operating history, financial software such as *QuickBooks* or *Microsoft Office Accounting* can help you get started.

Business people use different types of financial projection analysis and tools, all meant to give them information and help in making decisions about the future. Below are common examples.

Break-Even Analysis

Using a break-even analysis, you calculate how much revenue you'll need each week or month to break even—that is, not lose money. To calculate your break-even number, you need to know two pieces of information: your "overhead" and your "profit percentage." Overhead includes expenses that don't vary much each month, such as rent and insurance—you must pay these expenses no matter what is happening in the business.

To determine your profit percentage, start by calculating the total cost of a typical product. For example, if you sold bicycles, the cost would be the price you paid for a bicycle plus any shipping charges or the value of any labor that you spent to repair or tune it up. Let's say that the total cost is $75. Next, subtract that total cost from the selling price of the bicycle. So, if you sold it on eBay for $125, you would subtract $75 (cost) from $125 (selling price), and the difference would be $50. That's your gross profit.

To determine your profit percentage, divide your gross profit ($50) by the selling price ($125). Your profit percentage would be 0.40 or 40%.

Calculating Profit Percentage

Selling price (price at which the item sold on eBay) $ _____

Cost of item (price you paid plus associated costs to acquire
and sell the item) $ _____

Gross profit (subtracting cost of item from selling price) $ _____

Profit percentage (divide gross profit by selling price) $ _____

If you sell several different types of products, or make different amounts on each one, you need to average the various profit percentages to determine your business's overall profit percentage. To improve your accuracy, you should weight your results. For example, if you sell twice as many children's bikes as adult ones, you'll need to reflect that in your average. You can also save yourself some time and just work with the lowest or most conservative profit percentage.

Calculate your break-even amount by dividing your monthly overhead expenses by your profit percentage. For example, if your eBay bicycle store has fixed monthly costs of $500, and your profit percentage is 40%, then you need sales of $1,250 a month to break even ($500 divided by .40). If this amount is below your anticipated sales revenue, then you're facing a loss—and you'll need to lower expenses or increase sales to break even.

Calculating Monthly Break-Even Amount
(Monthly Sales Needed to Break Even Each Month)

Total monthly overhead expenses	$_____
Profit percentage (see above)	$_____
Monthly break-even amount (divide monthly overhead expenses by profit percentage)	$_____

Profit and Loss Forecast

In your profit and loss forecast, you refine the sales and expense estimates that you used for your break-even analysis into a formal, month-by-month projection of your eBay business's profit for one or two years of operation. It's basically a spreadsheet that details your expected monthly expenses and revenue.

To determine estimated profits, you plug in your estimates of monthly revenue and of expenses such as phone service, depreciation, and shipping.

If you have a spreadsheet program that can read *Excel* (.xls) spreadsheets, fillable spreadsheets are provided on the disc to help you prepare your monthly sales revenue forecast and a profit and loss statement. Sample templates are shown below.

Sales Revenue Forecast

Year 1: _____ , 20 _____ to _____ , 20 _____

	Month	Units (if applicable)	Revenue
Month 1	_____	_____	$ _____
Month 2	_____	_____	_____
Month 3	_____	_____	_____
Month 4	_____	_____	_____
Month 5	_____	_____	_____
Month 6	_____	_____	_____
Month 7	_____	_____	_____
Month 8	_____	_____	_____
Month 9	_____	_____	_____
Month 10	_____	_____	_____
Month 11	_____	_____	_____
Month 12	_____	_____	_____
Year One Total:		_____	$ _____

Year 2: _____ , 20 _____ to _____ , 20 _____

	Month	Units (if applicable)	Revenue
Month 1	_____	_____	$ _____
Month 2	_____	_____	_____
Month 3	_____	_____	_____
Month 4	_____	_____	_____
Month 5	_____	_____	_____
Month 6	_____	_____	_____
Month 7	_____	_____	_____
Month 8	_____	_____	_____
Month 9	_____	_____	_____
Month 10	_____	_____	_____
Month 11	_____	_____	_____
Month 12	_____	_____	_____
Year Two Total:		_____	$ _____

	Units (if applicable)	Revenue
Year One Total	_____	$ _____
Year Two Total	_____	_____
Total of Years One and Two	_____	_____

Profit and Loss Forecast: Year One

for _____

Month:	1	2	3	4	5
Sales Revenue					
Less: Cost of Sales					
Plus: Shipping and Handling Revenue					
Gross Profit					
Fixed Expenses:					
Wages/Salaries					
eBay Fees					
Collection Fees (PayPal, Credit Card)					
Payroll Tax					
Rent/Lease					
Marketing & Advertising					
Insurance					
Accounting/Books					
Interest Expense					
Depreciation					
Utilities					
Telephone					
Supplies					
Bad Debts					
Freight					
Miscellaneous					
Less: Total Fixed Expenses					
Profit/(Loss)					

Date Completed: _____

6	7	8	9	10	11	12	Year Total

Cash Flow Projection

Simply put, the money that comes in and goes out of your eBay business is your cash flow. Where the other types of projections predict long-term profitability, the cash flow projection focuses on day-to-day operations. Can you survive in those in-between times when you must pay bills but there are no eBay sales for that week? For example, the cash flow for the first few months of any business is often negative. In order to survive, you may need to borrow money during that period. Cash flow projections are useful for every business, but they're particularly helpful if you have not yet opened.

To make your cash flow projection, you'll have to prepare a spending plan, setting out items your business needs to buy and expenses you will need to pay. You then feed these numbers, along with information from your profit and loss forecast, into a spreadsheet. A fillable spreadsheet is provided on the disc to help you estimate your cash flow. A sample template is shown below.

A business plan guide can also help you with this task—for example, _Business Plan Pro_ or Mike McKeever's _How to Write a Business Plan_ (Nolo) can simplify this procedure. (The financial forms included with this kit are from _How to Write a Business Plan_, and are used with permission.) If you have more money to spend on financial projections ($200 to $1,000), you may want to consider paying a bookkeeper with small business experience to help you polish your forecasts.

Cash Flow Forecast: Year One

for _____

	Month:	1	2	3	4	5
Profit/(Loss) [P & L line 6]						
Less: Credit Sales _____% of Sales on Credit x Sales Revenue [P & L Line 1]						
Plus: Collections of Credit Purchases Received _____ Months After						
Plus: Credit Purchases _____% of Purchases on Credit x Cost of Sales [P & L Line 2]						
Less: Payments for Credit Purchases Paid _____ Months After						
Plus: Withholding _____% of Total Wages (if Paying Taxes Quarterly)						
Less: Quarterly Withholding Payments (if Paying Taxes Quarterly)						
Plus: Depreciation						
Less: Principal Payments						
Less: Extra Purchases						
Other Cash Items In/(Out)						
Monthly Net Cash						
Cumulative Net Cash						

Date Completed: _____

6	7	8	9	10	11	12	Year Total

Business Licenses and Permits

EIN: IRS Form SS-4, Application for Employer
Identification Number 252

Local Business License 253

DBA: Register Your Fictitious Business Name 253

Get a Seller's Permit... 255

Make Sure You Meet Local Zoning Requirements... 256

F irst, the bottom line: You may believe that it's better to "fly below the radar" and avoid registering your business with federal, state, and local agencies. Understandably, you may worry that filing registrations may result in more paperwork, more taxes, and more obligations, and also raise zoning issues. That decision is up to you, but ignoring licensing and registration requirements is risky and, if discovered, may interfere with your ultimate goal of building a thriving eBay business. Keep in mind that these registration requirements are easy to meet—you just have to fill out a few simple forms. This chapter explains how to find and file the basic forms required for any eBay business.

EIN: IRS Form SS-4, Application for Employer Identification Number

Despite its name, this form is required for many businesses that don't have employees. You must file it to obtain an employer identification number (EIN): a nine-digit number that identifies your business for tax purposes, just as a Social Security number identifies an individual. Your business must have an EIN if you have at least one employee. Even if you have no employees, you must get an EIN if either of the following are true:

- You operate your eBay business as a partnership, limited liability company, or corporation (the EIN is necessary to identify your business on your tax returns).
- You are a sole proprietor and have a Keogh retirement plan (a plan for self-employed people), buy or inherit an existing business, or file for bankruptcy.

Finding the forms. The IRS has made it easy to apply for an EIN. You can download the fillable Form SS-4 ("fillable" means that you can complete the form on screen instead of printing it out and completing it), then mail or fax it to the IRS, or you can fill out the Form SS-4 online at the IRS website and submit it electronically. You can also apply by phone at 800-829-4933. If you file electronically or by phone, you will immediately receive a provisional EIN, which will become your permanent EIN once the IRS verifies your application information. Don't forget to write the number down and store it someplace safe; if you file online, print a copy of the form for your records.

Local Business License

Many cities and counties require those that do business within their limits to file a registration form—this form may be called a tax registration certificate, business license, business tax application, or something similar. No matter what the form is called, its purpose is the same: to tax your business. You may have to pay a flat fee or a rate that depends on your annual revenue. If your eBay business is small (as measured by its revenues), you may be exempt from a city or county licensing requirement.

Finding the forms. If you do business in a city, contact your city government to find out about licensing requirements and get the necessary forms. If you do business in an unincorporated area, contact your county government. Many local governments have websites—and some post information for small businesses and make their forms available online. You can find a comprehensive list of links to online local government agencies at State and Local Government on the Net. If you're looking for county ordinances online, you can find them at the website of the National Association of Counties.

DBA: Register Your Fictitious Business Name

If your eBay business operates under a fictitious name (often called a "DBA," for "doing business as"), you probably have to register that name with your state or county government. A fictitious name does not refer only to a completely made up moniker, such as Xerox or Kodak. Any name that doesn't precisely match your corporate, partnership, or limited liability company name is considered fictitious. If you are operating as a sole proprietor, any name that doesn't include your last name (or, in some states, your full legal name) or seems to suggest that other people are involved in your business (such as John Brown & Associates) is fictitious.

In most places, DBAs are registered with your county government. Registration typically requires filing a registration certificate (along with a fee, of course) with the county. You may also have to run a statement in a local newspaper for a set period of time, stating your DBA and your true name.

The state wants you to register your name so it can track you down if your business does something wrong, such as ripping off consumers or skipping out on loans or bills. But there's plenty in it for you, too. For starters, registering a DBA puts other companies on notice that the name is taken—and stakes your claim to use the name as of the registration date. Registering a DBA does not provide trademark protection, however. Read <u>Registering Your Business Name</u> to understand the difference.

There are other practical reasons to register a name. For example, some banks require a registration certificate in order to open a business bank account under a business's fictitious name. And you may not be able to enforce a contract you signed in the name of the business unless you can show that the name was registered properly.

Finding the forms. For information on registering a fictitious name, go to your county clerk's website (you can probably find a link to it at <u>State and Local Government on the Net</u>). If the information you need is not there, check your state's website.

Get a Seller's Permit

In most states, you need a permit from the state authorizing you to sell goods to, and collect sales tax from, customers within the state. As the seller, you are responsible for charging sales tax on purchases made from your eBay store or via an eBay auction if the goods ship to a location within your state. For more, review Chapter 22, *Paying Your Taxes.*

In some states, the seller's permit also allows a seller to buy items from wholesalers (for resale to customers) without paying sales tax. This is a real money-saver if you are a seller who buys wholesale lots from jobbers or liquidation sales within your state that you plan to resell on eBay. Some states call this a seller's permit; others call it a resale permit or something similar. (Note: You might need a permit even if your state doesn't have a sales tax. Even in the handful of states that don't impose a sales tax— Alaska, Delaware, Montana, New Hampshire, and Oregon—local governments sometimes impose sales taxes, which you may be required to collect and submit to the appropriate agency.)

If your state requires a seller's permit, don't make sales unless and until you get one. Getting caught doing business without a permit will likely result in you having to pay the sales tax you should have collected from your customers, along with a fine.

Finding the forms. You can find information (and in some cases, forms) on seller's permit requirements at your state tax agency's website. To find a link to that website, check the list provided on the <u>Small Business Administration</u> website, on the <u>Multistate Tax Commission</u> website, or among the <u>state links</u> at the IRS website.

Make Sure You Meet Local Zoning Requirements

When you register for a local business license, your local government will almost certainly check to make sure that your eBay business meets the zoning requirements for the address you provide for your business. If your business is not in compliance—perhaps because it has too many employees, or because it has frequent deliveries and pickups—you will not get a license. What's more, you can probably expect a city or county inspector to drop by and start issuing citations (or perhaps even shut you down) in fairly short order. Ignoring the registration requirements will not work, either, because you can be sure that a neighbor will report you after the UPS truck blocks his driveway a few times. Deal with your business location right away—if the zoning is not right for your business, find another location or facility where you can store, pack, and ship your goods without hassle.

Paying Your Taxes

This *Does* Apply to You..258

What Taxes Your eBay Business Will Have to Pay 259

What About Sales Outside the U.S.? 261

How Business Income Is Taxed..261

Paying Estimated Taxes...263

First, the bottom line: If you are a typical owner of a small eBay business you will need to pay income taxes, self-employment taxes, employment taxes (if you have employees), and sales tax (if your state imposes sales tax on the goods or services you sell). If this sounds imposing, the good news is that an excellent tax preparation program exists to handle at least the income and self-employment taxes.

This *Does* Apply to You

Do not assume that because you are a casual eBay seller you don't have to report income from your sales. Regardless of whether you think of your eBay activities as a hobby or a business, you must report all income on your tax return. Failure to do so can lead to severe fines and penalties.

Keep in mind that eBay businesses already arouse some suspicion when it comes to IRS auditing decisions. The IRS computer analysis known as the discriminate function system (or "DIF") looks for red flags (information that the IRS believes taxpayers are likely to lie about) in a tax return, and one of those flags is the tax return item "losses from an activity that could be viewed as a hobby, rather than a business." eBay businesses, which often have a pleasure, leisure, or enjoyment component—for example, an eBay business that trades in Hummel figurines—can raise a red flag for an IRS auditor.

Can the IRS get your records from eBay? Yes, although most tax experts admit that a routine tax audit will likely not reach that level of investigation. But keep in mind that is exactly what happened in Australia, where the Australian Taxation Office sought records for Australian eBay PowerSellers. Considering that 430,000 Americans make a significant portion or all of their revenue from eBay, it's not out of the question to expect the IRS to take a closer look at eBay sales. This is all to say: Keep good records and report your income!

What Taxes Your eBay Business Will Have to Pay

There are four types of taxes a typical self-employed person running an eBay business might have to pay.

Income taxes. You will have to pay income taxes on the net profit your eBay business earns. The federal government imposes an income tax, as do the governments of most states (with the exception of Alaska, Florida, Nevada, South Dakota, Texas, Washington, and Wyoming). Some local governments (both county and city) also get into the act by taxing businesses within their jurisdictions; a few use an income tax, while others use some other method (an inventory, payroll, or business equipment tax, for example).

Self-employment taxes. If you are self-employed, you are responsible for paying your own Social Security and Medicare taxes. Unlike employees, whose employers are legally required to chip in for half of these amounts, you will have to pay the entire bill—currently, a 12.4% Social Security tax and a 2.9% Medicare tax on all of your taxable income from self-employment (although there is an earnings maximum amount subject to Social Security—$102,000 in 2008).

However, you are entitled to deduct half of these taxes from your gross income for purposes of calculating your income tax. To report and pay self-employment taxes, you must file IRS Schedule SE, *Self-Employment Tax*, along with your annual tax return. Even if you have a salaried job, and Social Security and Medicare are deducted from your paycheck, you still have to pay those taxes on amounts you earn from the eBay business you run in your spare time.

Employment taxes. If you have employees, you will have to pay half of their Social Security and Medicare taxes, as well as unemployment tax and perhaps temporary disability tax (to your state taxing authority). You'll also have to withhold taxes from your employees' paychecks and deposit them with the IRS. To report and pay unemployment tax, you file IRS Form 940, *Employer's Annual Federal Unemployment Tax (FUTA) Tax Return*.

To report all withholdings and pay your share of Social Security and Medicare, you must file IRS Form 941, *Employer's Quarterly Federal Tax Return*. The rules for employment taxes can get pretty tricky, and many employers are required to make quarterly filings with the IRS. For more information, check out IRS Publication 15 (Circular E), *Employer's Tax Guide*, at the IRS website.

TurboTax does not calculate your employment tax, but you can set up your payroll through *QuickBooks*. Because of the frequent filings required for employment taxes, you might investigate payroll services before hiring employees. These services, which may be offered through your bank, online, or through payroll companies such as PayChex, take care of paying your employees and filing federal and state employment tax returns. Make sure to comparison shop as to both price and reliability. These options are also discussed in the discussion about payroll in Chapter 19, *Hiring Help*.

Sales taxes. Almost every state imposes a tax on the sales of goods. The basic principle for eBay sales tax is that you are responsible for collecting sales tax from any buyer in the state where your eBay business has a physical presence, such as where you have an office or warehouse. For example, if you operate in California and a California buyer purchases an item from you, you would be responsible for collecting California sales tax. eBay will add a sales tax calculation into your listing so that buyers in your state can calculate their sales tax. State sales tax rules vary considerably. For example, every state exempts certain sales from tax (that is, you don't have to collect or pay tax on the sale), but the list of what is exempt differs from state to state. Similarly, each state's rules vary about when and how to submit taxes you have collected to the state taxing authority. To find the rules in your state, your best bet is to go straight to your state tax agency for help. The Small Business Administration provides links to all state tax agencies, and Commerce Clearing House (CCH) has a thorough explanation of sales tax obligations at its website. Nolo also offers information about sales tax on the Internet. The rules can be complicated if you use a drop-shipper—a business that maintains the inventory and facilitates shipment—or run an eBay consignment shop—a business in which others provide you with inventory to sell on eBay for a fee.

What About Sales Outside the U.S.?

Assuming you only occasionally sell items internationally, you do not have to be concerned about paying value added taxes (VATs) to other countries.

How Business Income Is Taxed

How you pay taxes on your profits will depend on how you have structured your eBay business. As explained in Chapter 14, *Business Entities: What Kind of Business Should Your eBay Business Be?*, there are four basic business forms: sole proprietorship, general partnership, limited liability company (LLC), and corporation (both C and S type). For tax purposes, however, there are only two types: those whose owners pay tax on business income on their individual tax returns (called "pass-through" entities, because income and expenses pass through the business to the owners), and those that must pay their own taxes.

The vast majority of eBay small business owners are running a pass-through entity. Sole proprietorships, partnerships, LLCs, and S corporations (corporations that elect to be taxed like a partnership) are all pass-through entities. A pass-through entity does not pay its own taxes. Instead, its profits or losses are deemed to be the profits and losses of the individual owners, who must report those amounts on their personal tax returns. Keep in mind that owners of a pass-through entity categorize the entity's income as their own, whether or not they actually receive any money from the entity. C corporations are separate entities for tax purposes.

The basic rules for reporting income by the various business entities are as follows.

Sole proprietors report business income and expenses on IRS Schedule C, *Profit or Loss From Business*, which they must file along with their personal tax returns (IRS Form 1040).

Partners report their respective shares of partnership income and expenses on IRS Schedule E, *Supplemental Income and Loss*, which they must file along with their 1040s. In addition, the partnership itself must file an informational return (IRS Form 1065, *U.S. Return of Partnership Income)* and provide each partner with an IRS Schedule K-1, which lists each partner's share of income and expenses.

Shareholders in S corporations report their respective shares of the corporation's income and expenses on their personal tax returns (IRS Schedule C, *Profit or Loss From Business,* and IRS Form 1040). In addition, the S corporation must file IRS Form 1120S, *U.S. Income Tax Return for an S Corporation.* This return gives the IRS information about the S corporation, but you don't pay any taxes with it. Note that S corporations filing a calendar year income tax return usually have a filing date of approximately March 15, not April 15 as for individual returns. To assist you, here is a tax calendar.

LLC members report their income and expenses just like sole proprietors, if it's a one-member LLC. In a multimember LLC, members report their income and expenses just like partners. A multimember LLC also has to file IRS Form 1065, *U.S. Return of Partnership Income*, and issue an IRS Schedule K-1 to each member. (LLCs may, however, choose to be taxed as C corporations by filing IRS Form 8832, *Entity Classification Election*, in which case the LLC would file its own tax return and pay its own taxes on LLC income.)

Shareholders in C corporations only report the corporation's income to the extent the corporation pays it out to them. The C corporation, the form most large businesses take, is the only business form listed here that is not a pass-through entity. A C corporation must file its own tax return and pay its own taxes on corporate income. (It does so by filing IRS Form 1120, *U.S. Corporation Income Tax Return.*) Corporate shareholders have to report personal income tax on their IRS Form 1040 only on the corporation's business income that is paid out to them as compensation or dividends. This is where the potential tax-saving benefits of incorporating come from—that is, shareholders can decide how much corporate income to distribute and how much to retain in the corporation, thereby timing when they will receive taxable income. Note that corporations filing a calendar year income tax return usually have a filing date of approximately March 15, not April 15 as for individual returns. To assist you, here is a tax calendar.

Paying Estimated Taxes

When you have your own eBay business, the IRS wants to collect your tax dollars as the year progresses, rather than waiting for you to pay the whole tab on April 15. That's why any eBay owner who must pay more than $1,000 in taxes in any calendar year must pay estimated taxes. If you are operating a sole proprietorship, for example, your estimated taxes would be calculated on your estimated annual income and paid in four installments over the course of each year. These payments must include both estimated income tax and estimated self-employment taxes.

Estimated Tax Payment Schedule	
Income Received	**Estimated Tax**
January 1 through March 31	April 15
April 1 through May 31	June 15
June 1 through August 31	September 15
September 1 through December 31	January 15 of the following year

You don't have to pay estimated taxes until you earn some income. For example, if your eBay business doesn't bring in any income by March 31, you don't have to make an estimated tax payment on April 15.

Not everyone has to pay estimated taxes. You don't if any of the following are true:

You expect to owe less than $1,000 in federal tax for the year.

- You paid no taxes last year, if you were a U.S. citizen and your tax return covered the full 12-month period.
- Your business is a C corporation and you receive dividends or distributions of profits from your corporation on which you will owe less than $500 in tax for the year. (Assuming that the corporation is paying payroll taxes on your salary, you don't have to pay estimated taxes on salary you receive from your corporation; instead, you report that income and pay tax on it annually, on your personal tax return.)

But even if you don't have to pay estimated taxes, you might want to do it, anyway. Paying estimated taxes spreads your tax bill over the entire year, so you won't have to come up with all of the money at once. On the other hand, as long as you really have enough socked away to cover your bill, paying it later and all at once will give you longer period of time. ●

Tax Deductions

What's a Tax Deduction Worth? 266

Basic Categories of Tax Deductions 267

Operating Expense: Deducting Home Office Costs 269

Additional Tips: Home Office Deduction 273

Operating Expense: Deducting Vehicle Costs 274

Operating Expense: Deducting Travel Costs 275

Operating Expense: Deducting Meals and Entertainment Costs 276

Capital Assets: Deducting the Costs of Long-Term Assets 277

Section 179 277

Depreciation 278

    Does depreciation ever make sense? 279

Special Rules for Computers, Cell Phones, and Other Potential Toys 279

Inventory Expense: Deducting the Cost of Goods Sold 280

Commonly Overlooked eBay Deductions 282

Quicklist: Tax Deductions 283

First, the bottom line: Your eBay business may provide not only extra cash, but additional tax deductions as well.

You can substantially lower your taxes by deducting eBay expenses from your income. For example, you can deduct the cost of the eBay goods you have sold, the use of your home and car for eBay business, money you pay employees, business insurance costs, rent, interest, and many other expenses. After you factor in federal income taxes, state income taxes, and self-employment taxes, every dollar you spend on deductible business expenses could save you more than 40 cents on your tax bill.

Many eBay entrepreneurs miss out on valuable business deductions simply because they don't know which expenses they can deduct. You may already itemize deductions on your personal tax return, but once you start an eBay business, a whole new range of deductions becomes available—and it sure pays to spend some time learning what they are.

This chapter explains some of the deductions most commonly claimed by eBay entrepreneurs. Once you start racking up deductible expenses, however, you will likely need more detailed information about these and other deductions. Consider _Deduct It! Lower Your Small Business Taxes_ and _Home Business Tax Deductions_, both by Stephen Fishman (Nolo). Additionally, the IRS website provides a lot of tax guidance, including helpful advice about business expenses. The IRS also offers some great online classrooms that offer lessons on setting up a business and preparing taxes.

What's a Tax Deduction Worth?

A tax deduction is the cost or value of something that you can subtract from your gross income (all the money you earn) to determine your taxable income (the amount on which you have to pay tax). When you bought this product, did you save the receipt or any other proof of purchase? Good! Assuming you are starting or have an eBay business, you can deduct this expense from your income.

Few of us stop and consider what a great deal the government is offering when it comes to tax deductions. By letting you deduct your expenses, the government is essentially offering to pick up part of the tab for your venture. The offer is on the table; it's up to you to take advantage of it by claiming every tax deduction to which you're entitled.

A tax deduction is not a dollar-for-dollar proposition: You don't save in taxes the entire amount you paid for deductible goods and services. But because you don't have to pay tax on the amount of income you spent on a deductible item, a deduction can save you almost half of what you spend. The exact amount you'll save by taking a deduction depends on your tax bracket—the tax rate that applies to your income. The higher your bracket, the more every deduction is worth.

To illustrate how valuable a tax deduction can be, consider this hypothetical case: Simon has an eBay business selling taxidermy equipment. He spends $2,000 on a computer for his business. He's in the 25% federal income tax bracket. By deducting the cost of the computer, he doesn't have to pay tax on $2,000 of his income. That saves him 25% of $2,000, or $500. But that's not all. The state where Simon does business imposes a 6% income tax, so Simon saves an additional $120 there. And Simon doesn't have to pay self-employment taxes—the amount self-employed people have to chip in to fund their Social Security and Medicare—on this money, either. The self-employment tax rate works out to about 12%, for an additional $240 savings. Simon ends up saving $860 in taxes, almost half of what he paid for his computer.

Basic Categories of Tax Deductions

How much you can deduct and when you can take the deduction depend on the type of expense. Below are the four basic categories of deductions. Rules for specific types of operating expenses, capital asset deductions, and treatment of inventory costs are also discussed in more detail later in this chapter.

Operating expenses. Once your eBay business is operating—that is, you are making sales—you can deduct your day-to-day operating expenses. These might include expenses for storage rental, office supplies, shipping costs, employee salaries, travel, professional services, advertising, interest on business loans or purchases, and other expenses incurred in operating your business. As long as you aren't paying for something that you will use for more than a year (and you'll see that this restriction has many exceptions), you can deduct these expenses in the year you spend the money. The IRS has created special rules for operating expenses that it believes are often overstated or abused—home office, travel, vehicle, and entertainment expenses—and these are covered in more detail below.

Capital expenses. You can deduct the cost of items for your business that have a useful life of more than one year, such as a car, furniture, or machinery. You usually have the choice of either depreciating an asset's cost (deducting a portion of the cost for each year of its useful life, the length of which is determined by the IRS) or deducting its cost all at once. See "Capital Assets: Deducting the Costs of Long-Term Assets," below, for more information.

Inventory expenses. You can deduct the cost of inventory that you sell on eBay, but there are special tax rules for inventory that is not sold each year. This is why so many businesses are desperate to get rid of their inventory at the end of the year: They want to take a larger deduction, and they want to minimize their burden when it comes time to count inventory for tax purposes. We'll discuss inventory deductions in more detail later in this chapter.

Start-up expenses. Money that you spend before you start selling on eBay—for example, when buying computers, researching what kind of eBay business to start, or conferring with your accountant—are start-up expenses. When it comes to dealing with these expenses, you can do one of two things:

- **Treat them as part of your basis in the business.** "Basis" is the amount of money you have invested in your business, which has not been treated as a tax deduction. If you were to sell your business, the basis would be subtracted from the sale price to determine your capital gain or loss. If you treat a start-up expense as part of the basis, you cannot deduct that expense from your income.

- **Deduct them over time.** If all of your start-up expenses were incurred after October 23, 2004, you may deduct up to $5,000 of them right away. If you do so, you must then deduct the remainder of the expenses over the first 180 months you are in business. A different rule applies to start-up costs incurred before October 24, 2004: None are deductible right away. Instead, all must be spread equally over the first 60 months you are in business.

If you have already incurred start-up costs, you'll have to follow the rules laid out above. If you are just starting to do so, and you don't anticipate spending more than $5,000 on start-up expenses, you can simply deduct all of those expenses in the year they are incurred. However, if you believe you will spend more than $5,000 in start-up costs, there are ways to avoid spreading out part of your deduction over the next 15 years. The key is to start your business before you lay out significant amounts of money; that way, your expenses are usually immediately deductible. Your business is considered to start operating once you make items available for sale. For example, postpone major purchases until you're up and running. Once you start selling on eBay, you can buy that fancy computer system and office furniture, or shell out thousands of dollars for advertising.

Operating Expense: Deducting Home Office Costs

If you are like most eBay entrepreneurs, you are likely running your operation from home. If so, you may be able to claim as a business deduction a portion of your rent, utility bills, cleaning services, homeowner fees, and other home-related costs. Although commonly referred to as the "home office" deduction, this deduction actually applies to any home space you use for your eBay business, including a studio or workshop.

Meeting the test. To qualify for the home office deduction, you must use your home workspace exclusively and regularly for business, in addition to meeting other tests, listed below. The requirements to qualify for a home office deduction are slightly different if the home is used to store inventory (see below).

Exclusivity. You meet the requirement of exclusivity if you use the home workspace only for managing eBay matters, and not for personal or other purposes. You are not required to devote an entire room to your eBay business to qualify; you can use just a portion of one, so long as that portion is used exclusively for eBay business. If you mix business with personal matters—for example, you use your workspace to correspond with clients and handle business bookkeeping, but also to play online poker and pay household bills—then you do not qualify for the home office deduction.

There is some flexibility with regard to the exclusivity requirement if you're using your home to store inventory. If you use part of your home for storage of eBay inventory, you can deduct the expenses related to this business use of your home without meeting the "exclusivity" standard, provided you meet all of the following tests:

- You sell the inventory as part of your eBay business.
- You keep the inventory in your home for use in your eBay business.
- Your home is the only fixed location of your eBay business.
- You use the storage space on a regular basis.
- The space you use is a separately identifiable space suitable for storage.

Regular use. You must also use your home office regularly; that is, on a continuing basis and not just for occasional work. The IRS has never clearly explained exactly what it considers regular use. One court found 12 hours a week sufficiently regular, but no one really knows how low you can go.

It doesn't have to be a house. You don't have to live and work in a house to take the home office deduction. Apartments, condominiums, or even motor homes, houseboats, and other vehicles that double as your home and workspace can qualify, but you must meet the tests set out above. Simply owning a vehicle that you use as a residence and running a business are not enough, in themselves, to prove your entitlement to the deduction. You must also be able to demonstrate a business use of the vehicle.

Other requirements. If you use your home office exclusively and regularly for eBay business, you will qualify for the home office deduction if you meet one of these additional tests:

- **Your home office is your principal place of business.** If you do all or almost all of your eBay business in your home office, you meet this test. If you work in more than one location, however, you must show that you perform your most important business activities or carry out your administrative or management tasks at home. For example, if you sell used vinyl recordings on eBay but you spend a lot of time buying vinyl record collections—that is, traveling to other people's homes to examine collections—you will qualify for the home office deduction as long as you manage your eBay listings, billing, and other important business at home.

- **You use a separate freestanding structure on your property.** If you regularly and exclusively use a standalone building, such as a detached garage, cottage, or workshop, you may use the home office deduction for that space—even if that structure is not your principal place of business.

What can you deduct? Using the home office deduction, you can deduct a portion of your household expenses, including:

- rent
- mortgage interest and property taxes (the advantage of taking a portion of these costs as a business deduction rather than a personal deduction—as you are entitled to do on IRS Schedule A, *Itemized Deductions*—is that it reduces your business income and therefore your self-employment taxes)

- condominium or homeowners' association fees
- depreciation on a home you own
- utilities
- insurance
- maintenance and cleaning
- security costs, and
- casualty losses.

The exact percentage of these expenses you can deduct depends on how much of your home used for business. There are two ways to calculate this percentage:

- **Using the room method.** Divide the number of rooms you use for business by the total number of rooms in your home (not including bathrooms, closets, and other storage areas). For example, if you use the spare bedroom of your four-room home for business, you can deduct 25% of your household expenses.
- **Using the square footage method.** Divide the square footage of the area you use for work by the total square footage of your home (do not include stairways, hallways, landings, entries, attics, or garages in your calculations unless the attic or garage is part of your home office). For example, if you use a ten-foot-by-20-foot room as an office in your 1,000-square-foot home, your home office deduction percentage is 20%.

In addition to deducting a portion of overall household expenses, you may deduct 100% of any expense incurred solely for your home office. For example, if you pay someone to paint the entire interior of your home (including your work area), you may deduct only the home office portion of the cost. But if you hire a painter to paint just your home office, you can deduct the entire amount.

Additional Tips: Home Office Deduction

Plenty of eBay business owners do not take a home office deduction, because they believe it will trigger an audit. The IRS insists that such belief is misguided, but it never hurts to be cautious. Follow these tips to maximize your home office deduction—and minimize your chances of losing in an audit.

- **Devote a separate room exclusively to your eBay business.** While you may claim a home office deduction even if you use only a portion of a room for work, designating an entire room to your work is much easier for deduction purposes: The math is easier, you won't have to worry about physically separating your work from your personal space, and you'll have an easier time satisfying the IRS that you use your office exclusively for your business.

- **Figure out which method yields the highest deduction.** Of course it's easier to simply count rooms, but also take the time to measure the square footage devoted to your workspace. Depending on your home's layout, the square footage method may result in a higher deduction.

- **Create visual aids.** Take a picture of your home office, and draw up a simple diagram of your home's layout showing the space used for business. This evidence can help prove, if ever necessary, that you applied the correct percentage when calculating what portion of your home is used for work.

- **Keep a record of eBay home office activities.** If clients or customers visit, ask them to sign a log book. Note the time you spend on business in a datebook or calendar.

- **Use your eBay home office as your business address.** It will be easier to prove that your home is your principal place of business if you designate it as such. As long as you are comfortable with privacy issues—your address may become publicly available—have business mail delivered there and put your address on business correspondence, cards, and your letterhead.

- **Save those eBay business receipts (and other records).** When you take the home office deduction, you can claim other expenses that you might not think of as business-related, such as a portion of your rent, utility payments, or house-cleaning fees. Remember that you'll have to save bills and receipts for these expenses along with your other business records.

Operating Expense: Deducting Vehicle Costs

Most eBay business owners do some driving for business, whether to pick up supplies, acquire inventory, go to the post office, or, other tasks. If you're one of them, you have two methods to choose from in calculating your vehicle deduction—the standard mileage rate or the actual expense method.

- **Standard mileage rate.** Using the standard mileage rate, you can claim a set deduction for every mile driven on eBay business. For 2008, the rate is 50.5 cents per mile (the current rate can also be found at the IRS website). Certain additional expenses, including parking fees and tolls, can also be deducted. However, the cost of repairs, maintenance, gas, insurance, or other costs of operating your car cannot be deducted, because these costs are already calculated into the standard rate. You can use the standard rate only for a car that you own. If you don't use the standard rate in the first year you drive your car for business, you will not be able to use it for that car, ever.

- **Actual expense method.** Using the actual expense method, you can deduct all of the costs related to business use of your car, including interest payments, insurance, license fees, oil, gas, and repairs. You can also depreciate the car, which means you take a deduction each year to reflect the car's declining value. If you use the car for personal reasons, you can deduct only a pro rata portion of your expenses. Using the actual expense method is much more time-consuming than using the standard mileage rate. However, if you have an expensive car, the depreciation rate and possibly higher operating costs could result in a hefty deduction, so it might be worth the extra recordkeeping.

Whatever method you use, you must keep careful records. Because the IRS believes that taxpayers often overstate how much they use their cars for business, it has instituted some special rules for vehicle deductions. For instance, you must carefully track your business and personal mileage. The easiest way to do so is to keep a log in your car and record the odometer reading at the beginning and end of every business-related drive, as well as the readings at the beginning and end of every year. If using the actual expense method, you'll also need to keep records of all vehicle expenses for that tax year.

Operating Expense: Deducting Travel Costs

If you travel overnight for eBay business, you can deduct your airfare, accommodations, rental cars, and other travel expenses. Economy is not an issue for the IRS—you may fully deduct your costs, even if you stay at four-star hotels and enjoy the comforts of a first-class cabin.

However, most people do not travel to a distant city and spend every waking moment working—time may also be spent seeing the sights and visiting friends. The IRS has created a set of rules delineating what costs are deductible and how much of a trip must be business-related in order to deduct its costs. These rules depend on where you travel and how long you stay.

If you travel within the United States, transportation costs (air and cab fare, for example) are deductible as long as you spend at least half of your trip on business—for example, buying merchandise or meeting with manufacturers. On days when you are carrying out business, you may also deduct your "destination" expenses, such as hotel costs, 50% of your meal expenses (see below for more on this 50% rule), local transportation (including car rental), and telephone charges.

On days when you are not working, destination costs cannot be deducted. Similarly, the costs related to a spouse or other companion accompanying you cannot be deducted unless that person is your employee and is traveling for a reason genuinely related to your business.

If you travel outside the United States, the rules depend on the length of your trip. If your trip is shorter than seven days, you can deduct your transportation costs and the destination expenses for days you spend working. If your trip lasts more than seven days and you spend more than 75% of your time on business—for example, you spend eight of ten days at a business conference— the same rules apply. However, if you spend between 50% and 75% of your time on business, you may deduct only the business percentage of your transportation costs (you can still deduct destination costs for the days you spend working). And if you spend less than 50% of your time working, none of your costs are deductible.

Although these rules may already seem complicated, there are many more that are too detailed to cover here. Because there has been a lot of taxpayer abuse, the IRS has really gone to town in imposing restrictions on travel deductions. As a result, there are special rules for cruises, conventions, side trips, and more. For all the details, read IRS Publication 463, *Travel, Entertainment, Gift, and Car Expenses.*

Operating Expense: Deducting Meals and Entertainment Costs

If you host customers, advisers, suppliers, or other business associates, you may be able to deduct 50% of your entertainment costs. However, because taxpayers have abused the entertainment deduction, there are many specific rules about what expenses may be deducted and how to prove the meal or entertainment had a business purpose.

To claim a deduction, you must be hosting someone who can benefit your business in some way—for example, a supplier of inventory or a software consultant. You cannot deduct the cost of renting, buying, or building an entertainment facility (such as a fishing lodge or tennis court); club dues; membership fees; or the cost of nonbusiness guests. As may be apparent, deducting meals and entertainment expenses is another area where the rules can be complicated. For more information, see <u>IRS Publication 463, *Travel, Entertainment, Gift, and Car Expenses*</u>.

Capital Assets: Deducting the Costs of Long-Term Assets

Capital or long-term assets are items purchased for use in your business that have a useful life of more than one year (as determined by the IRS). These include computers, machinery, furniture, and other equipment. The tax laws offer two alternatives in deducting the costs of long-term assets:

- **Section 179,** deducting the costs of capital assets in the year they were purchased, if the requirements of Section 179 of the Internal Revenue Code are met, or
- **Depreciation,** deducting a portion of the cost of the item for each year of the item's useful life.

Section 179

Section 179 of the Internal Revenue Code allows a business to deduct the costs of long-term assets in the year they are purchased. The amount of the deduction cannot be more than your total taxable income from the active conduct of any trade or business (that includes employee and spouse's wages, sole proprietorships, partnerships, and S corporations).

Any unused deduction under Section 179 may be carried over to a future year, when business is better and there is more income to cover the deduction. Assuming your eBay business is doing extremely well, you may deduct up to a current limit of $102,000 in costs for capital assets per year.

Section 179 only applies to the purchase of tangible personal property—you can't use it to deduct the cost of land, buildings, or intellectual property such as patents and copyrights. To take the deduction, you must use the item for business more than half of the time in the year you buy it. This means that if you buy an item (such as a computer or desk) for personal use and then start using it in your business more than one year later, you cannot deduct it under Section 179.

It also means that if you use an item at least half of the time for personal (nonbusiness) purposes, you can't take the deduction. If you use the item more than half of the time for business, you may deduct only a percentage of what you paid based on the time you use it for business. For example, if you paid $2,000 for a computer that you use 75% of the time for business, you may deduct $1,500 of the total cost.

Depreciation

Depreciation spreads the deduction for the cost of a long-term asset over its useful life, which the IRS considers to be three to seven years, at least for most business equipment and electronics. Rather than deducting the entire cost at once, you take the deduction in installments, according to one of several formulas accepted by the IRS. The depreciation rules are complicated; the IRS guide to the subject (Publication 946, *How to Depreciate Property*) is more than 100 pages long and is full of exceptions, limits, and traps for unwary deduction claimers. If you are required or plan to use the depreciation method, get some accounting assistance.

Does depreciation ever make sense?

Unless you buy more than $102,000 worth of business property in a single year, you'll probably be allowed under Section 179 to deduct the costs of long-term assets in their year of purchase. So why would anyone ever choose to depreciate these costs?

Generally, they wouldn't. In a couple of situations, however, spreading the cost of a capital asset over several years makes sense:

- **You need to show a profit.** If you're pushing up against the IRS's hobby-loss rule (see Chapter 3, *Is eBay Your Hobby or Your Business?*) in a particular year, you may need to show positive net income to prove you are really running a business, not playing at a hobby. Depreciation will decrease the deduction for an item for that year, which might mean the difference between a profit and a loss.

- **You expect to earn more in the future.** If you expect to be in a higher tax bracket in later years, you might want to depreciate. Because the value of a tax deduction depends on your tax rate, a deduction will save you more in taxes if your earnings are higher.

Special Rules for Computers, Cell Phones, and Other Potential Toys

The IRS has created special rules for deducting the cost of items that can easily be used for personal purposes, including computers, vehicles, cell phones, stereo equipment, and cameras. For these types of property (called "listed" property), you are required to keep a log proving that you use the item for business, even if you use it only for business and never for fun. The only exception is computers: If you use your computer exclusively for your eBay business, you don't have to keep a log. The moral of the story? Many eBay entrepreneurs find it more sensible to buy a separate computer solely for eBay use than to go through the hassle of noting every use.

Inventory Expense: Deducting the Cost of Goods Sold

Each year, you can deduct the cost to you of all of the items you sold on eBay. For example, if you purchased 400 troll dolls for $800 and you sold half of these, you can deduct $400 as your "cost of goods." For eBay businesses that sell hundreds or thousands of items each year, the calculation can become very complex, especially if the goods are handmade or manufactured specifically for sale on eBay. In the latter case, several costs must be calculated in order to determine the cost of goods.

The cost of goods sold is calculated on Schedule C of your tax return. The IRS illustrates this calculation on its website—see <u>lines 35 through 42</u> of a sample Schedule C. In summary, the lines are completed as follows:

- **Line 35.** If you are buying and selling merchandise, list the cost to you of the inventory of merchandise on hand at the beginning of the year. Usually, this amount is identical to the prior year's closing inventory. If it isn't, you must explain why to the IRS. If this is your first year of operations, beginning inventory would be zero. If you are a manufacturer or producer of goods—for example, you manufacture hand-made clothing for sale on eBay—include the total cost of raw materials, work in process, finished goods, and materials and supplies used in manufacturing the goods, but only those that were part of inventory at the beginning of the year. The IRS provides an <u>explanation on valuing inventories</u> at its website.

- **Line 36.** Here you provide the cost of all merchandise you purchased during the year. If you manufactured goods for sale, include the costs of all raw materials you purchased in the year that were necessary to manufacture those goods. Subtract the cost of any items withdrawn for personal use.

- **Line 37.** If you manufacture goods for sale, calculate labor costs: the amounts paid to employees for manufacturing. Do not include any amounts paid to yourself. If you are simply reselling merchandise and not creating new products, you will not have labor costs associated with your inventory. Of course, if you have employees that are not involved in manufacturing items for sale, their labor costs will be deducted elsewhere on the tax return and are not included in the cost of goods sold.

- **Line 38.** If you manufacture goods for sale, list the amount paid for materials and supplies, such as hardware and chemicals, used in manufacturing the goods.
- **Line 39.** If you manufacture goods for sale, you can list additional costs such as containers and packages that are part of the manufactured product, costs of freight to bring in supplies, and overhead expenses—for example, rent, heat, light, power, insurance, depreciation, taxes, and maintenance—that are direct and necessary manufacturing expenses.
- **Line 40.** Add lines 35 through 39, which will represent the total cost of inventory your business held in the year.
- **Line 41.** On line 41, you enter the value of the inventory unsold at the end of the year. Keep in mind that the value of the remaining inventory is not the price you plan to sell it for; it is the amount you paid for it or, if you are a manufacturer, invested in it. This amount will become your beginning inventory for the next year—that is the number you will use on line 35 of the following year's tax return. Note that most businesses do a "physical" inventory at the end of the year—that is, actually count and record the type and number of each remaining inventory item. The results of this work will provide the basis for the year-end inventory calculation. Physical inventories also allow you to inspect and discard inventory that is damaged or of no value, thereby "writing it off" of year-end inventory and increasing the costs of goods sold deduction. A physical count also will alert you to items missing from your inventory.

- **Line 42.** On line 42, you subtract the amount listed on line 41 (ending inventory) from line 40 (all inventory costs). The result is the amount you claim as your cost of goods deduction.

Because of the potential complexity in managing inventories, especially manufacturing inventories, many eBay entrepreneurs use software such as *QuickBooks* or *Microsoft Office Accounting* in conjunction with spreadsheets or auction management software (see Chapter 11, *Auction Management Tools*).

Commonly Overlooked eBay Deductions

While the types of business deductions discussed above can be somewhat complicated, the deductions below are more straightforward. Nevertheless, they are often overlooked by eBay entrepreneurs when tax time comes.

- **Casualty losses.** If your storage area is damaged or destroyed by fire, vandalism, flood, or some other sudden, unexpected, or unusual event, you can claim the amount of the loss as a deduction—but only to the extent that the loss isn't covered by insurance.
- **Dues, subscriptions, and fees.** You can deduct membership dues, subscriptions, and other fees related to your business. For instance, if you subscribe to stamp-collecting journals or belong to philatelic organizations, you can deduct these expenses from your eBay income, provided your business sells stamps or philatelic supplies.
- **Education expenses.** If you buy books or guides (like this one), take a seminar or attend an <u>eBay University</u> college course, or attend a convention to keep up with the latest trends in your field, you can deduct your costs. As long as the expenditure either improves your business-related skills or is required to maintain your professional status (like continuing legal education for lawyers), it's deductible.

- **Phone bills.** If you have a separate business line in your home office, you should deduct not only the costs associated with that phone, but also the cost of occasional business calls you make from your cell phone or personal phone line.
- **Retirement plans.** You can deduct the money you contribute to most types of retirement plans that you set up for yourself or your employees. And if you qualify, you can deduct some of the start-up and administrative costs of a pension plan you establish for your employees. (See IRS Form 8881, *Credit for Small Employer Pension Plan Startup Costs*, for more information.)
- **Federal and state tax credits.** Tax credits may be available to eBay businesses that support particular civic goals—for example, by hiring employees through a welfare-to-work program, doing business in designated "empowerment" or "renewal" zones (communities that are struggling economically), or using solar energy. You can find information on federal credits in IRS Publication 334, *Tax Guide for Small Business*; for information on state credits, contact your state taxing authority.

Quicklist: Tax Deductions

The following Quicklist will help you formulate your deductions. Keep in mind that this is just a starting point; you will need to confirm whether you qualify for each of these deductions by reviewing the material in this chapter.

Tax Deduction Basics		
Did you have any startup expenses?	☐ Yes ☐ No	
Do you have a home office?	☐ Yes ☐ No If so, what is your:	
	Rent	
	Mortgage interest	
	Property taxes	
	Homeowners' association fees	
	Depreciation	
	Utilities	
	Insurance	
	Maintenance and cleaning	
	Security costs	
	Casualty losses	
Did you use your vehicle for eBay business purposes?	☐ Yes ☐ No	
Did you travel for your eBay business?	☐ Yes ☐ No	
Did you spend money on meals or entertainment for your eBay business?	☐ Yes ☐ No	
Did you acquire any goods for your eBay business including office equipment, computers, cell phones, or other items needed to operate your eBay business?	☐ Yes ☐ No	

Tax Deduction Basics (continued)	
Did you acquire any capital assets?	☐ Yes ☐ No If so, do you want to: ☐ Deduct the costs of capital assets in the year they were purchased (Section 179), or ☐ Depreciate the costs (that means deducting a portion of the cost of the item for each year of the item's useful life).
Do you want to deduct the cost of goods sold (inventory deduction)?	☐ Yes ☐ No
Did your eBay business have any casualty losses?	☐ Yes ☐ No
Did you pay any dues, subscriptions, or fees related to your eBay business?	☐ Yes ☐ No
Did you have any education expenses for your eBay business?	☐ Yes ☐ No
Did you have any phone expenses for your eBay business?	☐ Yes ☐ No
Did you put money into any retirement plans associated with your eBay business?	☐ Yes ☐ No
Did your eBay business have any federal or state tax credits?	☐ Yes ☐ No

How to Use the CD-ROM

Installing the Files Onto Your Computer..289

Where Are the Files Installed?..290

Using the HTML Version of This Book...290

Using the Word Processing Files to Create Documents....................291

Opening a File...291

Editing Your Document 292

Printing Out the Document 292

Saving Your Document..292

Using the Spreadsheets..293

Files on the CD-ROM 295

P lease read this appendix and the ReadMe.htm file included on the CD-ROM for instructions on using it.

In accordance with U.S. copyright laws, the CD-ROM and its files are for your personal use only.

The CD-ROM can be used with Windows computers. It is not a standalone software program. It installs files that use software programs that need to be on your computer already.

Three types of files are included:

1. The contents of the book in HyperText Markup Language (HTML) that you open with your browser with clickable links to helpful websites (see "Using the HTML Version of This Book," below)

2. Word processing (RTF) forms that you can open, edit, print, and save with your word processing program (see "Using the Word Processing Files to Create Documents," below), and

3. Spreadsheets in *Microsoft Excel* format (XLS) that you can use with *Excel* and other spreadsheet programs that read XLS files (see "Using the Spreadsheets," below).

See the end of this appendix for a list of forms, their file names, and their file formats.

Note to Macintosh users: This CD-ROM and its files should work on Macintosh computers. Please note, however, that Nolo cannot provide technical support for non-Windows users.

How to View the README File

To view the file ReadMe.htm, insert the CD-ROM into your computer's CD-ROM drive and follow these instructions:

Windows 2000, XP, and Vista

(1) On your computer's desktop, double click the My Computer icon; (2) double click the icon for the CD-ROM drive into which the CD-ROM was inserted; (3) double click the ReadMe.htm file.

Macintosh

(1) On your computer's desktop, double click the icon for the CD-ROM that you inserted and (2) double click the ReadMe.htm file.

Installing the Files Onto Your Computer

Before you can do anything with the files on the CD-ROM, you need to install them onto your computer.

Insert the CD-ROM and do the following:

Windows 2000, XP, and Vista

Follow the instructions that appear on the screen.

If nothing happens when you insert the CD-ROM, then (1) double click the My Computer icon; (2) double click the icon for the CD-ROM drive that you inserted the CD-ROM into; (3) double click the file Setup.exe.

Macintosh

If the eBay Business Start-Up Kit window is not open, open it by double clicking the eBay Business Start-Up Kit icon.

(1) Select the eBay Business Start-Up Kit folder icon and (2) drag and drop the folder icon onto your computer.

Where Are the Files Installed?

Windows 2000, XP, and Vista

The HTML file that you use to access the HTML version of this book is index.html. The files it links to are installed by default to a folder named HTML in the \Program Files\eBay Business Start-Up Kit folder of your computer.

RTF files are installed by default to a folder named Forms in the \Program Files\eBay Business Start-Up Kit folder of your computer.

XLS files are installed by default to a folder named Spreadsheets in the \Program Files\eBay Business Start-Up Kit folder of your computer.

Macintosh

The HTML file that you use to access the HTML version of this book is index.html. The files it links to are in the HTML folder.

RTF files are located in the Forms folder.

XLS files are located in the Spreadsheets folder.

Using the HTML Version of This Book

The contents of the eBay Business Start-Up Kit book is on the CD-ROM in HTML format. In this format, there are links to helpful online information. (The only HTML file that you will work with is index.html.) It contains links to all the other book pages, found in the HTML folder.

There are three ways to open the book in HTML format.
1. Windows users can open a file by selecting its shortcut. (1) Click the Windows "Start" button; (2) open the Programs folder; (3) open the eBay Business Start-Up Kit folder; (4) click the icon for The eBay Business Start-Up Kit.
2. Both Windows and Macintosh users can open the HTML version of the book by double clicking the main index file.

Use My Computer or Windows Explorer (Windows 2000, Vista, or XP) or the Finder (Macintosh) to go to the eBay Business Start-Up Kit folder you installed on your computer. Then, double click the file named index.html.

Using the Word Processing Files to Create Documents

The CD-ROM includes word processing files that you can open, complete, print, and save with your word processing program. All word processing forms come in Rich Text Format and have the extension ".RTF." For example, the form for Quicklist: Before You Bid, discussed in Chapter 6, is in the file Q_BuyinganItem.rtf. RTF files can be read by most recent word processing programs including *Microsoft Word*, Windows *WordPad*, and recent versions of WordPerfect.

The following are general instructions. Because each word processor uses different commands to open, format, save, and print documents, refer to your word processor's help file for specific instructions.

Do not call Nolo's technical support if you have questions on how to use your word processor or your computer.

Opening a File

You can open word processing files in three ways:

1. Windows users can open a file by selecting its "shortcut." (1) Click the Windows "Start" button; (2) open the Programs folder; (3) open the eBay Business Start-Up Kit folder; (4) open the Forms subfolder; (5) click the shortcut to the form you want to work with.

2. Both Windows and Macintosh users can open a file by double clicking it. (1) Use My Computer or Windows Explorer (Windows 2000, XP, or Vista) or the Finder (Macintosh) to go to the eBay Business Start-Up Kit folder, (2) open the Forms folder, and (3) double click the file you want to open.

3. Windows and Macintosh users can open a file from within their word processor. (1) Open your word processor; (2) go to the File menu and choose the Open command. This opens a dialog box where (3) you will select the location and name of the file. (You will navigate to the version of the eBay Business Start-Up Kit folder that you've installed on your computer.)

Editing Your Document

Here are tips for working on your document.

- Refer to the book's instructions and sample agreements for help.
- Underlines indicate where to enter information, frequently including bracketed instructions. Delete the underlines and instructions before finishing your document.
- Signature lines should appear on a page with at least some text from the document itself.

Printing Out the Document

Use your word processor's or text editor's Print command to print out your document.

Saving Your Document

Use the Save As command to save and rename your document. You will be unable to use the Save command because the files are "read-only." If you save the file without renaming it, the underlines that indicate where you need to enter your information will be lost, and you will be unable to create a new document with this file without recopying the original file from the CD-ROM.

Using the Spreadsheets

This section concerns the spreadsheet files, which are in *Microsoft Excel* format and have the extension ".XLS." For example, the financial statement spreadsheet discussed in Chapter 12 is in the file FinancialStatement.xls. They can be opened and edited with *Microsoft Excel* and other spreadsheet programs that read XLS files.

The following are general instructions. Because each spreadsheet program uses different commands to open, format, save, and print documents, read your spreadsheet program's help files for specific instructions. Nolo's technical support department is unable to assist with your spreadsheet software.

To complete a spreadsheet, (1) open the file in a spreadsheet program that is compatible with XLS files; (2) fill in the needed fields; (3) print it out; (4) rename and save your revised file.

Opening a File

There are three ways to open the spreadsheets.

1. Windows users can open a file by selecting its shortcut. (1) Click the Windows "Start" button; (2) open the Programs folder; (3) open the eBay Business Start-Up Kit folder; (4) open the Spreadsheets folder, and (5) click on the shortcut to the spreadsheet you want to work with.

2. Both Windows and Macintosh users can open a file by double clicking it. Use My Computer or Windows Explorer (Windows 2000, Vista, or XP) or the Finder (Macintosh) to go to the eBay Business Start-Up Kit folder you installed on your computer. Then, double click on the Spreadsheets folder and double click the file you want to open.

3. Windows and Macintosh users can open a file from within your spreadsheet program. To do this, (1) start your spreadsheet program; (2) go to the File menu and choose the Open command. This opens a dialog box where (3) you will

select the location and name of the file. (You will navigate
to the eBay Business Start-Up Kit folder that you installed on
your computer.)

Entering Information Into the Spreadsheet

Here are a couple tips:

While you are filling in information, you can consult the
instructions and sample spreadsheets in the book for help.

Some spreadsheets are created to perform automatic calculations
as you fill the cells.

Printing Out the Spreadsheet

Use your spreadsheet program's Print command to print out your
document.

Saving Your Spreadsheet

After filling in the form, use the Save As command and rename
the file. You will be unable to use the Save command because the
files are "read-only." If you were to save the file without renaming
it, it would overwrite the original spreadsheet, and you would
need to recopy the original file from the CD-ROM to create a new
document.

Files on the CD-ROM

The following files are in Rich Text Format (RTF):

Form Title	File Name
Quicklist: Is eBay Your Hobby or Your Business?	Q_HobbyorBusiness.rtf
Quicklist: What Will You Sell?	WhattoSell.rtf
Quicklist: How to Prepare for an eBay Listing	ListinganItem.rtf
Quicklist: Before You Bid	Q_BuyinganItem.rtf
Quicklist: Should You Open an eBay Store?	Q_Open a Store.rtf
Quicklist: Software Tools	AuctionManagement.rtf
Quicklist: Tax Deduction Basics	TaxDeductions.rtf
Online Auction Buyer Demand Letter	OnlineAuctionBuyer.rtf
Promissory Note	PromissoryNote.rtf

The following spreadsheets are in Microsoft Excel Format (XLS):

Form Title	File Name
Cash Flow	CashFlow.xls
Financial Statement	FinancialStatement.xls
Profit and Loss Forecast	ProfitForecast.xls
Sales Revenue Forecast	SalesRevenue.xls

Index

A

About Me page, 18, 150

Account Guard spoof protection (eBay), 77

Accounting. *See* Record keeping and accounting

Accounting Assistant software (eBay), 198

Accounts payable/receivable, 196

Accrual method accounting, 200

Acronyms (eBay), 22, 57, 59

Actual expense method, for vehicle deductions, 274–275

Administration for Children and Families, 236

Adobe Photoshop Elements photo editing software, 61

Advanced search (eBay), 51

Advertisements, 14, 152

Affiliate programs (eBay), 153

Airfare expense deductions, 275

Alternative tax treatment, 174

Amazon.com, 81, 82

Announcement boards (eBay), 6

Answer center (eBay), 6

AOV (average order value), 149, 150

Apartments, home office deduction for, 271

Apple *Safari* Internet browser, 21

Appraisal services, 59

Articles of incorporation, 177

Articles of organization (LLC), 175

ASP (average sale price), 149

Assets, capital, 268, 277–279

Assets, protection of personal, 172–173

Auction, Dutch, 20, 66

Auctionblacklist.com, 114

AuctionBytes website, 62, 87, 88, 114, 140, 147

Auction Hawk auction management tools, 139

Auction items, in eBay stores, 91, 93

Auction listings. *See* Listing an item

Auction management tools
  accounting, 194, 198
  choosing the tool you need, 135–138, 140–141
  description templates, 64
  desktop or web-based, 134
  for handling photos, 61, 62
  list of popular programs, 138–141
  overview on, 21–22, 134–135, 139, 140
  PayPal integration with, 107–108
  for prioritizing /automating work, 221

for tracking inventory, 196
    utilized by PowerSellers, 148
Auction photography software, 61
Auction Sentry, 88
Auction Software Review website, 140
Auctiva auction management tools,
    140
Audits, 29, 194, 195, 201–203, 258, 273
Authentication and Grading Services
    (eBay), 59
Authenticity questions, auction item,
    82
Auto insurance, 186–187, 190
Automobile expense deductions, 195,
    202, 271, 274–275, 279
Auto shippers, 129
Average order value (AOV), 149, 150
Average sale price (ASP), 149

B

Backup withholding, 232
Bad debts, 200
Bank loans, 154
Bankruptcy, 156, 173
Banner ads, 152–153
Banner Space ad space agents,
    152–153
Basis, business, 268–269
Bid Alert feature (eBay), 77
BidderBlock software, 141
Bidding
    being outbid, 84, 86
    bid shielding, 113
    list of tasks, 79–82

placing a bid, 83–86
    process overview, 83–88
    proxy bidding, 86, 87
    retracting a bid, 79, 83, 111, 113
    shill bidding, 112
    sniping, 87–88
    tracking your bids, 87
    unwelcome, 112
    watching before, 77
BIN (buy it now price), 66, 68
Bizrate shopping website, 81
BizyMoms work-at-home tips, 218
Blackthorne software tools (eBay), 68,
    139
Bookkeeping and accounting. See
    Record keeping and accounting
Books, listing for sale, 61
BOP (business owners' policy)
    insurance, 189
Borrowing money, 154–156, 240
Break-even analysis, 240–242
Brick-and-mortar retail store, 34, 41,
    127–128, 154
Broadband connection, 10–11, 219
Budgeting
    and deciding to quit your day job,
        158
    personal financial statement for,
        161–169
    preparing a spending plan, 246
Building cost deductions, 278
Business assets, 268, 277–279
Business bank account, as proof of
    business activity, 30
Business basis, 268–269

Business classification, 28–32, 258
Business entities
   C corporations, 173–174, 176–178, 181, 261–264
   corporations, 173–174, 176–178, 222, 252–254, 262–263
   general partnerships, 172, 178–181, 222, 252
   and limited liability, 172–174
   limited partnerships, 180, 182
   LLCs *vs.* corporations, 173–175
   pros and cons of various, 180–182
   S Corporations, 180, 182, 261, 262
   taxes for various, 181–182, 259–263
   See also LLCs (limited liability companies); Partnerships; Sole proprietorships
Business equipment deductions, 277
Business equipment insurance, 185, 186, 190
Business form conversion, 175
Business interruption coverage, 187
Business licenses, 253
Business owners' insurance policy (BOP), 189
Business plan guides, 247
Business Plan Pro guide, 247
Business tax application, 253
Buyer demand letter, 116–117
Buyer protection, PayPal, 81, 108, 118
Buying an item
   on eBay Motors, 76, 128–129
   insurance for eBay transactions, 187–188
   item not received, 115, 118
   outside of eBay, 111
   overview on, 19, 79–82
   purchase protection, 118, 128
   registering to, 76
   research before, 79
   software tools, 141
   unwelcome buying/bidding, 112
   using the toolbar, 76–77
   Want It Now listings, 77–78
   See also Bidding
Buy it now (BIN) price, 66
Buy-It-Now items (fixed price listings), 20, 91, 94, 95, 100–101, 126
BuySafe bonding service, 81, 114, 188

C

Cab fare deductions, 275
Cable Internet connection, 219
California refund policy laws, 212, 213
Camera expense deductions, 279
Capital expenses, 268, 277–279
Capital gain/loss, 269
Car expense deductions, 195, 202, 271, 274–275, 279
Car insurance, 186–187, 190
Cash flow projections, 246–249
Cash method accounting, 199–200
Cash value insurance policy, 185
Casualty loss deductions, 272, 282
Categories, item listing, 49, 54–55
C corporations, 173–174, 176–178, 181, 261–264
CC&R (covenants, conditions, and restrictions) on home offices, 216, 217

CD-ROM instructions, 7, 288–295

CDs, listing for sale, 61

Cell phone cost deduction, 279

Chat rooms/boards, 6, 59, 111, 213–214

Children as customers, special rules for, 214

Child support, new hire reporting laws and, 235–236

Civic goal tax credits, 283

Cleaning cost deductions, 272

Click-N-Ship system (USPS), 208

Click-throughs, 96, 153

Club dues, as nondeductible, 277

CNET website, 10–11, 82, 220

Cohan rule, on deductible expenses, 195

Coins, selling collectible, 46, 59

Commercial space leasing, 221–223

CommissionJunction marketing assistant, 153

Commissions, third-party sales, 153

Community building, for increases web traffic, 151, 153

Community content policy (eBay), 111

Community property states, spouse co-owners in, 179

Community resources (eBay), 6, 147

Community values (eBay), 4–6

Comparison pricing, 24, 81

Computer, as basic equipment, 10

Computers, deducting cost of, 277–280

Computer software tools. *See* Software tools

Condition of sales items, 58–59

Conditions of sale, 71, 213–214

Condominiums, home office deduction for, 271, 272

Consignment sales, 41, 261

Contact us page (eBay), 22

Content, to attract web traffic, 151

Content theft, 61

Contracts, in partnerships, 178

Convention expense deductions, 276, 283

Conversion rate (CR), 150

Conversion to an LLC, 175

Cool eBay Tools newsletter, 147

Copyright costs, deducting, 278

Copyright infringement, website insurance against, 187

Copyright notices, 214

Corporate bylaws, 177, 178

Corporations, 173–174, 176–178, 180–182, 222, 252–254, 262–263

CoStar Group commercial leasing information, 222

Cost of goods sold deduction, 39, 280–282

Costs. *See* Fees (eBay)

Craigslist, 219, 222, 231

CR (conversion rate), 150

Credit card loans, 155

Credit cards, business *vs.* business/ personal use, 200, 201

Credit/merchant card account, 11, 52

Cruise expense deductions, 276

Customer privacy, 213

Customers, rules on children as, 214

Customer satisfaction. *See* Feedback

Customer satisfaction rating, 73

D

Data management, hiring professionals for, 227

Day job. *See* Quitting your day job

Dazzle shipping software, 209

DBA (doing business as) registration, 253–254

Debt liability, 156, 178

Debts, deducting bad, 200

Deductions. *See* Tax deductions

Depreciation of long-term assets, 32, 202, 274, 275, 278–279

Depreciation on your home, deducting, 272

Descriptions, item, 50, 63–65, 82

Detached garage, for home office deduction, 271

Detailed seller ratings (DSRs), 73, 124, 144

Digital camera/scanner, as basic equipment, 11

Disability insurance programs, 236, 259

Disclaimers, 213

Discounts, multiple sales, 150

Discussion boards (eBay), 6, 111, 147

Dispute resolution, 58, 112, 114–119, 187–188

Dispute resolution services, 118

Dissolution, creditor, 173

Domestic travel deductions, 275–276

Drop-shipping, 209–212, 260–261

DSL connection, 10, 219

DSRs (detailed seller ratings), 73, 124, 144

Dues, deducting, 282

Duration of auction, 67

Dutch auctions, 20, 66

E

eBay auction management tools, 138–139

eBay Business portal, 10

eBay companies, 23–25

eBay Express, 23

eBay features/services. *See* Features/services (eBay)

eBay Groups, 6, 111, 147

eBay insurance, 118

eBay Motors
  buying on, 128–129
  Dealer Center, 128
  overview on, 126
  selling on, 126–128, 130–132
  special feedback review of, 118
  vehicle history report option, 126

eBay university, 22, 282

eB Calc fee calculator, 69, 141

Education expense deductions, 282–283

EIN (employer identification number), 233, 252–253

Email, rules on unsolicited, 112

Email threats, prohibition on, 111

Employees
  benefits for, 188
  deducting retirement plan costs, 283
  employee-related insurance, 188, 189

finding the right, 230–231

friends/family members as, 229–230

handling payroll, 197, 259–260

income withholding for, 235, 236, 259

legal and paperwork requirements for hiring, 235–236

preparing to take on, 233–235

spouses as, 179

tax credits for welfare-to-work, 283

trading rules for, 111

vs. independent contractors, 226–229

zoning/homeowners' association restrictions on, 216, 217

Employer, respecting your current, 159–160

Employer identification number (EIN), 233, 252–253

Employment, current. *See* Quitting your day job

Employment notices, 234

Employment taxes, 197, 259–260

Empowerment zone tax credit, 283

Endicia shipping solutions, 209

Enhancements, listing, 56, 68

Entertainment expense deductions, 195, 202, 276–277

Entertainment facilities, as nondeductible, 277

Equipment, insurance for business, 185, 186, 190

Equipment, shipping, 206

Equipment cost deductions, 277

Escrow services, 114

eSnipe "hosted" services, 88

Established retail business, 34, 41, 127–128, 154

Estimated taxes, 263–264

Eviction, commercial space, 223

Excel spreadsheet software, 135, 158, 197, 242, 247

Exclusive use, for home office deduction, 270–271

Expenses, capital, 268, 277–279

Expenses, daily. *See* Operating expenses

Expenses, start-up, 268–269

Expertise, benefit of personal, 30, 31, 40, 146

Extortion, feedback, 113, 123–124

F

False contact information, 111

Family, borrowing money from, 154

Family members, hiring, 229–230

FAQs (frequently asked questions; eBay), 22, 90, 96, 144–145

Fast Photos photo editing software, 61

Features/services (eBay)

About Me page, 18, 150

Account Guard spoof protection, 77

affiliate programs, 153

Authentication and Grading Services, 59

a-z index, 22

Business portal, 10

customizable toolbar, 76–77

discussion boards, 111, 147

eBay community resources list, 6
frequently asked questions, 22, 90, 96, 144–145
glossary, 20, 22
help resources, 22–23, 147
Home Page, 12–15
ID verify process, 11, 17, 66
for item photos, 60–62
Keep It Simple listing method, 49–52
Learning Center, 22, 23, 147
Listing Designer, 64
market research, 34–39, 66, 79
My eBay page, 14, 21–22, 87
other eBay companies, 23–25
Popular Products page, 39
Reviews and Guides section, 6, 59, 82, 88, 147
selling methods, 20
Standard Purchase Protection Plan (eBay), 118
toolbar, 76–77
Trust and Safety Team (eBay), 118
tutorials, 76, 81
Want It Now want-ad service (eBay), 77–78
Watch List/Bid Alert, 77
See also Search feature; Stores
Federal laws, mail/telephone order rule, 211–212
Federal laws, on employment notices, 234–235
Federal tax credit deductions, 283
Federal tax debts, 173
FedEx shipping solutions, 209

Fee calculators, 69–70, 141
Feedback
    as accessible from the toolbar, 77
    for BIN pricing, 66
    changing posted, 122
    and DSRs (detailed seller ratings), 73, 124, 144
    entering, 121–123
    extortion threats, 113, 123–124
    feedback ratings, 122
    mutual feedback withdrawal, 118
    to open a eBay store, 97
    poor packaging and, 11
    in PowerSeller criteria, 144
    private feedback profiles, 123
    rules on negative buyer, 110, 119–121
    and safe payments, 73
    when buying an item, 81, 123–124
Fees, deducting membership, 282
Fees (eBay)
    double listing (insertion), 55
    on eBay Motors, 128
    fee calculators, 69–70, 141
    final value fees (FVF), 68, 96, 111, 115
    insertion fees, 55, 68, 95, 128
    ProStores, 101
    store, 91, 95–96
    subtitle, 56
    tracking, 68–69
Fictitious business name registration, 253–254
Final value fees (FVF), 68, 96, 111, 115

Finances. *See* Budgeting; Personal
   finances; Record keeping and
   accounting
Financial forecasting
   break-even analysis, 240–242
   cash flow projections, 246–249
   profit and loss forecast, 195,
      242–246
   and quitting your day job, 158
   sales revenue, 243
Financing, eBay Motors purchases,
   128
Financing Center (eBay Motors), 128
Financing your eBay business,
   154–156
Fixed price listings (Buy-It-Now
   items), 20, 91, 94, 95, 100–101, 126
Fixed price listing with best offer, 20
Flash player, 76
Florida refund policy laws, 213
Form I-9: *Employment Eligibility
   Verification,* 235
Form of business. *See* Business entities
FotoKiss photo editing software, 61
Fraud, 81–83, 113, 114, 178
Freight charges, in costs of goods
   sold, 281
Frequently asked questions (eBay), 22,
   90, 96, 144–145
Friends, borrowing money from, 154
Friends, hiring, 229–230
Froogle shopping website, 81
FTC (U.S. Federal Trade Commission),
   211, 214
Furniture, office, 218–219, 277

FUTA (Federal Unemployment Tax
   Act), 259
FVF (final value fees), 68, 96, 111, 115

G

Gas expense deduction, 274
General partnerships, 172, 178–181,
   222, 252
Getting started
   becoming an eBay member, 15–18
   deducting expenses of, 268–269
   essential items for, 7, 10–11
   learning about eBay, 5–7, 12–15,
      18–23
   other eBay companies, 23–25
   registering your business, 233,
      252–256
Gift expense deductions, 195
Gift items, strategies for selling, 40
Glossary (eBay), 20, 22
GMS (gross merchandise sales), 149,
   150
"Good 'Til Canceled" listings, 91, 95
GoToMyPC remote access software,
   134
Grading an item, 58–59
Gross leases, 222
Gross profit, 241
Guarantees, seller, 81

H

Half.com bargain center, 24
Hammertap's Fee Finder calculator,
   70, 141
Handling charges, 51, 72

Hazard insurance, 185, 217
Health insurance coverage, 145, 159
Help (eBay), 22–23, 147
High speed Internet connection, 10–11, 219–220
High-volume sellers, 21
Hiring help
    classifying workers, 226–229
    friends or family members, 229–230
    getting started as an employer, 233–235, 252–253
    ICs (independent contractors), 226–229, 232–233
    legal/paperwork requirements for independent contractors, 232–233
    recruiting, 230–231
    See also Employees
Hobbyists, IRS rules on, 28–32, 258, 279
HomeFurnish, for office furniture, 219
Home improvement deductions, 272
Home office
    advantages of, 223
    handling distractions, 218
    if you outgrow your, 221–223
    insurance for your, 185, 186, 188, 217
    restrictions on your, 216–217
    tips for maximum efficiency, 218–221
    tracking listed property use, 202
    use logbook for, 273
    and your neighbors, 217
Home office deduction, 269–274
Homeowners' association, restrictions on home offices, 216, 217

Homeowners' association fees, deducting, 272
Homeowners insurance, for business coverage, 185, 186, 188, 217
Home page (eBay), 12–15
Houseboats, home office deduction for, 271
HTML code, 63, 64, 99

I

ICs (independent contractors), 226–229, 232–233
ID verify process (eBay), 11, 17, 66
Illegal activity, 46, 81–83, 113, 114, 123–124, 178
Imports, sales strategies for, 41
Income, accounting of, 194, 202
Income forecasting, 158
Income taxes, 174, 196, 197, 259
Incorporation services, 176
Independent contractors (ICs), 226–229, 232–233
In-home business insurance policy, 188
InkFrog auction management tools, 140
Insertion fees, 55, 68, 95, 128
Insurance
    basic terminology, 184
    business equipment insurance, 185, 186, 190
    business interruption coverage, 187
    business owners' policy (BOP), 189
    car insurance, 186–187, 190, 274
    considering riders (endorsements), 184, 190

coverage through your homeowners' policy, 185, 186, 188, 217

deducting cost of, 272, 274

employee-related insurance, 188, 189, 234, 236

health coverage, 145, 159

liability insurance, 186, 190

lowering eBay insurance costs, 184, 189–191

making claims, 191

overview on basic coverages, 185–188

property insurance, 185–186, 189

reviewing exclusions, 184, 187, 191

shipping, 188, 206

specific to eBay transactions, 81, 114, 118, 187–188

understanding deductibles, 184, 190

web insurance policies, 187

for your home office, 185, 186, 188, 217

Insurance Information Institute, 188

Insurance underwriter, 184

Intellectual property cost deductions, 278

Intellectual property protection, 112

Interest payment deductions, 274

International sales, 46, 111, 261

International Society of Appraisers, 59

International travel deductions, 276

International wholesaler sources, 41

Internet browsers, tabbed, 21

Internet connections, high-speed, 10–11, 219–220

Internet Movie Database (IMDb), for spotting trends, 40–41

Inventory

conducting a "physical," 281–282

deducting cost of, 268, 280–282

eBay store fees for, 95

home office deduction for storage of, 270

ideas for choosing, 39–42

professionals to set up and manage, 227–228

profit and, 150

prohibited and restricted items, 20, 45–47, 112, 113

property insurance for, 185–186

record keeping of, 196

software for managing, 138–140

valuing, 280

writing off damaged, 282

IRS Form 8832, *Entry Classification Election*, 262

IRS Form 1120, *U.S. Corporate Income Tax Return*, 174, 176, 263

IRS Form 1120S, *U.S. Income Tax Return for an S Corporation*, 262

IRS Form 5213, *Election to Postpone Determination As to Whether the Presumption Applies That an Activity Is Engaged In for Profit.*, 32

IRS Form 940, *Employer's Annual Federal Unemployment Tax (FUTA) Tax Return*, 259

IRS Form 941, *Employer's Quarterly Federal Tax Return*, 260

IRS Form SS-4, *Application for Employer Identification Number,* 252–253

IRS Form 1040, *U.S. Individual Income Tax Return,* 262, 263

IRS Form 1099-MISC, *Miscellaneous Income,* 233

IRS Form 1096, *Annual Summary and Transmission of U.S. Information Returns,* 233

IRS Form 1065, *U.S. Return of Partnership Income,* 262

IRS Form W-4, *Employee's Withholding Allowance Certificate,* 235

IRS Form W-9, *Request for Taxpayer Identification Number,* 232

IRS Form W-2, *Wage and Tax Statement,* 236

IRS (Internal Revenue Service)
    audits, 29, 194, 195, 201–203, 258, 273
    classifying workers, 227–229
    discriminate function system (DIF) red flags, 258
    postponing IRS profit determination, 32
    record keeping rules, 194, 195, 201–203
    rules on business *vs.* hobby classification, 28–32, 258
    tax guidance from, 266

IRS Schedule A, *Itemized Deductions,* 271

IRS Schedule C, *Profit or Loss From Business,* 262, 280–282

IRS Schedule E, *Supplemental Income and Loss,* 262

IRS Schedule K-1 (Form 1065), 178, 262

IRS Schedule SE, *Self-Employment Tax,* 259

ISBN number, for listing books/CDs, 61

Item not received, 115, 118

J

JPG format, for item photos, 61

Judgments, enforcing, 119

Jurisdiction, small claims court, 119

K

Keep It Simple listing method (eBay), 49–52

Keogh retirement plans, 252

Keywords, 37–39, 56, 57, 151–152

Kijiji classified ad site, 24

L

Label printers, 206

Labor costs, in costs of goods sold, 281

Land costs, deducting, 278

Lawsuits, 119, 223

Learning Center (eBay), 22, 23, 147

Lease restrictions, on home offices, 216–217

Leasing commercial space, 173, 221–223

Legal requirements, in hiring help, 232–233, 235–236

Liability, 172–174, 178, 186, 190, 213–214, 222

License fees, deducting auto, 274

Licensing laws, selling multiple autos, 127

LifeOrganizers office organization tips, 220

Limited partnerships, 180, 182

Links, and website search ranking, 151

LinkShare marketing assistant, 153

Listed property, 202, 278–280

Listing an item
  buying enhancements, 56, 68
  categories in, 49, 54–55
  creating descriptions, 50, 63–65
  customizing your listing, 54
  on eBay Motors, 126
  fast method for ("Keep It Simple" choice), 49–52
  grading the condition, 58–59
  multiple quantity selling, 139
  overview on, 48, 53
  payment methods, 52, 72–73
  photos, 50, 58, 60–63, 126
  pricing, 24, 51, 65–66, 81, 126–127, 148
  prohibited and restricted items, 20, 45–47, 112, 113
  reviewing and submitting, 73
  revising or terminating, 74, 126–127
  the "rule of 55," 56
  safe payment requirement, 73, 81
  setting quantities, 66
  shipping costs, 51, 72
  starting price, 65, 68
  terms and conditions, 71
  timing and duration, 67, 91, 95
  titles, 49, 56–57
  tracking fees, 68–70
  weighing before, 206
  See also Getting started

Listing Designer (eBay), 64

LLCs (limited liability companies)
  converting to a, 175–176
  creating, 175
  EINs for, 252
  fictitious business names and, 253–254
  as pass-through entities, 180, 261
  pros and cons of, 181
  reasons to form, 172–173, 222
  taxes on, 262
  vs. corporations, 173–176

Loans, 154–156, 173, 240

Local business licenses, 253

Local fictitious business name registration, 254

Local government agency information, 253, 254

Local taxes, 259

Local transportation deductions, 275, 276
  See also Vehicle expense deductions

Local zoning restrictions/ requirements, 216–217, 222, 255–256

Lodgings expense deduction, 276

Logbook, for business mileage, 275

Logos, 108, 112, 144, 145

Long-term assets, 268, 277–279

LoopNet commercial leasing information, 222

M

Machinery, as capital asset, 277

Macromedia Flash player, 76

Mail or telephone order merchandise rule, 211

Maintenance cost deductions, 272

Manufacturing goods, in cost of goods sold, 281

Marketing, 148, 150–153, 206, 212

Marketing software, 141

Marketplace Research service (eBay), 34–36, 66, 79

Market research, 34–39, 79–82, 141

Marketworks auction management tools, 140

Meal expense deductions, 195, 202, 276–277

Mediation services, 118

Medicare taxes, 259, 263, 267

Medium-volume seller, 21

Membership, establishing eBay, 11, 15–18

Membership fees, as nondeductible, 277

Merchandise. *See* Inventory; Selling an item

Merchant card account, 11, 52

MicroPlace social investing site, 24

Microsoft *Internet Explorer* 7 Internet browser, 21

Microsoft Office Accounting program, 194, 197, 198, 237, 240, 282

Microsoft Outlook email software, 107, 198, 209

Mileage logbook, 275

MIMP (Mint in Mint Package), 59

"Mitigation of damages," 223

MNB (Mint No Box), 59

Monthly break-even amount, 240–242

Moonlighting, 159–160

Mortgage payment deductions, 271

Motor homes, home office deduction for, 271

Motor vehicle expenses, 195, 202, 271, 274–275, 279

Motor vehicle insurance, 186–187, 190

Mozilla *Firefox* Internet browser, 21

Multimember LLC, 262

Multiple eBay seller accounts, 17

Multiple item auction listing, 20, 66

Multiple listings, on eBay Motors, 127

Multiple quantity selling, 139

Multistate Tax Commission website, 255

My eBay page, 14, 21–22, 87

MYOB accounting software, 197

N

"Named peril " insurance policy, 185

National Association of Counties, 253

Navigation bar (eBay), 13

Negligence claims, 173

Neighbors, and your home-based business, 217, 256

Net GMS (gross merchandise sales), 149

Net leases, 222

New York refund policy laws, 212, 213

Niche products, 153

Noncompete agreements, 160

Nontaxable income accounting, 194, 202

NPB (nonpaying bidder) rate, 149

O

Office Accounting program (Microsoft), 194, 197, 198, 237, 240

Office ergonomics, 219

Office furniture, 218–219, 277

Office supplies, 159–160

Oil, deducting auto, 274

One-of-a-kind items, selling, 40, 139, 153

One-owner/member LLC, 174, 262

OnlineOrganizing office organization tips, 220

Operating expenses
deducting, 268–272, 274–277
in manufacturing of goods, 281
overhead, 240–242, 281
in profit and loss forecast, 242, 244
record keeping of, 195, 202

Outlook email software, 107, 198, 209

Overhead, 240–242, 281

Ownership structure. *See* Business entities

P

Paperwork, hiring requirements, 232–233, 235–236

Parking fee deductions, 274

Partnerships
automatic formation of, 172
converting to an LLC, 175
EINs for, 252
fictitious business names and, 253–254
general partnerships, 172, 178–181, 222, 252
limited partnerships, 180, 182
partnership agreements, 179
as pass-through entities, 174, 261
taxes on, 262

Pass-through tax entities, 174, 180, 261

Patent costs, deducting, 278

Paychex payroll service, 197, 237, 260

Paycycle payroll service, 236

Payment methods, for eBay sales, 52, 72–73, 82, 128

PayPal
basics of, 11, 24, 104
billing with, 107
buyer protection plan, 81, 108, 118
for eBay Motors deposits, 128
for eBay stores, 97
as essential to eBay businesses, 104
fee calculator, 69
fees associated with, 106–107
integration with auction tools, 107–108, 139
payment services fees, 69
PayPal Shopping Cart system, 104

as preferred payment choice, 52
shipping solutions, 207–208
spoofs, 113
three account types, 104–106
Payroll services, 197, 236–237, 260
Payroll taxes, 197, 259–260
Peachtree accounting software, 197
Personal asset protection, 172–173
Personal finances
creating a budget and, 161–169
effect of quitting your day job on, 158
keeping separate from business, 200–201
Personal guarantee, when leasing, 222–223
Personality, selling an item and, 4–7, 18, 40
Personal liability, 172–174, 178, 222
Phising, 113
Phone bill expense deductions, 283
PhotoImpact photo editing software, 61
Photos, eBay item, 50, 58, 60–63, 126
Photos, for proof of home office percentage calculations, 273
Photo studios, mini, 60
Photo tutorial (eBay), 60
Physical inventory, 281–282
Picasa photo editing software, 61
Picture Manager (eBay), 62
Picture Pack (eBay), 62
Popular keywords, 37–38
Popular Products page (eBay), 39

Postage scales, for business shipping, 206
Poster compliance requirements, for employers, 234–235
PowerSellers
auction management tools for, 134
characteristics of, 145–150
financing for, 154–156
levels of, 144–145
qualifications and benefits of, 144–145
revocation of status, 110
tips for increasing web traffic, 150–154
warning on overspending, 156
PriceGrabber shopping website, 81
Pricing, 24, 51, 65–66, 81, 126–127, 148
Principal place of business requirement, for home office deduction, 271, 273
Privacy policies, 17, 213
Product liability coverage, 186
Product placement, 148
Profanity, eBay rules against, 111
Profit, 29–32, 39, 240–242, 279
Profit and loss, 138, 154, 174, 179, 195, 242–246
Profit percentage, 240–242
Profit test, IRS, 29–31
Prohibited and restricted items, 20, 45–47, 112, 113
Promissory notes, 154
Promotion, 148, 150–153, 206, 212
Property insurance, 185–186, 189

Property use records, 202, 278–280
ProStores (eBay), 24, 101
Proxy bidding, 86, 87
Publishing notice, of business filing, 175
Pulse page (eBay), 36–37
Purchase protection, 118, 128

Q

Quantity sales, 66
QuickBooks accounting software
   as comprehensive record keeping tool, 194, 196–198, 240
   downloading shipping costs to, 208
   exporting from auction management programs to, 141
   integration with PayPal, 107
   inventory and sales information integration with, 135, 282
QuickBooks payroll service, 197, 236, 237, 260
Quitting your day job
   avoiding problems with your current employer, 159–160
   evaluating your personal finances, 161–169
   points to consider before, 158–159
   tips before quitting, 159

R

Record keeping and accounting
   audits and, 201–202, 258
   choosing an accounting method, 199–200
   with eBay accounting software, 197–198
   getting organized, 220
   hiring a professional for, 227–228
   keeping receipts, 203, 274
   overview on, 194–197
   PowerSellers knowledge of, 149–150
   as proof of business *vs.* hobby, 30, 31
   separating business/personal finances, 200–201
   time limit on keeping records, 203
Referral credits, eBay store, 96
Refunds, 108, 212–213
Registering your business, 233, 252–256
Regular use, for home office deduction, 270–271
Regular work habits, hobby *vs.* business classification and, 30, 31
Remote computer access, 134
Renewal zone tax credit, 283
Rent, deducting, 271
Rent.com rental properties/roommate site, 24
Renter's insurance, coverage for your home business, 217
Renting, home-business restrictions while, 216, 217

Renting a commercial space, 221–223

Repairs, deducting auto, 274

Replacement cost insurance policy, 185–186

Reputation, eBay seller, 206, 212, 227

Resale permit, 255

Resale purchases, 255

Research, market, 34–39, 79–82, 141

Reserve price, 65, 68, 87, 126

Restricted and prohibited items, 20, 45–47, 112, 113

Retail business, 34, 41, 127–128, 154

Retirement plans, 158, 252, 283

Retracting a bid, 79, 83, 111, 113

Return merchandise authorization (RMA) number, 212

Returns, 71, 212–213

Reviews and Guides section (eBay), 6, 59, 82, 88, 147

Revising your listings, 74, 126–127

Risk management, 189–190

RMA (return merchandise authorization) number, 212

Room method, home office deduction percentage calculation, 272, 273

Rules and guidelines
 About Me page, 18
 on community content policy, 111
 content and picture theft, 61
 for dispute resolution, 58, 114–119, 187–188
 on excessive handling charges, 72
 on item condition, 58
 PowerSellers mastery of, 147
 table of, 112–113
 values behind, 110

S

Safe payments, 73, 81

Sales
 knowledge and tracking of, 149–150
 observing seasonal trends, 40–41
 in PowerSeller criteria, 144
 in profit and loss forecast, 242, 244
 profits from, 29–32, 39, 240–242, 279
 record keeping of, 196
 Sales Revenue Forecast worksheet, 243
 taxable and nontaxable, 196
 wholesale, 255

Sales fees, 68, 96, 111, 115

Sales statistics, 149–150

Sales tax, 71, 112, 196, 254–255, 260–261

S corporations, 180, 182, 261, 262

Search engine ranking, 151–152

Search feature (eBay)
 advanced search, 51
 for auction items, 13
 for bid research, 81
 DSRs impact on, 124
 eBay Motors, 128, 129
 help topics, 22
 leveraging misspellings, 57
 for pricing research, 51
 researching common frauds, 114
 Shop eBay Stores, 95
 store inventory sales in, 91
 title selection and the, 56–57
 Top Category keywords, 37–38

Section 179 deductions, 277–278
Secured loans, 154, 155, 173
Security cost deductions, 272
Security deposits, 223
Self-employment taxes, 259, 263, 267
Self-help evictions, under a
  commercial lease, 223
Seller performance
  BuySafe bonding service, 114
  DSRs (detailed seller ratings), 73,
    124, 144
  impact of personality on, 4–7, 18,
    40
  reputation and, 206, 212, 227
  rules and guidelines on, 112
  safe payments and, 73, 81
  See also Feedback
Seller protection, PayPal, 81, 108
Seller's Assistant Basic/Pro software
  tools (eBay), 139
Seller's permit, 254–255
Selling an item
  About the Seller function, 91
  buyer backs out, 68
  choosing merchandise, 39–42, 149
  collecting sales tax, 260
  consignment sales, 41, 261
  dealing with unpaid items (UPI),
    111, 112, 115, 120–121, 123
  drop-shipping, 209–212, 260–261
  on eBay Motors, 126–128, 130–132
  fees associated with, 68, 96, 111,
    115
  fixed price listings (Buy-It-Now
    items), 20, 91, 94, 95, 100–101, 126

fraud in, 113
handling returns, 71, 212–213
niche products, 153
offering guarantees, 81
one-of-a-kind items, 40, 139, 153
outside of eBay, 111
overview on, 19–20
prohibited and restricted items, 20,
  45–47, 112, 113
researching buying trends, 34–39
role of personality in, 4–7, 18, 40
selling formats, 19, 20
selling strategies, 39–42, 148
store inventory sales, 91
terms and conditions, 71, 213–214
tracking costs, 39
See also Auction management
  tools; Inventory; Listing an item;
  PowerSellers; Seller performance;
  Shipping; Stores
Selling Manager Pro auction
  management tool (eBay), 95, 138
Selling Manger auction management
  tool (eBay), 22, 68, 95, 138
Seminar cost deductions, 282
Service interruption, insurance against
  website, 187
Shareholders, corporate, 174, 180,
  262–263
Shill bidding, 112
Shipping
  calculators for costs, 51
  as critical to success, 11, 206
  drop-shipping, 209–212, 260–261
  for eBay Motors autos, 129

final transaction fees, 69
and handling charges, 51, 72
insurance for, 188, 206
legal rules on delays, 211–212
listing an item, 51, 72, 82
methods for handling, 207–209
packaging, 206–207
and returns, 71, 212–213
supplies for, 11, 206–207
terms and conditions associated
  with, 213–214
tips on, 206–207
Shopping.com comparison pricing, 24
Signature loans, 156
Significantly not as described (SNAD),
  115, 118
Site interference, 112
Site outage policy (eBay), 112
Skype, Internet-based long distance,
  24, 87
Small Business Administration, 190,
  255, 260
Small claims court, 119
SNAD (significantly not as described),
  115, 118
Sniping, 87–88, 141
Social Security taxes, 259, 263, 267
Software tools
  accounting, 194, 196–198
  for buyers, 141
  fee calculator, 69–70, 141
  marketing, 141
  photo editing, 61
  for remote computer access, 134
  sniping, 87–88, 141

spreadsheet, 135, 158, 197, 242, 247
tools for selecting/comparing,
  135–139, 141, 196
  See also Auction management tools
Solar energy tax credit, 283
Sole proprietorships
  automatic formation of, 172
  converting to a LLC, 175
  EINs for, 252
  fictitious business names for, 254
  leasing an office, 222
  as pass-through entities, 174, 261
  pros and cons of, 181
  spouses working in, 179
  taxes on, 262
Solution Finder software selection
  application, 141
Spam, eBay prohibition on, 112
"Special form " insurance policy, 185
Sponsored search results/links, 151
Spoofs, 77, 113
Spouses, 179, 200–201, 230, 276
Spreadsheet software, 135, 158, 197,
  242, 247
Square footage method, home office
  deduction percentage, 272, 273
SquareTrade dispute resolution
  service, 117, 118
Stamps.com shipping solutions, 209
Standard auction with BIN listing, 20
Standard mileage rate, for vehicle
  deductions, 274
Standard Purchase Protection Plan
  (eBay), 118
Star icon (eBay), 122

Start up. *See* Getting started

Start-up expense deductions, 268–269

State agency information, 253, 254, 260

State filing fees, 176, 177

State laws

    articles of incorporation, 177

    creditor dissolution, 173

    employee withholding, 236

    employment notices, 234–235

    on LLC formation, 176

    new hire reporting, 235–236

    on refunds, 212–213

    sales tax, 71, 112, 196, 254–255, 260–261

    on selling multiple autos, 127

    worker's compensation insurance, 188, 189, 234

State tax

    credit deductions for, 283

    disability insurance programs, 236, 259

    owing debts of, 173

    sales tax, 71, 112, 196, 254–255, 260–261

State unemployment insurance agency, 228, 234

Stereo equipment, deducting cost of, 279

Stock certificates, corporate, 177, 178

Storage area deductions, 270, 282

Store referral credits (eBay), 96

Stores

    About the Seller function, 91

    auction items in, 91, 93, 100–101

    categories in, 98

    costs to create and run, 95–97

    customizing the appearance, 92–94, 97–99

    deciding whether to open, 90, 102

    eBay Stores home page, 91

    eBay Store toolkit, 98, 99

    fixed-price items in, 91, 94, 95, 100–101

    hiring someone to set up, 227

    how to open, 97–100

    important to PowerSeller status, 146–147

    inventory sales, 91

    overview on, 20, 23, 90–94

    ProStores, 24, 101

    sample store pages, 92–94

    subscription levels, 95, 97

StubHub entertainment ticket site, 25

StumbleUpon special interest service, 25

Subscription cost deductions, 282

Supplier information, 39

Supplies, office, 159–160

Supplies, shipping, 11, 206–207

Suspended users (eBay), 111, 120

T

Tabbed browser benefits, 21

Tax bracket/rate, 267, 279

Tax calendar, 262, 263

Tax credit programs, 283

Tax debts, 173

Tax deductions

    commonly overlooked, 282–283

depreciation, 32, 202, 274, 275, 278–279

hobby loss rule, 28, 279

home office deduction, 269–274

inventory expenses (cost of goods sold), 268, 280–282

listed property, 202, 278, 279–280

long-term assets, 268, 277–279

meals and entertainment, 195, 202, 276–277

operating expenses, 268–272, 274–277

overview on, 266–269, 283–285

record keeping for, 195, 196, 202

Section 179 deductions, 277–278

start-up expenses, 268–269

travel costs, 195, 275–276

vehicle expenses, 195, 202, 271, 274–275, 279

Taxes

corporate, 174, 176–177

employee withholding, 235, 236, 259

fines and penalties for avoiding, 258

hiring independent contractors and, 232, 233

on international sales, 261

LLC alternative tax treatment, 174

local business, 253

in partnerships, 178

pass-through tax entities, 174, 180, 261

paying estimated, 263–264

sales tax, 71, 112, 196, 254–255, 260–261

tax calendar, 262, 263

value added taxes (VATs), 261

in various business forms, 181–182, 259–263

Taxpayer ID, 232

Tax policy (eBay), 112

Tax registration certificate, 253

Telephone bill expense deductions, 283

Telephone order merchandise rule, 211

Temporary agencies, employees from, 231

Theft, website image, 61, 187

30-day cure, for late rent, 223

30-day rule, on fulfilling orders, 211

Three-out-of-five years profit test, 29–31

Toll expense deductions, 274

Top Category keywords (eBay), 37–38

Tracking bids (eBay), 87

Trademarks, use of eBay, 112

Trading assistants (eBay consignment sales), 41, 261

Transaction interception (eBay), 113

Transaction interference (eBay), 112

Travel expense deductions, 195, 275–276

Trust and Safety Team (eBay), 118

Turbo Lister auction management tool (eBay), 66, 138, 139

TurboTax tax preparation software, 196–198, 260

Tutorials (eBay), 76, 81

Typohound (auction typos), 57

U

Unemployment, worker classification and, 228

Unemployment taxes, 234

Unique items, selling, 40, 139

Unpaid items (UPI), 111, 112, 115, 120–121, 123

Unpaid rent, 30-day cure for, 223

Unsolicited email, eBay prohibition on, 112

UPS shipping solutions, 206–208

U.S. Department of Health and Human Services, 236

U.S. Department of Labor, 234

U.S. Federal Trade Commission, 211, 214

USCIS (United States Citizenship and Immigration Services) Form I-9: *Employment Eligibility Verification,* 235

User ID (eBay), 17

USPS (United States Postal Service) shipping solutions, 206–209

Utility expense deductions, 272

V

Valuation of inventory, 280

Value added taxes (VATs), 261

Vehicle expense deductions, 195, 202, 271, 274–275, 279

Vendio auction management tools, 139

Virginia refund policy laws, 213

Virgin Money loan facilitation business, 154–155

W

WAHM (Work at Home Moms) work-at-home tips, 218

Want It Now want-ad service (eBay), 77–78

Watch List, bidding (eBay), 77

Web insurance policies, 187

WebMomz, for work-at-home tips, 218

Websites (individual), 146–147, 213–214, 227

Website traffic, tips on increasing, 150–153

Welfare-to-work program, 283

WhatsItWorthtoYou.com appraisal service, 59

Wholesale sales, 255

Withholding, employee, 235, 236, 259

Worker's compensation insurance, 188, 189, 234

Workflow prioritization, 220–221

Work-for-hire agreements, 232–233

Work habits, hobby *vs.* business classification and, 30, 31

Working from home. *See* Home office

Workshop, for home office deduction, 271

WowBanners banner ad design, 152

Z

Zoning restrictions/requirements, 216–217, 222, 255–256 ●

Get the Latest in the Law

(1) **Nolo's Legal Updater**
We'll send you an email whenever a new edition of your book is published!
Sign up at **www.nolo.com/legalupdater**.

(2) **Updates at Nolo.com**
Check **www.nolo.com/update** to find recent changes in the law that
affect the current edition of your book.

(3) **Nolo Customer Service**
To make sure that this edition of the book is the most recent one, call us at
800-728-3555 and ask one of our friendly customer service representatives
(7:00 am to 6:00 pm PST, weekdays only). Or find out at **www.nolo.com**.

(4) **Complete the Registration & Comment Card ...**
... and we'll do the work for you! Just indicate your preferences below:

Registration & Comment Card

NAME _____ DATE _____

ADDRESS _____

CITY _____ STATE _____ ZIP _____

PHONE _____ EMAIL _____

COMMENTS _____

WAS THIS BOOK EASY TO USE?   (VERY EASY)   5   4   3   2   1   (VERY DIFFICULT)

☐ Yes, you can quote me in future Nolo promotional materials. *Please include phone number above.*

☐ Yes, send me **Nolo's Legal Updater** via email when a new edition of this book is available.

Yes, I want to sign up for the following email newsletters:

　☐ **NoloBriefs** (monthly)
　☐ **Nolo's Special Offer** (monthly)
　☐ **Nolo's BizBriefs** (monthly)
　☐ **Every Landlord's Quarterly** (four times a year)

☐ Yes, you can give my contact info to carefully selected
partners whose products may be of interest to me.

EBIZ1

Send to: **Nolo** 950 Parker Street Berkeley, CA 94710-9867, Fax: (800) 645-0895, or include all of
the above information in an email to regcard@nolo.com with the subject line "EBIZ1."

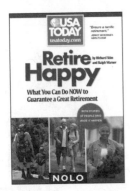

MEET YOUR NEW ATTORNEY

"Loves walking in the rain and drawing up prenuptial agreements."

Brent
San Francisco

"Enjoys fine wine and creating living trusts."

Juliana
Phoenix

"Spends time gardening and doing trademark searches."

Ron
Seattle

Start a great relationship
(you can skip the walks on the beach)

You don't need just any attorney. You need that "special someone" – someone whose personality puts you at ease, whose qualifications match your needs, whose experience can make everything better.

With Nolo's Lawyer Directory, meeting your new attorney is just a click away. Lawyers have created extensive profiles that feature their work histories, credentials, philosophies, fees – and much more.

Check out Nolo's Lawyer Directory to find your attorney – you'll feel as if you've already met, before you ever meet.

Visit us and get a free eBook!
http://lawyers.nolo.com/book

Meet your new attorney   **NOLO'S LAWYER DIRECTORY**

The attorneys listed above are fictitious. Any resemblance to an actual attorney is purely coincidental.